THE DRACULA DILEMMA

New Directions in Tourism Analysis

Series Editor: Dimitri Ioannides, E-TOUR, Mid Sweden University, Sweden

Although tourism is becoming increasingly popular as both a taught subject and an area for empirical investigation, the theoretical underpinnings of many approaches have tended to be eclectic and somewhat underdeveloped. However, recent developments indicate that the field of tourism studies is beginning to develop in a more theoretically informed manner, but this has not yet been matched by current publications.

The aim of this series is to fill this gap with high quality monographs or edited collections that seek to develop tourism analysis at both theoretical and substantive levels using approaches which are broadly derived from allied social science disciplines such as Sociology, Social Anthropology, Human and Social Geography, and Cultural Studies. As tourism studies covers a wide range of activities and sub fields, certain areas such as Hospitality Management and Business, which are already well provided for, would be excluded. The series will therefore fill a gap in the current overall pattern of publication.

Suggested themes to be covered by the series, either singly or in combination, include – consumption; cultural change; development; gender; globalisation; political economy; social theory; sustainability.

Also in the series

Emotion in Motion
Tourism, Affect and Transformation
Edited by David Picard and Mike Robinson
ISBN 978-1-4094-2133-7

Tourism Enterprises and the Sustainability Agenda across Europe
Edited by David Leslie
ISBN 978-1-4094-2257-0

Social Media in Travel, Tourism and Hospitality
Theory, Practice and Cases
Edited by Marianna Sigala, Evangelos Christou and Ulrike Gretzel
ISBN 978-1-4094-2091-0

Tourists, Signs and the City
The Semiotics of Culture in an Urban Landscape
Michelle M. Metro-Roland
ISBN 978-0-7546-7809-0

The Dracula Dilemma
Tourism, Identity and the State in Romania

DUNCAN LIGHT
Liverpool Hope University, UK

Routledge
Taylor & Francis Group

LONDON AND NEW YORK

First published 2012 by Ashgate Publishing

2 Park Square, Milton Park, Abingdon, Oxon OX14 4RN
711 Third Avenue, New York, NY 10017, USA

Routledge is an imprint of the Taylor & Francis Group, an informa business

First issued in paperback 2016

British Library Cataloguing in Publication Data
Light, Duncan, 1965–
The Dracula dilemma : tourism, identity and the state in Romania. — (New directions in tourism analysis)
1. Tourism—Romania—History. 2. Tourism—Government policy—Romania. 3. Transylvania (Romania)—In literature. 4. Economics and literature—Romania. 5. Dracula, Count (Fictitious character)
I. Title II. Series
338.4'791498–dc23

Library of Congress Cataloging-in-Publication Data
Light, Duncan, 1965–
The dracula dilemma : tourism, identity and the state in Romania / by Duncan Light.
    p. cm. — (New directions in tourism analysis)
Includes bibliographical references and index.
ISBN 978-1-4094-4021-5 (hardback : alk. paper)
1. Tourism—Social aspects—Romania. 2. National characteristics, Romanian. 3. Vlad III, Prince of Wallachia, 1430 or 31–1476 or 7—Influence. I. Title.
G155.R78L55 2012
914.9804—dc23

ISBN 978-1-4094-4021-5 (hbk)
ISBN 978-1-138-27474-7 (pbk)

Contents

Contents

List of Figures and Tables

List of Figures and Tables

Acknowledgements

There are many people who have helped me with the research that forms the basis of this book. I would especially like to thank Nicolae Păduraru, President of the Transylvanian Society of Dracula, who on many occasions shared with me his unparalleled knowledge of Dracula tourism as well as introducing me to many other people who were able to help me. Nicolae was one of the few Romanians who really understood the Western fascination with Transylvania and like many people I was greatly saddened to hear of his death in 2009. I would also like to thank Alexandru Misiuga (who also died in 2009) and Andrei Raiescu who each granted me several interviews but also gave me access to their personal archives of material about Dracula. I also thank those other people who agreed to be interviewed and who shared with me their thoughts about Dracula and Dracula tourism: Ştefan Andreescu, Stefan Andrei, Alex Harris, Narcis Dorin Ion, Sabina Ispas, Codrea Marinescu, Ion Mânzat, Ioan Prahoveanu and Valer Sîmihaian.

Outside Romania, Elizabeth Miller answered many of my questions and also sent me copies of some of her own resources, as well as commenting on a draft of Chapter 2. A number of people also shared their experiences on the Dracula trail in Romania including Jeanne Keynes Youngson, Dave Hawley, Bruce Wightman and other members of the British Dracula Society. A number of other people also assisted me with ideas and information including Michael Bayley Hughes, Lucian Boia, Dennis Deletant, Jessica Douglas-Home, Alin Todea and David Turnock. David Phinnemore and Janet Speake commented on early drafts of some of the chapters. Craig Young played a vital role in encouraging me not to give up on this project altogether. Thanks also to Anya for providing critical encouragement throughout.

To undertake a research project such as this it was necessary to spend a lengthy period of time in Romania and I am grateful to the Leverhulme Trust for the award of a Research Fellowship which enabled me to spend 2004 in the country. I thank my friends in the Department of Human and Economic Geography at the University of Bucharest – particularly Liana, Paul, Mirela and Nic – who made me welcome and who followed this project with a mixture of interest and bemusement. Thanks also to those Geography students from the University who took part in my focus group and especially Cristian Ciobanu and Vali Chivu who volunteered their services as unpaid research assistants and provided me with invaluable help (thanks also to Cristian for permission to use some of his photographs in this book). I must also mention the students – Alin, Bogdan, Iustina and Cătălin – in the upstairs flat in Drumul Taberei where I was staying. They were more than surprised to find an English Geographer in their midst but they took a keen interest in what I was doing and in return I learnt from them a lot about Bucovina and its traditions.

Finally I owe a special thanks to Daniela Dumbrăveanu of the University of Bucharest. There were parts of this project that I couldn't have done without her but she already knows that!

List of Abbreviations

CMJ	Company of Mysterious Journeys
DUHR	Democratic Union of Hungarians in Romania (*Uniunea Democrată Maghiară din România*)
EU	European Union
FDTS	Sighişoara Fund for Tourism Development (*Fondul pentru Dezvoltare Turistică Sighişoara*)
NATO	North Atlantic Treaty Organisation
NGO	Non-Governmental Organisation
NSF	National Salvation Front (*Frontul Salvării Naţionale*)
NTO	National Tourist Office
ONT	*Oficiul Naţional de Turism 'Carpaţi'* (the socialist-era national tourist office)
PSDR	Party of Social Democracy of Romania (*Partidul Democraţiei Sociale din România*)
RCP	Romanian Communist Party (*Partidul Comunist Român)*
RDC	Romanian Democratic Convention (*Convenţia Democrată Română*)
SDP	Social Democratic Party (*Partidul Social Democrat)*
TSD	Transylvanian Society of Dracula
UNESCO	United Nations Educational, Scientific and Cultural Organization

Introduction

Mention Romania and, for many people, one name springs to mind: Dracula. Whether Romania likes it or not, Count Dracula is the best known Romanian (Boia 2001a). There are many who know little (if anything) about Romania but they do believe that it is the place that Dracula comes from. And who, exactly, is this Dracula? In this sense we are talking about the sinister, shadowy, monstrous Count Dracula, an undead, predatory vampire who thrives on the blood of the living. Brought to life by Bram Stoker in 1897, Count Dracula has proved to be one of the most enduring and recognizable literary creations. The novel *Dracula* is known throughout the world: it has never been out of print and has been translated into numerous foreign languages. And its eponymous vampire has come to be almost synonymous with Romania: in the Western popular imagination, Romania is the 'land of Dracula'. It is difficult to think of another country that is so immediately identified with a literary character – and a villain at that.

Dracula's home is, of course, Transylvania, a place that has an extraordinary resonance in the West. There are many people who have never been near Transylvania but they have a clear idea in their minds what it is like: 'In the West, the very word *Transylvania* conjures up images of howling wolves, midnight thunderstorms, evil-looking peasants, and the thick, courtly accent of Count Dracula, as portrayed by Bela Lugosi' (Kaplan 1994: 149). A powerful 'place myth' has developed around Transylvania. The region is imagined as being a strange, remote, fairytale land, a place of surprise, magic and enchantment, but also a place of uncertainty, menace and danger. It is a place somewhere on the very edge of Europe, close enough to be recognizable but sufficiently unfamiliar to be threatening. It is also inseparable from vampires. As a result, Transylvania has come to exist in the West more as a fantasy than as a real place (Gelder 1994). I can remember looking at an atlas during an A level Geography lesson and being surprised and a little startled to discover that Transylvania really existed. I'm sure I'm not the only person to have reacted in this way.

When Stoker published *Dracula*, Transylvania was part of the Austro-Hungarian Empire. Romania gained the territory at the end of the First World War and in so doing it also unconsciously acquired the Dracula myth (Boia 2001b). Of course, if *Dracula* had remained an obscure piece of nineteenth-century fiction none of this would matter very much. But *Dracula* has become one of the world's bestselling books. It has also been the inspiration for numerous films, plays, television programmes, cartoons, comics and even brands of food and drink. In the process, Count Dracula has become an international icon, the world's best known vampire. Moreover, Stoker's *Dracula* has been the starting point for a thriving and lucrative genre of vampire literature and cinema so that the figure of the vampire is now ever present within Western popular culture. Over time, Count Dracula has become a powerful cultural myth – meaning, in this sense, something that is not strictly 'true' or 'real' but which nevertheless has meaning and significance for many people. And the seemingly natural home of the vampire continues to be Transylvania.

In a world that is characterized by restlessness and mobility, affluent tourists are now able and prepared to travel around the world to pursue their interests. Transylvania has long had a special allure to fans of the Dracula myth and for more than four decades enthusiasts have visited Romania on their own searches for Dracula in Transylvania. Some are literary tourists on the trail of the places described in Stoker's novel. Others are 'film-induced' tourists searching for what they have seen represented in films. Still others are hunting vampires or are seeking an experience of the supernatural, the spooky and the ineffable in Transylvania. Their motives, expectations and behaviour are diverse and, although their numbers have never been huge, they make up a significant part of Romania's tourist demand.

However, this is a form of tourism that has long presented Romania with a quandary. No country would especially welcome being so closely associated with a predatory villain intent on destroying Western civilization! Similarly, many countries might be unhappy at being regarded by the West as the home of vampires (which are unknown in Romanian folklore) and the supernatural. The West's view of Romania has, in large part, been shaped by Stoker's novel but this is starkly at odds with the way that Romania sees itself and wishes to be seen by others. For this reason Romania has long resisted the Western Dracula myth. To complicate things further, Romanians have a Dracula of their own, in the form of a medieval prince, Vlad III. Known as 'Dracula' during his lifetime, Vlad is regarded by Romanians as a heroic leader who fought to bring justice to his country and preserve its independence from the Ottoman Empire. However, in the West, Vlad III – known as Vlad the Impaler – has been promoted as the inspiration for Stoker's Count Dracula. There is nothing to associate Vlad with vampirism and in fact little evidence that Stoker knew anything much about him. But Romanians are not surprisingly resentful to see one of their national heroes appropriated in the West as the archetype for a fictional vampire.

Thus, 'Dracula tourism' has become a problem for Romania. It is a predicament which can be described as 'identity versus economy' (Tunbridge 1994: 127, Light 2000). On the one hand this form of tourism has the potential to attract Western visitors to Romania and to generate revenue. Such is the global popularity of Dracula that Romania would have little difficult promoting (even branding) itself to tourists as the 'home of Dracula'. Indeed, Dracula could easily become Romania's unique selling point, something no other country can lay claim to. But on the other hand, Dracula tourism fundamentally collides with Romania's sense of its own cultural and political identity. It is a form of tourism that is founded on (and perpetuates) a Western image of Romania as a strange, remote and backward place haunted by vampires and the supernatural. However, this has nothing in common with the way that Romania sees itself. During the communist (or socialist) period (up to 1989) Romania was a rapidly modernizing state founded on the materialist principles of Marxism. Dracula tourism, with its focus on discredited superstitions and the supernatural was therefore totally discordant with the country's self-image. After 1989, Romania has been remaking itself as a modern, democratic, European state with aspirations for membership of the European Union (EU). In this context, it has been striving to demonstrate its cultural and historical ties with Europe and its allegiance with European political and economic values. Again, there is no place for vampires in this project. However, Romania has not been able to prohibit tourists visiting in search of Dracula. Instead, it has had little choice but to accept such tourism and seek to manage it on its own terms.

This book is a historical-cultural study of 'Dracula tourism' – by which I mean the visiting of sites and places in Romania associated with both the fictional Count Dracula and the historical Vlad the Impaler. I follow Franklin (2003) in seeing tourism as being as much a cultural activity as a commercial exercise. As such, I am not concerned with the economic significance (or impacts) of Dracula tourism, neither do I consider issues of destination/attraction management, or the organization of the tourist experience. Instead, I focus on the cultural politics of Dracula tourism. In particular, I examine what has enticed Western tourists to Transylvania and the ways in which the Romanian state has responded to this form of tourism. It is an obvious (if sometimes overlooked) aspect of tourism that nation-states make choices about what sorts of tourism they do (and do not) want to encourage, and will support tourism development that allows them to present themselves to Others on their own terms. But nation-states can sometimes have to contend with unwanted forms of tourism and Dracula tourism is one such case. As such, I focus on the ways that the Romanian authorities have attempted to negotiate what has been a problematic and undesirable form of tourism.

The time period covered by this study is from the mid-1960s up to the present day. During this time Romania has undergone a dramatic change in political organization and orientation. Before 1989 Romania was a socialist state (characterized by Communist Party leadership and a centrally planned economy). Since 1989 Romania has remade itself as a multiparty democracy with a free market economy. Therefore as the nature of the state itself has changed dramatically so too has the context in which Dracula tourism has unfolded. A central theme of my analysis is to examine the differences between the socialist and the post-socialist eras in terms of the nature of Dracula tourism and the way that the state (through its various institutions) has responded to it.

Sources and Methods

The data for this study is derived from a combination of secondary documentary sources and interviews with key individuals associated with Dracula tourism. An obvious starting point for examining Dracula tourism during the socialist era would be policy documents and plans produced by the Ministry of Tourism. However, locating such materials has proved a challenge. In conversations with current Ministry employees there was widespread agreement that such an archive probably existed 'somewhere' but nobody I spoke to had any idea of its whereabouts. On the other hand, a number of people (including some former employees of the tourism ministry) told me privately that the archive no longer existed. According to some accounts it had disappeared, while others claimed that it had been deliberately broken up after 1989. The most plausible account that I heard (from a number of people) was that the archive had been transferred to a building that was subsequently destroyed by fire (and according to some versions of the story the fire had been started deliberately). Despite extensive enquires I have not succeeded in locating the Ministry's archive and I am doubtful that it still exists. There may be other materials relating to Dracula tourism in other archives from the socialist period (for example, the records of meetings of the Romanian Communist Party are now publicly available in the National Archives in Bucharest). However, the search would be something like looking for a needle in a haystack. In addition, Romanian law permits access only to documents that are more than 30 years old (Tismăneanu 2003) so that even if there are materials that record the state's response to Dracula tourism these are unavailable from the 1980s onwards.

In the absence of primary documentary sources it was necessary to reconstruct socialist Romania's stance towards Dracula tourism in other ways. The first was through in-depth interviews with a number of former employees of *Oficiul Naţional de Turism* (ONT), the national tourist office, along with other individuals who were able to comment on the state's position regarding Dracula tourism during the socialist era. Interviews were conducted (in both English and Romanian) with the following people: 1) Professor Ştefan Andreescu, Nicolae Iorga Institute of History, Bucharest; 2) Ştefan Andrei, Foreign Minister of Romania, 1978–85; 3) Codrea Marinescu, architect at the Ion Mincu Institute of Architecture, Bucharest; 4) Alexandru Misiuga, former director of the ONT office in the county of Bistriţa-Năsăud; 5) Colonel (retired) Ion Mânzat, former head of the *Securitate* for the county of Bistriţa-Năsăud; 6) Nicolae Păduraru, former ONT guide and founder of the Transylvanian Society of Dracula; 7) Ioan Prăhoveanu, former custodian of Bran Castle; 8) Andrei Raiescu, former head of the Romanian National Tourist Office in New York. In addition a telephone interview was undertaken outside Romania with Alexander Harris, Chairman of General Tours (New York). In each case I explained fully the nature of my research and each interviewee gave their permission to be identified and quoted.

These interviews were supplemented and triangulated as much as possible with reference to published materials about tourism from the socialist era. In particular, I consulted a range of tourism promotional materials that were archived in the library of the Romanian Academy. These included: 1) *Holidays in Romania*, a monthly colour magazine for foreign tourists, published in English and a number of other European languages from 1965 onwards. It was written by a dedicated team of staff working in a department for 'external propaganda'; 2) *Almanah turistic*, a tourism yearbook published annually from 1960 in Romanian. This contained a range of articles about Romanian tourism, including occasional policy statements from the Ministry of Tourism; 3) *România pitorească*, a monthly tourism magazine published in Romanian from 1972 onwards, which contained a range of articles, many written by the members of the same team that produced *Holidays in Romania*. Socialist Romania practised a strict form of censorship (Ficeac 1999, Troncotă 2006) in which any forms of publication were expected to conform to state ideology. Moreover, anything intended for an external audience was likely to be carefully monitored (particularly from the 1970s onwards when socialist Romania was seeking to raise its international profile and present itself to the wider world as an independently-minded socialist state). Therefore, although they may initially appear to be trivial, tourist promotional materials can be treated as sources that mirror the 'official' position of the state. As such they offer an indirect indication of socialist Romania's approach to Dracula tourism. These materials were supplemented with reference to newspaper reports (particularly from *Scînteia*, the official paper of the Romanian Communist Party) which again were strictly censored so as to accord with state ideology.

Investigating Dracula tourism in the post-socialist era presented its own challenges. The notion of government documents being in the public domain was, until recently, poorly developed in post-socialist Romania. Therefore it proved difficult to locate any materials produced by the Romanian Ministry of Tourism (in its various guises) that dealt with tourism policy and development strategies. However, I was again able to infer the government's position regarding Dracula tourism through looking at a wide range of 'official' promotional materials produced over the 1990–2011 period. Even this was far from easy since the run of *Holidays in Romania* in the Romanian Academy Library stops in the early 1990s. The magazine is now produced by a private company but I was refused access to its archive of issues from 1990 onwards. Further material about developments after 1989 was obtained from interviews with Nicolae Păduraru and Alexandru Misiuga. Additional interviews were undertaken with Professor Sabina Ispas, Head of the Institute of Ethnography and Folklore, Bucharest; Narcis Dorin Ion, then director of Bran Castle Museum; and Valer Sîmihaian, director of Coroana Travel in Bistriţa. Once again, all the interviewees gave permission to be quoted. In addition, various newspapers (particularly *Adevărul, Cotidianul, Evenimentul zilei and România liberă*) were consulted regarding Romania's approach to Dracula tourism in the post-socialist period. Newspapers were also the main source of information about the Dracula Park project. In the following analysis, all translations from Romanian are mine unless otherwise indicated.

Structure and Organisation of this Book

In Chapter 1 I introduce the academic context for this study. In particular I review the relationship between tourism and the making and projection of national identities, with reference to the role of the state in this process. I also consider the nature of literary and film-induced tourism and the significance of literary/ cinematic myths and their contemporary importance. Any readers who have picked up this book to find out more about Dracula can skip this section.

Chapters 2 and 3 consider the Dracula phenomenon in order to establish a context for the later discussion of Dracula tourism. Chapter 2 examines Bram Stoker's famous novel *Dracula* and its role in creating a place myth of Transylvania as the home of vampires and the supernatural. This chapter then considers the reaction in Romania to Bram Stoker's novel. Chapter 3 considers the 'historical' Dracula, Vlad the Impaler. It reviews the significance of this Prince (or Voievode) for Romanian history and examines how he has been regarded by Romanian historians. It then goes on to examine the well-worn claim that Vlad the Impaler was the inspiration for Bram Stoker's Count Dracula and considers the Romanian response to these claims.

In Chapters 4 and 5 I review the development of Dracula tourism during the socialist period (from the mid-1960s until 1989). Chapter 4 examines the early growth of Western interest in visiting Transylvania and socialist Romania's response. Romania was reluctant to promote Dracula as a tourist attraction and adopted a strategy of tolerating Dracula-themed tourism without doing much to encourage it. Nevertheless, there were local developments (particularly in Bistriţa) intended to cater for Dracula fans although these appear to have taken place without the knowledge of the central authorities. Chapter 5 considers the pervasive myth of 'Castle Dracula' and its special appeal to Dracula fans. It then examines the three places in Romania – Bran Castle, Poienari Citadel and Hotel Tihuţa – that have come to be known in this way. In the cases of Bran and Poienari, a Romanian building has come to be known as Castle Dracula without any encouragement or approval from the Romanian authorities. The third case was another local initiative intended to cater for Dracula enthusiasts, but about which the central authorities appear to have been in the dark.

Chapters 6 and 7 examine Dracula tourism in the post-socialist period. Chapter 6 is a broad overview of Romania's changing relationship with Dracula after 1989 and seeks to situate the development of Dracula tourism within the context of broader post-socialist political and economic restructuring. Tourists have continued to visit Romania on the Dracula trail and this segment is increasing in significance. However, while the private sector has been eager to exploit the commercial possibilities of Dracula the Romanian state has continued to be reluctant to engage with, or promote, Dracula tourism. The one exception was the proposal in 2001 to build a theme park based on the Dracula myth and Chapter 7 reviews the rise and fall of the 'Dracula Park' project. This was a government initiative that was intended to revitalize the country's tourism industry and promote a positive message about Romania as an energetic and self-confident state that was willing to exploit Dracula on its own terms. However, the Dracula Park project was poorly conceived and quickly became an international embarrassment for Romania. As a result the original proposal was substantially modified and later abandoned altogether. Finally, the conclusions consider the future potential of Dracula in creating a tourist brand for Romania.

Chapter 1
Tourism, Identity and Popular Culture

This book focuses on the development of 'Dracula tourism' in Romania and the responses of the Romanian authorities to this form of tourism However, before examining the whole Dracula phenomenon and the travel that it has generated, this chapter provides an academic contextualization of the key concepts and issues that will be explored in later chapters. The first section examines the relationship between tourism and identity, with particular reference to the ways that tourism is implicated in the construction and projection of national identities. The discussion also considers the role of the state in tourism development to establish a context for considering the Romanian's state's responses to Dracula tourism. The second section examines the nature of literary and film-induced tourism, focusing on the myths about places that are created and diffused through literature and cinema. This provides a framework for understanding Dracula tourism as a form of literary or screen tourism.

Tourism and Identity

The concept of identity – how we define ourselves, whether individually or collectively – has risen to the forefront of social science research in recent decades. Contemporary thinking rejects essentialist notions of identities as somehow given, coherent and static. Instead, identities are treated as being socially constructed in diverse and dynamic contexts – and as such 'senses' of identity are fluid, situational and sometimes contradictory (S. Hall 1996, Grossberg 1996). The notion of a single unified identity has been superseded by the recognition that identities are multiple. We can define ourselves in many different ways depending on the context in which the defining takes place. In a sense identities are like hats that an individual can change to suit the particular circumstances in which he or she happens to be (Palmer 2005). Similarly, senses of identification also exist at a variety of (sometimes overlapping) scales – from personal identities to group, regional and national identities. Rather than being fixed and stable, identities can be conceptualized as dynamic and created through continuous performance. Moreover, however they are defined, identities are also incomplete, fragmented and constantly in the process of change (Curticapean 2007).

A key aspect of any discussion of identity is the notion of the Other. Identities are relational and oppositional: almost all identities are in some way defined with reference to (or in opposition to) what we are not, as much as by what we are. As such, identities are underpinned by difference. As S. Hall (1996: 5) notes 'identities can function as points of identification and attachment only *because* of their capacity to exclude, to leave out, to render "outside"'. Defining or constructing an identity implies defining someone (or somewhere) else as different, as not the same as me/us. Any identity is therefore a simultaneous 'process of expression and exclusion' (Abram and Waldren 1997: 6).

Given the current level of academic interest in questions of identity it comes as no surprise that there has been increasing attention over the past decade to the relationship between tourism and identity. In particular, there is a widespread recognition that issues of identity are ever present in discourse about tourism (Lanfant 1995) and that tourism plays a key role in the formation of both individual and collective identities in a globalized world (Burns and Novelli 2006, C.M. Hall 2005, Wearing et al. 2010, White and Frew 2011).

On one level, there has been considerable interest in the significance of tourism for senses of personal identity. One research strand takes as its starting point the position that, in contemporary societies, senses of personal identity are constructed less through work but instead through practices of consumption (Urry 1994). In this context, travel is one form of consumption that can be used as a means of self-expression and self-definition. The choice of holiday type and destination is another way to make a statement about what sort of person we are. Indeed, travel has long been an expression of taste and discernment, and a way of affirming class status (Mowforth and Munt 2009). Over the past two decades, various groupings within the middle classes have increasingly rejected mass tourism and have turned instead to individual travel and/or various 'alternative' tourisms. The explosive growth in new types of holiday – including the rise of numerous forms of niche 'tourisms' (Novelli 2005) – in new destinations has been the response of the global tourist industry to the rise of what has been termed post-tourism or postmodern tourism (Munt 1994, Urry 2002). Recent studies have argued that participation in alternative tourisms is used by the 'new middle classes' as a way of acquiring cultural capital in order to articulate and define class identities (Munt 1994, Mowforth and Munt 2009).

Another research strand has focused on the transformative character of tourism for senses of personal identity. Rejecting the suggestion that tourists themselves are passive collectors of signs and experiences, Franklin (2003) argues that tourists are seeking a sense of personal growth, change and transition. Travel and holidaymaking are conceptualized as an occasion for self-actualization and self-discovery (Wang 1999, Urry 2002) and an opportunity for making and remaking senses of self-identity (Wearing et al. 2010). A number of recent studies have examined these issues in the context of what can be broadly termed adventure tourism. In a study of British travellers in Peru, Desforges (2002) noted that many of his interviewees started travelling at moments of uncertainty or crisis in their lives when self-identity was open to question. For such people travel was an opportunity to construct a new biography and to make a new sense of self for the future. Clarke's (2004) study of working holidaymakers in Australia established that such holidays were opportunities for self-development and argued that many participants returned home having developed confidence, new skills and stronger personal narratives.

At a different scale, there has been increasing attention to the relationship between tourism and national identities. Such senses of belonging and allegiance are complex and multifaceted. National identity arises in tandem with nationalism, an ideology that asserts the primacy of the nation-state as a form of social and political organization. Nationalism promotes and mobilizes the idea of a shared national consciousness in order to foster social cohesion and secure allegiances to the ideal of a nation-state with its own defined territory. Once again this process is founded on difference and exclusion and the formation of national identities involves the simultaneous identification of Others, those (both internal and external to a state) with competing beliefs and aspirations who do not qualify for membership (Graham 2000).

Nevertheless, there is a widespread acceptance that national identities are not innate, timeless and static (despite the claims to the contrary by some nationalist politicians) but instead, like many other identities, are socially constructed at particular times and in particular contexts. Indeed, nations and national identities are as much imaginative constructs as material realities (Gruffudd 1994). For example, Anderson (2006: 6) has famously defined the nation as an 'imagined political community', something composed of individuals who will never encounter all the other members of the nation but nevertheless believe that they share something with them. The nationalist project works to create a shared sense of 'who we are' – or in Anderson's words, a 'deep, horizontal comradeship' (2006: 7) – among people who have never met and who may otherwise have little in common. Moreover, once created, such a shared identity is not inherently stable, but instead is something that needs to be continually renewed, so that nation-building is an ongoing project (A.D. Smith 1991). However, national identities rarely achieve hegemonic status. Instead, as Graham (2000) notes their resonance is compromised by competing allegiances derived from, for example, religion, class, gender, region and ethnicity. Moreover, national identities may be further fractured by individuals or groups within a nation-state who may contest or circumvent dominant inscriptions of nationhood or evoke alternative versions of national identity (Edensor 1998). Overall, then, despite the best efforts of nationalists, national identities are not stable and all-embracing but instead are fluid, dynamic and contextual. Nevertheless, however fragmented and unstable they may be, national identities remain a powerful form of group allegiance and show little sign of weakening in a globalizing world (Pryke 2009).

In order to construct a shared identity, nation-states embark on a process of socialization that is intended to inculcate a collective public culture. This is achieved through, for example, the creation of national institutions, the existence of a mass media and a standardized and publicly funded mass education system (A.D. Smith 1991). Moreover, nation-states seek to anchor themselves in time and space through writing (or inventing) a 'national' past and promoting popular attachments to the national territory. In so doing, certain locations are inscribed and celebrated as being places of 'national' significance (Edensor 2002, Franklin 2003). Such places include historic buildings, monuments or battlefield sites associated with key events in the nation's past along with statues, landscapes, landforms, national parks and other sacred sites (A.D. Smith 1988).

However the resonance of national places will be limited unless the wider population understands their significance. This is where the role of tourism in nation-building becomes apparent: there is no better way to appreciate the significance of a national place than by travelling to it. Consequently, as Franklin (2003) argues, nation-states have explicitly used travel and tourism as a means of promoting senses of citizenship and national identity. The growth of the railways in the nineteenth century was something that facilitated travel, enabling people to develop a greater awareness of the national territory and reinforce a sense of belonging to an entity that was larger than the locality. Thus, domestic tourism became an opportunity to 'perform' national identity (Edensor 2002). By visiting places of national significance (including national museums) tourists were able to make (and reflect upon) the connection between themselves and the nation (Palmer 1999). Through travel and tourism, national places became sites for affirming collective (national) memory and building popular allegiances (Johnson 1994, Edensor 1997). Far from being trivial or insignificant, tourism is arguably one of the key processes of modernity (Franklin 2003).

Tourism remains important for nation-building in the twenty first century. Nation-states continue to promote domestic travel and tourism as a means for renewing and reproducing senses of national allegiance and identity (Franklin 2003). Indeed, tourism is an established component of the public culture of the modern nation-state (see Horne 1984): it continues to be 'one of the defining activities of the modern world, shaping the ways in which one relates to and understands self and other, nation and nationness' (Palmer 2005: 8). The relationship between domestic tourism and the making (and remaking) of national identity is attracting increased academic attention and recent studies have explored this issue in contexts as diverse as America (Pretes 2003); Croatia (Goulding and Domic 2009); England (Palmer 1999, 2003, 2005); India (Edensor 1998); Korea (Park 2010); Scotland (Edensor 1997, 2002); Thailand (Peleggi 1996); and Wales (Pitchford 2008).

In addition to cultivating and building a sense of national identity among their own populations nation-states also seek to project their sense of themselves – their identity – outwards to Others. This is identity-building for an external rather than an internal audience (Light 2001, Pitchford 2008, Kaneva and Popescu 2011). All states seek to present a positive image of themselves to the wider world and to ensure that their unique character and cultural identity is appreciated and respected by other states: this is an affirmation of self on behalf of Others (Lanfant 1995). The interactions with these Others is not a trivial matter. As O'Connor (1993: 68) argues 'the way in which we see ourselves is substantially determined by the way in which we are seen by others'. As a result nation-states make considerable efforts to project themselves – on their own terms – to the rest of the world. This project can include material objects such as postage stamps, banknotes and coins, iconic buildings and monuments and national stadia (Cresswell 2004, Raento and Brunn 2005, Unwin and Hewitt 2001). Similarly, nation-states can seek to join international organizations – for example, the United Nations or the European Union – as means of declaring their adherence to particular values. Similarly, many states seek to host international meetings, congresses or sporting events as a way of presenting their 'best face' to the international community. We only have to look at the enthusiasm with which Estonia, Latvia, Ukraine and Turkey hosted the Eurovision Song Contest in the early 2000s. For these aspirant members of the European Union, the contest was a means to showcase themselves as modern, European countries and to legitimate their claims for future membership (see Szondi 2007).

Tourism is also an important way through which nation-states seek to project their cultural and political identity to the wider world. At this point, the role of the state in the development and promotion of tourism merits fuller consideration (see Light 2007a). Although the political dimensions of tourism have long been neglected (C.M. Hall 1994) there is increasing attention to the role of the state in shaping the nature and character of tourism that takes place within its territory. A state may intervene in the operation and development of tourism in many ways (C.M. Hall 2000, 2005, Harrop and McMillan 2002, Jeffries 2001). For example, through policymaking and planning a state can support and encourage the development of particular forms of tourism in particular locations. Similarly, it may introduce legislation and regulation to provide a framework within which the tourism industry can operate. States may directly provide facilities and infrastructure essential for a successful tourism industry (such as roads or hotels). In addition, most states engage to some degree in the activity of tourism promotion. Such is the importance of tourism that many nation-states have established a government ministry with responsibility for tourism planning and development.

However, the involvement of the state in tourism is not merely confined to 'technical' processes of legislation, planning and policy formulation: there is also a cultural politics of tourism development (Burns 2005, Light 2007a). States may use tourism to fulfil particular political agendas (C.M. Hall 1994, Morgan and Pritchard 1998). For example, the choices of which forms of tourism development will (and will not) be encouraged, and for whom, are not neutral or value free. Instead, through such decisions the state assumes the role of the arbiter and definer of cultural meanings (Wood 1984, Cano and Mysyk 2004, Yan and Bramwell 2008, Goulding and Domic 2009). A state will support the development and promotion of those forms of tourism that accord with its sense of political and cultural identity. In addition, states will seek to show off their achievements to their visitors (see Sanchez and Adams (2008) in the case of Cuba). The choice of what will be celebrated for tourism is therefore an ideological one that constitutes a statement of national identity (Wood 1984, Morgan and Pritchard 1998). Through its policies for tourism development and promotion a nation-state can also make a declaration about itself to the wider world and seek to raise its international profile and prestige (Morgan and Pritchard 1998). For this reason many states encourage cultural and heritage tourism, as much for foreign tourists as for their own citizens, as a means to project their history, values and identity to an international audience. More broadly, states can use tourism as an element of their foreign policy and international relations (C.M. Hall 1994, Franklin 2003).

Such is the potency of tourism in projecting a national or cultural identity to the wider world that many states undertake considerable investment in external tourism promotion (C.M. Hall 2000). Indeed, many nation-states are actively attempting to create a unique brand for themselves (Anholt 2010, Pitt et al. 2007). This activity is usually undertaken by a dedicated state agency, most often a National Tourist Office. These organizations do not sell holidays directly but instead aim to create a unique profile for the destination (see Peleggi 1996) and to contribute to economic development through attracting foreign tourists. But the activities of a National Tourist Office are underpinned as much by political as economic imperatives. One of their roles is to present and project a nation-state to the world in a way that flatters and affirms national identity (Lanfant 1995). As such, state-sponsored promotional materials are not value free representations of the particular destination but instead are constructs that are imbued with official (and therefore ideological) viewpoints (Peleggi 1996, Ateljevic and Doorne 2002). Official promotional materials can be 'read' as expressions of cultural and political identity (Pritchard and Morgan 2001). They make an overt statement of 'this is who *we* are' and 'this is how *we* want *you* to see *us*' (Light 2001: 1055). The same hegemonic narratives of history, culture and identity that are mobilized for domestic nation-building are now articulated for the consumption of an external audience (Peleggi 1996).

Romania is a good example of how state-sponsored tourism promotion can be used for ideological ends. During the socialist era the Ministry of Tourism produced a monthly tourist magazine, available in various foreign languages, the English edition of which was entitled *Holidays in Romania*. The magazine presented Romania's diverse attractions for tourism but was also imbued with messages about Romania itself. Many articles asserted Romania's identity as a socialist state and highlighted the agenda and achievements of socialism. In addition, the overtly nationalist narratives of Romanian history and identity that were dominant during the socialist era (such as an emphasis on indigenous rather than Western influences as the key to understanding Romania's historical development) were frequently emphasized. Tourist promotion was even employed to exalt the policies and achievements of Nicolae Ceauşescu, the Secretary General of the Romanian Communist Party and later state president.

Since the collapse of Ceauşescu's dictatorship, Romania's state-sponsored tourism promotion has been underpinned by a different agenda but one that is equally ideological in nature. In common with the other formerly socialist states of Central/Eastern Europe, Romania has sought to remake itself as a modern, democratic and European state. Tourism promotion has been used to project this new political identity to the West, particularly an image of 'Europeanness' that legitimates aspirations for EU entry (see Morgan and Pritchard 1998, D. Hall 1999, 2001, 2010, Szondi 2007, Smith and Puczkó 2011). Unsurprisingly, Romania's post-socialist tourism promotion is imbued with messages about the 'new' Romania and its aspirations (Light 2006, Kaneva and Popescu 2011). Romania now stresses what it shares with the rest of Europe. There is a major emphasis on historical and cultural ties with Western Europe that predate state socialism and that are being resumed in the post-socialist era. Romania is now presented as having a firmly Latin and European heritage, and cultural and architectural links with France are particularly highlighted. There is also a stress on rural traditions and heritage that are presented as having survived four decades of socialism relatively intact. Through such messages, Romania is seeking to project its new identity to the West and ameliorate its image among Western public opinion.

Yet while nation-states may endeavour to encourage particular forms of tourism and promote these to the wider world this project may be subject to contestation. Whether it likes it or not, each nation-state is situated within much broader historical, political and cultural discourses that structure the ways in which particular peoples and places are perceived in the wider world (Morgan and Pritchard 1998, Pritchard and Morgan 2001, Echtner and Prasad 2003, Yan and Santos 2009). Such discourses are grounded in (and reinforce) existing asymmetric power relations, and some states – predominantly those from the West – have more power to represent than others. The result can be 'representative dissonance' (Bandyopadhyay and Morais 2005) where a people or place may be represented, not as they would choose to represent themselves, but as more powerful states in the West choose to portray them, frequently in terms of clichés, myths or cultural stereotypes (Echtner and Prasad 2003, Yan and Santos 2009). The reiteration of such stereotypes in tourist brochures (or other forms of popular culture) may, in turn, generate particular forms of externally driven tourism demand and practice that may be unwelcome to the host community (Morgan and Pritchard 1998). Such tourism may even compromise or collide with the cultural and political identity that the state wishes to present to the wider world (see Burns 2005). On the other hand, a state can resist or contest the way that it is represented (Bandyopadhyay and Morais 2005). Hence, tourism may become a site of struggle between a nation-state's attempts to project itself on its own terms and the ways in which it is represented by Others (Morgan and Pritchard 1998).

Romania faces exactly this dilemma with Dracula tourism (Light 2007a). As I shall discuss in the following chapter, Romania has long been subject to particular 'ways of seeing' in the West that construct the country as Other. The novel *Dracula* is itself founded on a 'place myth' of Transylvania as a remote, backward and sinister region where vampires and the supernatural run wild. This place myth is something that has considerable appeal to some Western tourists who travel to Transylvania in search of Otherness generally and the supernatural in particular. But this is a form of tourism that has been (and remains) problematic for Romania. In particular, Dracula tourism is starkly at odds with Romania's sense of its own identity and the way in that it wishes to be seen by the wider world. In the later chapters I will examine the ways in which Romania has attempted to manage and negotiate Dracula tourism on its own terms.

Literature, Film and Tourism

Travel and literature are closely linked. Robinson and Andersen (2002a) point out that much tourism is based on the written word while many tourists themselves are inspired by what they read. In the first instance there are some forms of writing that are overtly related to tourism: travel guides and guidebooks aim to interpret places to their potential or actual visitors and play an important role in signposting the gaze of the tourist. Similarly there are distinct forms of literature essentially based on tourism. The best example is travel writing in which an author writes of their experiences as a traveller (rarely as a tourist!) usually in faraway locations (see Dann 1999). But in addition there are many works of fiction (novels, prose and poems) which, although not specifically about travel or tourism, are set in, or evoke, real places and landscapes. This visiting of places associated with works of fiction (or their authors) has become known as literary tourism. This is a form of niche tourism or special interest tourism, although it is also treated as a subset of heritage or cultural tourism (Herbert 2001, M.K. Smith 2009).

The relationship between literature and travel and tourism is long established, especially in Britain (Aitchison et al. 2000). From the eighteenth and nineteenth centuries onwards writers played a significant role in creating 'ways of seeing' places and landscapes that, in turn, had considerable allure to tourists. For example, up until the eighteenth century few people visited the English Lake District. However, the idealized and nostalgic celebrations of the region's natural beauty in the poetry of William Wordsworth and other Lakeland poets played a vital role in popularizing the Lakes as the object of the tourist gaze (Newby 1981, Squire 1988). Similarly, the novels and poetry of Walter Scott played a major role in establishing the Scottish Highlands as a land of Romance and mystery (Aitchison et al. 2000, Inglis and Holmes 2003). Thus, literature does more than simply evoke or describe particular places and landscapes: instead, it can play a highly important role in creating these places (Crang 1998) and in subsequently constructing them as the focus of the tourist imagination.

While early literary tourism was centred on the sights and sites associated with the authors of 'classic' fiction (such as Shakespeare, Dickens, Hardy and Brontë) this form of tourism has broadened significantly in recent decades. As part of the 'de-differentiation' that characterizes postmodern societies (Urry 2002) the distinction between 'high' and popular culture has largely collapsed. As a result all sorts of locations associated with popular fiction have also become the focus of tourist interest. One example is the development of tourism in the northeast of England centred on the life and works of Catherine Cookson, a writer of popular romantic fiction (Pocock 1992). The development of tourism in Romania inspired by Bram Stoker's Dracula (and the whole genre of vampire fiction that followed) is also part of this trend.

Literary tourism takes various forms (Herbert 1996, 2001, Robinson and Andersen 2002a). In the first place, some tourists are interested in the biography of a particular writer and choose to visit places associated with his/her life and work. There are many buildings with literary associations that have been carefully preserved and opened as tourist attractions. These may include the building in which an author was born (such as Shakespeare's birthplace) or where they lived and worked (such as Chawton, a former home of Jane Austen). In some cases (for example, Poet's Corner in Westminster Abbey) an author's grave may also become the focus of tourist interest. A visit to such places affords the opportunity to 'connect' in some way with the life of the author and gain an insight into the circumstances in which he or she lived and wrote (Robinson and Andersen 2002a). Such tourism – particularly in the context of 'classic' literature – has been described as a form of pilgrimage (Pocock 1987). Indeed, the notion of the literary pilgrim – the dedicated scholar and enthusiast – is a well-established (if exaggerated) idea (Herbert 2001). This 'personality-based' form of literary tourism (Robinson and Andersen 2002b) is, in fact, little different from other forms of heritage tourism that involve visits to buildings or places associated with famous historic figures.

Another form of literary tourism entails visits to those places or landscapes that are depicted in, or form the backdrop to, a particular novel. Many writers set their novels in specific locations or were inspired to varying degrees by real places and landscapes. In some instances, the geographical setting is an essential component of the novel: we only have to think of how central Transylvania is to the plot of Bram Stoker's *Dracula*. Through their imaginative writing many authors have been instrumental in creating and circulating ideas about places and landscapes that have considerable allure to tourists. For some literary tourists the simple act of viewing the landscape may be sufficient to gain a fuller appreciation or enjoyment of the novel. But for others, visiting such a landscape is an opportunity to connect with the imaginary world of the novel. Such is the level of interest in 'literary landscapes' (Rojek 1993) that numerous places in Britain – and throughout Europe – now promote and profit from their associations with a particular novel or its author. Literary trails have become commonplace (Rojek 1993) enabling tourists to visit a series of places associated with an author or their work. Furthermore, tourist boards, local authorities and other place promoters have enthusiastically embraced literary connections in the construction of place identities. Thus Britain has, among others, 'Brontë Country', 'Hardy's Wessex' and 'Catherine Cookson Country'.

However, in some instances, tourists may visit a literary landscape less out of interest in a particular author or their work but instead to engage with much broader cultural meanings, values and myths that may have little to do with the location itself. In a study of Beatrix Potter tourism in the English Lake District, Squire (1993, 1994) argued that tourists at Hill Top Farm (Potter's former home) were doing much more than just visiting a building associated with a particular author. Instead, their visit was a starting point for much wider forms of introspection and escapism. For some people, the visit was an occasion for nostalgia centred on idealized memories of childhood and family life. For others it was an occasion to reflect upon broader cultural myths and values surrounding rural life, the countryside, authenticity and the nature of Englishness. As such, literary tourism at Hill Top Farm was not so much about Beatrix Potter herself as about a much wider range of experiences and emotions that were evoked by her stories. In a similar way, a visit to Transylvania is an opportunity to engage with ideas of Otherness and the supernatural that go well beyond Bram Stoker's *Dracula*. Thus, visiting a literary landscape can also be an opportunity to perform identities (whether individual or collective) and affirm senses of self through reflecting on the nature of the Other (Robinson 2002).

Overall then, one of the defining characteristics of literary tourism (and something that sets it apart from many other forms of contemporary tourism) is that it takes place simultaneously in both real and imagined worlds. It is travel that takes place as much in the mind as in a material geographical setting. A visit to a literary place is an occasion where the boundaries between fiction and reality become increasingly blurred (Robinson and Andersen 2002a). Reading a novel is itself something that engages the imagination: it is an opportunity to suspend disbelief and to escape (temporarily) into other places with other people (Robinson 2002). In a similar way, a visit to a literary landscape is another opportunity to enter the imaginative world of a novel (Herbert 2001). Visits to literary places are opportunities to indulge in – and enact – speculation, fantasy and escapism (Squire 1994) as well as being occasions for fun and play. For example, studies of 'Brontë tourism' at Haworth have noted that imagining scenes and characters from the novels – particularly *Wuthering Heights* – was an important part of the experience for some visitors (Pocock 1987, Tetley and Bramwell 2002). Similarly visitors to Hotel Castle Dracula in Transylvania (see Chapter 5) described the excitement of hoping to encounter Dracula at some stage of their visit along with the thrill of being slightly scared whilst in Transylvania (Light 2009a). In short, literary tourism involves the fusing of real and imagined worlds (Herbert 2001) and each tourist defines their own boundaries between the two (Robinson and Andersen 2002a).

To recognize the imaginative dimension of literary tourism inevitably leads to the notion of myth (and in particular 'literary myths'). 'Myth' is a widely used but ambiguous word. In its original use 'myth' referred to ancient narratives (such as those from Greek mythology) involving heroic, supernatural or divine figures that had significance for the life of a particular community. However, more recently 'myth' has taken on a range of meanings and is now used to refer to anything that deviates to some extent from reality (Boia 2001b). Thus the term 'myth' is used as a label for ideas or stories that do not have a strictly factual basis but which are believed in some way. Myths have long been the focus of academic scrutiny and two broad perspectives can be identified (Johns and Clarke 2001). The anthropological approach treats myths as narratives or beliefs that are part of the realm of the imaginary (Overing 1997, Boia 2001b). This approach focuses on the uses of myths within the everyday lives of contemporary societies and the ways in which they frame daily practice in the material world (Overing 1997). In particular, myths can play an important role in structuring and underpinning our ways of thinking and behaving in the world. On the other hand, the linguistic approach (following the work of Roland Barthes) treats myths as a form of communication. Here I follow the anthropological approach in treating myths as a form of belief (see Dann 1996, Selwyn 1996, Hennig 2002, Buchmann 2006).

In the case of literary tourism, the blurring between fiction and reality is such that, in some cases, entirely fictional characters or places have taken on a life of their own in the material world. The term 'myth' or 'literary myth' is sometimes used to describe such situations. For example, Pocock (1987) talks of the Brontë myth at Haworth while Rojek (1993) analyses the myth of Sherlock Holmes. In this sense, literary myths are forms of belief that are grounded in the imaginary, and the 'truth' (or otherwise) of the myth is unimportant to many literary tourists. What is more significant is how the myth helps in explaining or describing reality (Buchmann 2006) or what it represents or offers in terms of ideals, dreams and fantasies. Moreover, such myths can shape or influence the practices of those who engage with them and a visit to a literary landscape offers a tourist the opportunity to enact or perform the myth. Such tourism is not so different from that involving visits to places associated with mythical historical figures. For example, Nottingham has a long tradition of attracting visitors in search of Robin Hood (Shackley 2001) even though there is limited evidence that the outlaw ever existed. Similarly, Tintagel in Cornwall has long drawn tourists in search of King Arthur (Robb 1998) even though the historical existence of Arthur is contested and his connections with Tintagel are unproven. In both cases, there are many tourists that are apparently happy to enjoy the myth or legend and its historical veracity is unimportant (Shackley 2001, Fowler 1992). What is significant is not the myth itself but instead what it means or represents to people.

Such is the resonance of some literary myths that spaces and places are being transformed to meet the expectation of tourists through a process that Robinson and Andersen (2002a: 15) describe as the 'commodification of the imagined'. For example, many Sherlock Holmes fans have sought the detective's home at 221B Baker Street. Like the character, the address belonged to the realm of fiction: indeed, the relevant part of the street did not exist when Arthur Conan Doyle wrote the Holmes stories (Herbert 2001). Nevertheless, this section of Baker Street became a focus of tourist interest and the level of demand was such that a Sherlock Holmes museum opened at '221B Baker Street' in 1990. Similarly in Denmark, Kronborg Castle in Helsingør has become known to tourists as 'Hamlet's castle', even though the 'historical' Hamlet lived elsewhere (Robinson and Andersen 2002a). In Tibet the region of Zhongdian was renamed as 'Shangri-La' in 2002 in order to cater for tourists on the trail of James Hilton's book of the same name (Gao *et al* 2012). In Romania, a castle entirely unconnected with Bram Stoker's novel (but which looks suitably Gothic) has come to be known (outside Romania) as 'Dracula's Castle' (see Chapter 5). There are many other examples, but each instance is the response of tourists demanding a meaningful experience of an entirely fictional place.

In addition, literature can play a hugely significant role in creating myths about the locations and landscapes that are represented in fiction. Thus, literature is engaged in circulating what Shields (1991) terms 'place myths' which themselves have especial importance for tourism. Place myths are essentially geographies of the imagination; culturally constructed ideas about the nature of other places (regardless of their character in reality). They are formed from images of the place that may be partial, exaggerated, incomplete or based on stereotypes or prejudices (Shields 1991). These myths are maintained and reproduced through a variety of means including literature (Urry 1995) and other forms of popular culture. Over time they may become embedded within popular consciousness as a particular discursive 'way of seeing' the place (Hughes 1992).

There are numerous locations around which a distinct place myth has developed. For example, through his writing, Wordsworth played a key role in shaping the place myth of the Lake District as a natural and unspoilt region, offering visitors the opportunity for solitude, contemplation and quiet recreation. This framework for imagining and experiencing the region remains pervasive today (Urry 1995). Similarly, the novels and poetry of Walter Scott played a major role in the creation of the place myth of the Scottish Highlands as a land of Romance, myth and mystery (Aitchison et al. 2000, Inglis and Holmes 2003). Harrogate in Yorkshire enjoys the place myth of a genteel spa resort characterized by discipline, order and sobriety (Cuthill 2004). As I shall examine in Chapter 2, Bram Stoker's *Dracula* give birth to a distinct place myth of Transylvania as a sinister, marginal place that is haunted by the supernatural. Thus, the creation of myths about places can also be a key component in the construction of identities for those places, especially in the cases of place myths that are founded on ideas of Otherness (Morgan and Pritchard 1998, Echtner and Prasad 2003).

Moreover, place myths (whether created through fiction or by other sources) are a strong influence on tourist practices since they influence the choice of holiday destination. A tourist will evaluate potential destinations on the basis of their promise to offer something new and original. However, the choice of destination is rarely made on the basis of prior experience of the place itself. Instead, the decision is framed by received beliefs and ideas about what the destination is 'like' – in other words its place myth. In addition, many place myths are founded on easily recognizable stereotypes about other places. As such they are widely utilized in tourism promotion (see Buchmann 2006). For example, the tourism promotion of Scotland draws extensively on the place myth of the Highlands created by Walter Scott (Hughes 1992). Since, as the earlier discussion noted, tourism marketing is grounded in global relations of power it can also play an active role in reinforcing existing place myths, particularly those founded on the Otherness of the place being represented (Selwyn 1996, Echtner and Prasad 2003).

While imaginative literature is important in shaping and transmitting our knowledge of places there are other forms of contemporary popular culture that have a much greater impact than the written word. Watching television is the dominant leisure activity in contemporary societies (Roberts 2004) and there are many people who have encountered literary classics not through the novels themselves but instead through televisual or cinematic adaptations (*Dracula* is one of the most obvious examples). Like many novels, films depict distinct geographical locations so that cinema plays an active role in the creation and circulation of place myths. In the same way as literary tourism, visitors are frequently drawn to places and landscapes that they have seen represented in a film or television program. Indeed, there is increasing evidence that the number of visitors to a place increases (sometimes significantly) after it has been represented in film or on television (Tooke and Baker 1996, Riley et al. 1998). This activity has been labelled variously as 'film-induced tourism' (Beeton 2005, Bolan et al. 2011), 'movie-induced tourism' (Riley 1994, Riley et al. 1998, Busby and Klug 2001), 'film tourism' (Roesch 2009, Buchman et al. 2010), 'cinematic tourism' (Tzanelli 2004), or 'screen tourism' (Connell and Meyer 2009) the latter being adopted in this study. It is a form of cultural tourism (M.K. Smith 2009) although it is also increasingly identified as a form of tourism in its own right. It includes any form of travel generated by the moving image in its widest sense (film, television, video and DVD) (Beeton 2005). This includes both visits to places where films were made and to places portrayed in film (Roesch 2009). There is much overlap between screen tourism and literary tourism and one writer has proposed the term 'media tourism' as an overarching term for tourism based on books and the moving image (Reijnders 2011a, 2011b).

Screen tourism can take a variety of forms (Busby and Klug 2001, Beeton 2005). It is less personality-based than literary tourism (Beeton 2005) and so rarely takes place at locations associated with a key individual involved in the creation of a film (although in some cases the houses of living actors have become attractions in their own right). In other instances production studios (and associated theme parks) have become the focus of tourist interest. A further widespread form of screen tourism involves visits to the places and landscapes associated with a particular film. As such, tourists are sometimes drawn to the locations where filming took place (see for example Graml 2004) but more usually they seek the places represented in a film and where filming is *believed* to have taken place (Tooke and Baker 1996, Busby and Klug 2001, Roesch 2009). One of the most often cited examples of such 'displacement' (Bolan et al. 2011) is Mel Gibson's *Braveheart* (1995). Although most of the filming took place in Ireland the film generated a significant increase in tourist visits to locations in Scotland portrayed in the film (Beeton 2005). Similarly, many Dracula fans and enthusiasts are eager to see Transylvania for themselves and are little concerned that none of the classic Dracula films was actually made in the region. For tourists, it is the meanings and values that are attached to a place represented in a film that turn it into a meaningful attraction for tourists (Kim and Richardson 2003, Reijnders 2010).

Clearly, like literary tourism, much screen tourism involves a fusing of the real and the imaginary (Busby and Klug 2001, Buchmann *et al* 2010, Carl et al. 2007, Reijnders 2010, 2011a) to the extent that it is difficult to disentangle the two. Film tourists are usually seeking to a visit a place as they believe it to be from its representation on screen. The visit to such a place is an occasion to make a connection with the imaginative world of that film. Once again, the visit is an opportunity for fantasy, escapism, dreamwork and play. Drawing on the work of Pierra Nora, Reijnders (2010, 2011a, 2011b) proposes the concept of the *lieux d'imagination* ('places of the imagination') for locations that provide an opportunity for media pilgrims to temporarily connect with (and briefly enter into) the imaginary world they have experienced through film or television. Gao *et al* (2012: 199) propose the similar concept of "phantasmal destinations", places that are fusions of real and imagined worlds.

A key characteristic of screen tourists is their willingness to suspend disbelief and give full reign to their imaginations (Reijnders 2011a). As such, it is a far from uncommon practice for some tourists to (re)enact iconic scenes from a film when they visit places associated with that film. For example, fans of *The Lord of the Rings* frequently take the opportunity to recreate moments, shots and scenes from the film trilogy when visiting New Zealand (Roesch 2009, Buchmann et al. 2010). Similarly, fans of *The Sound of Music* often break into song or dance when visiting a gazebo in Salzburg, Austria that featured in an iconic moment in the film (Graml 2004). And at key locations in Transylvania Dracula enthusiasts play at being in Castle Dracula (Light 2009a, 2012, Reijnders 2011a, 2011b). This sort of deliberate and self-aware playful behaviour – also known as ostention (Holloway 2010, Reijnders 2011a) – illustrates how screen/media tourism unfolds simultaneously in the 'real' world and in the world of the imagination.

Screen tourism, like literary tourism, can also be an occasion to engage with cultural ideas, values and meanings that go beyond the film itself. For example, Edensor (2002) argues that films can stimulate utopian desires and promise a transcendence of the everyday and commonplace. A visit to places in Scotland associated with, for example, *Braveheart*, can be an occasion to engage with such ideals and fantasies in a way that goes well beyond the story or geographical setting of the film itself. Graml (2004) notes that the success of *The Sound of Music* was largely because it articulated American nostalgic desires for order and harmony and projected them onto an idealized Austrian landscape (see Vansant 1999). Similarly, a visit to Transylvania is an opportunity for tourists to engage with broader Western fantasises of Otherness, particularly the enchantment promised by the region's association with the supernatural.

Film and television are as influential as literature in transforming places so that they accord more closely with the expectations of tourists. One of the best examples is Verona, famously the setting for Shakespeare's *Romeo and Juliet* (Williams 2002, Teller and Ratcliffe 2006). A Hollywood production of the play was released in 1936. The popularity of the film (which was nominated for four Academy Awards) led the Veronese city authority to develop some recognizable sights in the city to cater for tourists on the trail of Shakespeare's unfortunate lovers. The city purchased a house in the city centre in 1936 and added a balcony. Later, a statue of Juliet was set up below the balcony. Although neither Romeo nor Juliet had any existence outside fiction, the balcony is today Verona's biggest tourist attraction. Similarly, following the success of *Braveheart* a statue loosely modelled on Mel Gibson's portrayal of William Wallace was erected close to the Wallace Memorial in Stirling. It created an easily photographable site to link

Stirling and Wallace to the film (Beeton 2005). Moreover, the local tourist board was able to capitalize on the film by branding the surrounding area as 'Braveheart Country' (Edensor 2002).

In contemporary societies, literature, cinema and television play a decisive role in shaping the way that we think about places and the people that inhabit them. Books and films create and circulate portrayals of places and landscapes that, in turn, can lead to the construction of enduring place myths. Such myths can have a powerful allure for tourists. Literary and film-induced tourism are phenomena based on tourists visiting places that they have encountered previously through a literary or cinematic representation. Tourists' expectations of the 'real' place may be high but there always exists the possibility that a literary or cinematic place may disappoint and fail to live up to expectations. However, the nature of tourist demand is such that real places are increasingly being transformed by their representations in books or films. Places are remade so that they more closely resemble and accord with their literary or cinematic myths. Moreover, literary and cinematic landscapes are also remade through the ongoing performances of the tourists who visit them. Yet, host communities may not always welcome the way that they are represented in books or films and may attempt to resist demands that they be transformed into something which tourists expect. These issues are particularly relevant to Dracula tourism in Romania: this phenomenon is an example of literary and screen tourism that is generated outside the country and which Romania is reluctant to encourage.

Chapter 2
The Dracula of Literature

Bram Stoker's *Dracula*

In 1897 – the year of Queen Victoria's Diamond Jubilee – the London firm Archibald Constable and Company published the novel *Dracula*. Its author, Bram Stoker, had been born in Dublin in 1847 and, after studying mathematics at Trinity College, he worked as a civil servant. During his free time he started writing theatre reviews for local newspapers. One of these caught the attention of Henry Irving, later considered to be the greatest actor of the day, and in 1878 Stoker moved to London to work for Irving as manager of the Lyceum Theatre. He remained with the Lyceum until its closure in 1902. While working in London he also turned to writing novels and short stories with horror and romantic themes. In 1890 he embarked on a much larger work of vampire-based horror fiction. *Dracula* received mixed reviews after its publication, but over time achieved a fame which none of Stoker's other novels ever enjoyed: it came to be regarded as the definitive work of Gothic horror fiction, giving rise to one of the most enduring literary myths of the twentieth century (Leatherdale 1993). It was to bring Stoker worldwide fame, although not during the author's lifetime.

Beliefs in vampires and similar supernatural creatures exist in various forms throughout the world and can be traced back to ancient Egypt, Greece and Rome (Beresford 2008). However, it was writers of fiction during the nineteenth century that brought the vampire into popular consciousness. The first vampire novel dates from 1819 when *The Vampyre* by John Polidori was published (under Lord Byron's name). Other notable landmarks of nineteenth-century vampire fiction included James Malcolm Rymer's *Varney the Vampire* (1847) and Joseph Sheridan Le Fanu's *Carmilla* (1872). Thus, by the time that *Dracula* was published the vampire was a well-established figure in Gothic literature (Frayling 1991, McGrath 1997). However, Stoker took the genre to a new height introducing a vampire was far more sinister and menacing than anything that had appeared previously. Nevertheless, such was the popularity of Gothic and horror fiction in the late nineteenth century that, when it was published, *Dracula* appeared commonplace as another adventure story pitting Englishmen against foreign monsters (Auerbach and Skal 1997).

The plot of Dracula unfolds as follows: in May 1893 Jonathan Harker, a solicitor, travels to Transylvania to conclude the sale of various properties in England with a mysterious Hungarian aristocrat, Count Dracula. After a stay at the Golden Crown hotel in Bistritz (Bistriţa) he travels to Dracula's castle in the Borgo Pass (see Figure 2.1). Harker soon realizes that he is a prisoner in the castle and that Dracula is not entirely human. Dracula leaves Harker to his fate and travels by sea from Varna (in Bulgaria) to England. He arrives in Whitby in Yorkshire where he finds his first victim in Lucy Westenra (Lucy's closest friend, Mina Murray is coincidently Jonathan Harker's fiancée). Dr John Seward, a former suitor of Lucy, is called to provide medical assistance but is unable to diagnose Lucy's illness and instead summons his mentor, Dr Van Helsing, from Amsterdam. On his arrival Van Helsing recognizes Lucy's need for a blood transfusion, and over the coming weeks she receives blood from her fiancé Arthur Holmwood, Seward, Van Helsing himself and Quincey Morris (another of Lucy's former suitors). Despite these efforts, Lucy dies, but returns to life as an undead vampire. Van Helsing later ends her vampiric existence by driving a wooden stake through her heart. Meanwhile, Mina has married Jonathan Harker who had managed to escape from Castle Dracula. Van Helsing reads Jonathan's diary and calls together the various characters to explain the nature of the threat posed by Dracula. The group resolve to track down and destroy the Count. In the course of pursuing Dracula, Mina also becomes the vampire's victim. Tracked to London, Dracula realizes he has no choice but to flee to Transylvania. He is pursued in a chase through Romania that ends at Castle Dracula. In the climax of the novel Harker and Quincey Morris kill Dracula, Morris dies in the struggle, and Mina is released from the vampire's spell. The story ends with a return visit to Transylvania by the Harkers some years later when they reflect on the strange events which they had experienced.

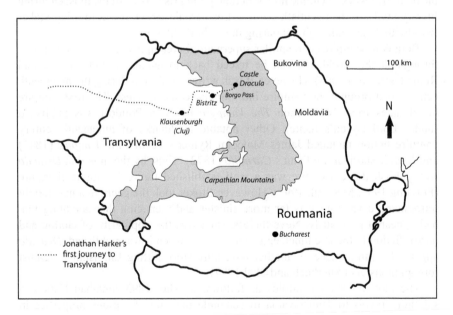

Figure 2.1   The Romanian setting of Bram Stoker's *Dracula*

Since its publication *Dracula* has enjoyed enormous success. The novel has never been out of print and has been translated into at least 29 other languages (Melton undated). Despite this apparent popularity it does not appear to be a widely read book. As Leatherdale (1993: 9) notes, a common response to the question 'Have you read Dracula?' is 'No, but I saw the film'. In fact, *Dracula* is 'probably the best-known unread novel in the world' (Miller 1997: 199). When, in 2003, the British Broadcasting Corporation invited the UK public to choose its 100 favourite books, *Dracula* was not among them.

Dracula was largely ignored in the academic world until the 1970s, from which time a 'veritable 'academic industry'' (Gelder 1994: 65) has grown up around the novel. The novel has generated a wealth of research studies and even has its own dedicated journal (*The Journal of Dracula Studies*). As Gelder (65) notes, *Dracula* enables a wide range of interpretations: 'It is ... a textually dense narrative, written from a number of perspectives or 'points of view', which brings together a multiplicity of discursive fields ... this is a novel which seems (these days, especially) to generate readings, rather than close them down'. Consequently, *Dracula* can be read in a variety of ways (see Carter 1988a, Leatherdale 1993, Miller 1997, 2000, Gibson 2006, Skal 2004): it can be viewed as a struggle between good and evil; a detective story; a Christian allegory (or parody); a critique of modernity; a tale of cultural xenophobia; a commentary on nineteenth century European politics; or as an analogy of the Cold War. The novel has been analysed from Psychoanalytical, Marxist, Feminist, Postcolonial, narratological and Darwinian perspectives. Literary critics have explored themes such as sexuality; class; backwardness versus modernity; superstition versus science; West versus East; perceived national decline in Imperial Britain; reverse colonization; and the personal and political influences on Bram Stoker himself. There are undoubtedly many new interpretations still to come. Consequently, there is, as Gelder (1994: 65) notes, no longer one *Dracula*, but many *Draculas*, which 'compete for attention in the academic/student marketplace'.

In this context, the role of tourism in *Dracula* has not been overlooked. This is hardly surprising since travel is a constant theme within the novel and the various characters are constantly on the move (see Pile 2005). Thus, Jonathan Harker is himself a business tourist in Transylvania, travelling from the West to the East while, to use Arata's memorable phrase (1990), Count Dracula himself is an 'Occidental tourist', travelling in the opposite direction. Van Helsing spends much of his time shuttling between Holland and England, while the various other characters are frequently on the move between Whitby, London and Exeter. Various diaries, journals and notes are written whilst travelling on the train. In this sense, *Dracula* is characterized by the restless mobility of the key protagonists. The visit by the Harkers to Transylvania that concludes the novel is a holiday overtly based on 'Dark' tourism!

Dracula and Transylvania

Dracula is inseparable from Transylvania. In fact, only six of the novel's 27 chapters are set there (Miller 2000) and most of the action unfolds in Victorian England. Nevertheless, Transylvania has come to be almost synonymous in the Western popular imagination with vampires. As Gelder (1994: 1) notes: 'One of the peculiarities of vampire fiction is that it has – with great success – turned a real place into a fantasy. It is impossible, now, to hear the name [Transylvania] *without* thinking of vampires; the very word invokes an image of something unbelievable'. One illustration of this is a survey of over 500 American students undertaken by Dresser (1989) in which half believed that vampires originated in Transylvania. Yet, Arata (1990: 627) reminds us that the seemingly 'natural' association of Transylvania with vampires is something that began with (rather than which predates) Stoker.

Such is the mythology that has grown up around Transylvania that many in the West are surprised to learn that Transylvania is a real place. In fact, Transylvania is one of three regions that make up contemporary Romania. Transylvania is a Latin word meaning 'The Land Beyond the Forest'. Romanians call the region *Ardeal* while it is also known as *Erdely* (in Hungarian) and *Siebenburgen* (in German). Transylvania is an upland plateau lying within the arc of the Carpathian Mountains (see Figure 2.1). Most of the region features rolling hills that are extensively utilized for agriculture and it is only those sections that border the Carpathians that are mountainous. Transylvania has long been an area of mixed population. The largest ethnic group is Romanians who claim continuity of settlement in the area since the Roman occupation in the first century AD. Transylvania was also settled by Magyars (Hungarians) in the ninth century and Germans (Saxons) were invited to the region in the twelfth century to defend the southern frontier. For much of its history Transylvania was under Hungarian rule and when Bram Stoker wrote *Dracula* the region was a part of the Austro-Hungarian Empire. In December 1918, following the collapse of the Empire at the end of the First World War, Transylvania became a part of Romania.

Bram Stoker had never visited Transylvania. Indeed, his working notes indicate that he had originally intended to locate *Dracula* in an area of eastern Austria known as Styria (Leatherdale 1987). In doing so, Stoker was following a well-established practice in Gothic fiction of locating evil and horror in marginal or peripheral locations (Goldsworthy 1998, Seaton 2000). However, at some stage in the early 1890s Stoker decided to move Dracula's home further eastwards to Transylvania. Miller (1997) suggests that he made this decision after reading an article about Transylvanian superstitions by Emily Gerard (1885). Gerard, the wife of an officer in the Hungarian army, lived in Transylvania for two years and enthusiastically researched local traditions and beliefs. She portrayed the region as a place where superstition was rife:

Transylvania might well be termed the land of superstition, for nowhere else does this curious crooked plant of delusion flourish as persistently and in such bewildering variety. It would almost seem as though the whole species of demons, pixies, witches, and hobgoblins, driven from the rest of Europe by the wand of science, had taken refuge within this mountain rampart, well aware that here they would find secure lurking places, whence they might defy their persecutors yet awhile. (1885: 128)

Gerard is also emphatic on the association of vampires with Transylvania: 'Most decidedly evil, however, is the vampire, or nosferatu, in whom every Roumanian peasant believes as firmly as he does in heaven or hell' (1885: 142). Yet, the source of her observations is not clear since, while vampire legends are widespread in Eastern Europe, the vampire as such is unknown in Romanian folklore. Transylvanian folklore instead knows the *strigoi* (which loosely translates as 'ghost'), an undead spirit and in no cases a drinker of blood. In fact, the word vampire (which is of Slavic origin) is almost unknown in Romania: the word entered Romanian from French in the nineteenth century and its use was largely confined to literary works. As for *Nosferatu*, the word has never been encountered in over 200 years of recording Romanian folklore.[1]

Gerard's account of Transylvania seems to have convinced Stoker that the region represented an ideal home for his vampire-Count. His working notes indicate that he subsequently read a number of travellers' accounts of the region, principally Boner (1865), Crosse (1878), Anon (1881) and Johnson (1885). All these works tend to treat Transylvania as a primitive, remote, but faintly exotic corner of Europe and to varying extents they were all prone to the sweeping generalizations which characterized English travellers' accounts of southeast Europe (Todorova 2009). Stoker liberally borrowed from these sources (in the absence of any personal experience of the region) to create his distinctive portrait of Transylvania. However, his knowledge of Transylvania and its people seems to have been, at best, superficial (Light 2005). Stoker was not a particularly meticulous researcher (Miller 1998) and did not question the accuracy of his sources (indeed, many of their inaccuracies found their way into his novel)

One of the most insistent themes in Dracula is that of a threat coming from the East. Thus, Count Dracula himself is an alien predator from the East, who is intent on contaminating and corrupting British society. He represents 'those forces in Eastern Europe which seek to overthrow, through violence and subversion, the more progressive, democratic civilization of the West' (Wasson 1966: 24). As such Stoker's novel expresses long established Western discourses about the periphery as the source of danger and moral invasion (Seaton 2000). However, Arata (1990) also interprets Dracula as an expression of a wider fear in late-Victorian Britain (itself plagued with anxiety about perceived national decline) that the 'civilized' world is prey for colonization by primitive and barbaric forces.

---

1   Sabina Ispas, Interview.

As such Stoker portrayed Transylvania as a suitable home for a monster. It is a remote and almost unknown place on the very edge of Europe, far removed from the 'civilized' West. Thus Jonathan Harker describes the Carpathian Mountains as 'one of the wildest and least known portions of Europe' (Stoker 1997: 10). Moreover, Transylvania is more explicitly located as 'beyond' the West. As Harker leaves Budapest he comments: 'The impression I had was that we were leaving the West and entering the East' (9). Harker's repeated exasperation over the lack of punctuality in the region – 'It seems to me that the further East you go the more unpunctual are the trains' (11) – underlines the shift from the orderliness of the West to the unpredictability of the East (Gelder 1994).

Stoker asserts the 'Easternness' of Transylvania in other ways. The region is represented as a place where Western rationality has not penetrated and which, instead, is ruled by superstition and the supernatural. Such a portrayal owes much to Gerard. Thus, Jonathan Harker states: 'I read that every known superstition in the world is gathered into the horseshoe of the Carpathians, as if it were the centre of some sort of imaginative whirlpool' (Stoker 1997: 10). Later he is told: 'It is the eve of St George's Day. Do you not know that tonight, when the clock strikes midnight, all the evil things in the world will have full sway?' (12). Similarly, Mina Harker describes the local people as '*very, very* superstitious' (312). Stoker was not alone in representing Transylvania in this way. Jules Verne's novel *The Castle in the Carpathians* published in 1892 (which Stoker may or may not have read) was also set in Western Transylvania and Verne was similarly insistent that the region was a primitive and backward place. For example, he described Transylvania as one of the most superstitious countries of Europe, and a place 'still much attached to the superstitions of the early ages' (1).

In writing *Dracula* Bram Stoker created a powerful and enduring place myth (Shields 1991, Urry 1995) of Transylvania. He portrayed the region as a marginal, backward and sinister place on the very edge of Europe where the supernatural reigns supreme (Light 2008). It is 'a land beyond scientific understanding – a netherworld' (Leatherdale 1993: 109). Yet, Stoker was not describing Transylvania (after all he had no firsthand experience to draw on): instead his Transylvania was an imaginative construct that expressed both the established traditions of Gothic fiction and well-embedded Western discursive myths about the periphery. In writing *Dracula* Stoker created a specific imaginative geography of Transylvania in the minds of his readers as 'a distinctly eastern portion of Europe where the laws and customs of the West do not apply' (Wasson 1966: 24). Stoker's Transylvania is emphatically pre-modern and non-Western. In other words, it is the social and spatial Other of Victorian Britain.

Such a representation of Transylvania can be situated within a broader context. In particular *Dracula* is grounded in – and reproduces – the seemingly natural division of Europe into East and West (Dittmer 2002/2003) whereby the eastern part of Europe is regarded as backward, underdeveloped and fundamentally different from the West. This way of thinking about the east of Europe has – perhaps unsurprisingly – its origins in Western Europe. Wolff (1994) argues that since the eighteenth century the West has sought to define itself as modern, developed and civilized. In affirming its own precedence in this way Western Europe simultaneously constructed other places as being somehow different or inferior to the West. Thus Western Europe invented its imaginative counterpart in Eastern Europe, a region that came to be regarded with ambivalence, suspicion and condescension. This idea of 'Eastern Europe' has proved extremely enduring and the belief in a Europe divided into two halves has gained a pervasive hold on the Western imagination.

Todorova (1997, 2009) extends this analysis with particular reference to southeast Europe, taking as her starting point Edward Said's celebrated analysis of 'Orientalism' (1995). Said focused on the practices within colonial contexts through which the West has constructed myths about non-Western people and places so as to construct them as Others. In particular, Said examined Western ways of representing the Orient (defined not as a specific geographical location but as a more vaguely imagined 'East' in the minds of Westerners) and argued that as the West sought to define itself as being modern, rational and progressive, the Orient was represented as somewhere exotic and mysterious, but also static and backward. While European identities have typically been constructed with reference to 'the East' as Other (Neumann 1999), different areas of the 'East' have been treated in different ways. In particular, Todorova argues that Balkanism – the ways in which the West has dealt with and represented southeast Europe – is something different from Orientalism. She argues that while Orientalism 'is a discourse about an imputed opposition, Balkanism is a discourse about an imputed ambiguity' (2009: 17). The Balkans (by which we can also understand southeastern Europe more generally) is a region evoked as a 'bridge' or 'crossroads' (15). It is a liminal space (Bjelić 2002), a region that is characterized by its 'in-betweenness' (Todorova 2009: 18) and its transitional status between West and East. As southeast Europe came to be regarded as the Other of Western Europe it was at the same time the Other 'within' (Todorova 2009: 188). It is a region that is in Europe but not 'fully' European (Wolff 1994, Dittmer 2002/2003).

Dracula is clearly an early expression of the Balkanist discourse. The novel is insistent on a clash between West and East (Gibson 2006) and highlights the opposition between 'Western progress and Eastern stasis, between Western science and Eastern superstition, between Western reason and Eastern emotion, between Western civilization and Eastern barbarism' (Arata 1990: 637). Stoker's Transylvania is 'one of the wildest and least known portions of Europe', but it is part of Europe nonetheless. Although peripheral, Transylvania is a distant part of the Austro-Hungarian Empire, and is connected with the rest of Europe through a modern (if slow) rail network. It is a region where the local population speaks German further underlining connections with Central Europe. Count Dracula, who speaks 'excellent German' (Stoker 1997: 18), is an Austro-Hungarian nobleman with many of the usual attributes of a European aristocrat (Leatherdale 1993). His spoken English is near perfect (and much better than that of the Dutchman, Van Helsing) and he has little difficulty in passing unnoticed in London society.

Both Todorova (2009) and Goldsworthy (1998) highlight the role of popular fiction in constructing 'Eastern Europe' as being strange, backward and 'different'. *Dracula* is no exception. Indeed, as one of the earliest and most influential novels set in this region, *Dracula* has played a central role – perhaps *the* central role – in this respect. Throughout the twentieth century (and particularly since Hollywood discovered vampires) *Dracula* has continued to structure the ways in which Transylvania – and Romania more generally – is viewed in the Western popular imagination. Transylvania exists as an extraordinary place and the seemingly natural home of strangeness and the supernatural. For example, Brokaw (1976: 12) enthuses: 'What other land calls up such mystical visions of shrouded, misty forests; of driverless coaches pounding up treacherous, uncharted trails to hidden castles; of black-cloaked figures stalking across moonlit cemeteries in the chill of night?'.

Popular fiction in the twentieth and twenty first centuries has continued to equate Transylvania with vampires (although, as Skal (1996: 194) wryly observes, the region has also become a 'pop culture dumping ground for just about every monster under the sun'). For example, in Anne Rice's *Interview with the Vampire* (1976) two American vampires travel to Eastern Europe in search of their roots. There they encounter local people who are 'savages' compared to Westerners (195), while Transylvanian vampires are mindless animated corpses and 'monstrous creatures' (265) compared with the elegant and urbane vampires of Paris. Similarly, in J.K. Rowling's Harry Potter series, Romania (and Eastern Europe more widely) is the home for some of the strange creatures that Harry encounters (see also Shandley et al. 2006). In *Harry Potter and the Philosopher's Stone* (1997), Ron Weasley announces that his brother is in Romania studying dragons,[2] while Professor Quirrell's classroom smells 'strongly of garlic, which everyone said was to ward off a vampire he'd met in Romania and was afraid would be coming back to get him one of these days' (100).

However, it is not only popular fiction that portrays Transylvania in this way. Instead the Balkanist discourse is present in many contemporary forms of popular culture. One of these is tourism promotion, an activity well known for appropriating and reinforcing cultural stereotypes (see Morgan and Pritchard 1998). Thus, it is not surprising that many tourism representations portray Romania/Transylvania as a remote and magical place offering excitement and enchantment that cannot be found at home. For example, one guidebook stated that that 'Romania is a country of crazy superstitions and fantastic legends' (Williams and Wildman 2001: 13). Another states: 'Transylvania … is famed as the homeland of Dracula, a mountainous place where storms lash medieval hamlets, while wolves – or

---

2   In the Romanian edition of *Harry Potter and the Philosopher's Stone* Ron announces that his brother is in Romania studying 'vampires and dragons' (Rowling 2001: 79) although there is no such mention of vampires in Rowling's original. Why did the translator add this reference to vampires for a Romanian readership? It may indicate a recognition in Romania that, for contemporary English readers, Romania is synonymous with vampires.

werewolves – howl from the surrounding woods. The fictitious image is accurate up to a point' (Burford and Longley 2011: 123). Similarly, websites and tourist brochures (especially those produced by Western companies) promoting holidays in Romania continue to evoke the region in language that directly echoes *Dracula* (see for example Hovi 2008a). One brochure has described Transylvania in the following terms:

> Transylvania! The very word conjures up romantic images of a mysterious land where myths and legends are closely woven into the fabric of everyday life. Wooded forests line the slopes of the Carpathian mountains – home, rumour has it, to werewolves and vampires! Towering castles with fairytale turrets grace the skyline … And is Count Dracula man or myth – we'll let you decide! (Shearings Holidays 2001: 127)

Another states:

> Romania is a magical country, full of surprises and with breathtaking scenery … We can't include Romania in our brochure without mentioning Dracula. Legend has it that he lived in a castle in Transylvania … So if you can tear yourself away from the slopes for a few hours the visit to Dracula's castle is well worth it. (Balkan Holidays 2004: 44)

Thus, the continuing resonance of Bram Stoker's portrayal of Transylvania, more than a century after *Dracula* was published is unmistakeable. In addition to his immortal vampire-Count, Stoker's most enduring legacy has been the creation of a particular 'way of seeing' Transylvania. As a result of Stoker's novel, Transylvania exists as an immediately recognizable metaphor for Otherness in the Western popular imagination. It is a form of *lieux d'imagination* (Reijnders 2010, 2011b) a location anchored in the collective imagination that is the point of entry into an imagined world of vampires and the supernatural. Needless to say, this way of thinking about Transylvania is deeply unwelcome in Romania; yet it is also something over which Romania has little control. I shall return to this theme in later chapters.

Dracula in Western Popular Culture

Although *Dracula* is a nineteenth-century novel it was during the twentieth century that it made its mark (Auerbach and Skal 1997). Over the course of the twentieth century and beyond, *Dracula* has become an enduring element of popular culture, especially in America where Count Dracula has become as iconic a figure as the Big Mac (Dresser 1989). Theatre and especially cinema were quick to recognize the dramatic possibilities of Stoker's novel and were instrumental in introducing Dracula to a wider audience. The first cinematic version was apparently a Hungarian production made in 1921 (Skal 2004), but it is F.W. Murnau's *Nosferatu* of 1922, loosely based on Stoker's novel, which is the most acclaimed early production. Considered to be a masterpiece of German expressionism (Brown 1997), Max Schreck played the villainous Count Orlock, complete with bald head, pointed ears and long sinister fingernails. From the outset, the film departed from Stoker's novel since it introduced the now familiar motif of the vampire being killed by sunlight (something which does not appear in the novel).

The first stage play based on the novel opened in 1924 and ran for three years in English provincial theatres before transferring to London where it enjoyed considerable success. The play's director, Hamilton Deane, made further changes to the image of Dracula, conceiving the Count as a 'kind of devilish vaudeville magician in evening dress and an opera cloak' (Skal 1997: 377). A revised version of the production opened in America in 1927 with the Hungarian actor Bela Lugosi taking the title role. Lugosi had been born in 1882 in the Banat (a region which was at that time a part of the Austro-Hungarian Empire but which was transferred, along with Transylvania, to Romania after the First World War). He emigrated to America in 1920 where, despite experiencing difficulties in learning English, he found success as an actor (Cremer 1976, Lennig, 2003).

Lugosi starred in the first cinematic version of Dracula to be made in America. Universal Studio's *Dracula*, made in 1931, is another widely acknowledged classic. Lugosi introduced Deane's portrayal of Dracula to a wide audience and in many ways created the definitive image of the vampire in the modern popular consciousness (Brown 1997). Lugosi's Dracula was less a sinister predator and more a suave and elegant (and fangless) European aristocrat, dressed in black cape, with sleek, swept-back black hair and speaking in heavily accented English (Skal 2004). But this Dracula lacked most of the menace of Stoker's character: consequently, he was 'almost immediately absorbed by American culture and transformed into a meaningless pop icon no more threatening to society than Tinkerbell or Donald Duck' (Brown 1997: 273). Universal's *Dracula* was a big success and brought the studio its first profit for two years (Skal 2004) and it paved the way for Hollywood's future engagement with horror films.

In the late 1950s Count Dracula appeared in a series of films produced in the UK by Hammer Films. The first of these films, titled *Dracula* (released in America under the title *The Horror of Dracula*), was produced in 1958. Starring Christopher Lee as Dracula and Peter Cushing as Van Helsing it departed from Stoker's novel and presented the story as a struggle between the forces of good and evil (Melton 2011). Lee redefined the central character, making Dracula more menacing (partly through the addition of fangs) while emphasizing the Count's sexual ferocity (Gelder 1994). Hammer films produced seven Dracula films and a further six vampire films and reputedly saved the British film industry (Gelder 1994). Christopher Lee was to play the Count for over 15 years.

The late 1970s saw another surge in the production of Dracula and vampire films, particularly in America (Karg et al. 2009). Universal Studios remade *Dracula* in 1979 and a series of large budget vampire films followed in the 1980s.

One of the most notable productions was Francis Ford Coppola's lavish *Bram Stoker's Dracula* of 1992, which sought to return to the novel for inspiration. By 2010 more than 350 films had been made that featured Count Dracula in some way (Browning and Picart 2011); the Count is the second most frequently represented character in film after Sherlock Holmes (Skal 2004). Such has been the success of cinema in circulating the image of Dracula throughout the world that the Count 'is best known to the public as a quintessential Hollywood icon, and only secondarily as the fictional creation of Bram Stoker' (Skal 1997: 371).

From cinematic beginnings a much broader vampire subculture emerged in America. This began to take off in the 1970s which, as Auerbach (1995: 131) argues was the 'halcyon decade for vampires when they not only flourished but reinvented themselves'. Thus, within American popular culture, vampires took on a vigour of their own that was increasingly independent of Dracula. Again cinema played a key role and by 1995 more than 500 vampire films had been made globally, over a third of them in America (Skal 1996). Among the most popular recent examples are the films of the *Twilight* series (based on the novels by Stephanie Meyers) that have enjoyed huge global success.

Similarly, vampires have thrived on television (Karg et al 2009, Miller 2003). In addition to made-for-television versions of Dracula, particular landmarks include two situation comedies, *The Addams Family* and *The Munsters,* both broadcast for the first time in 1964. A soap opera called *Dark Shadows* broadcast in America between 1966 and 1971 saw its ratings increase dramatically after a vampire was introduced into the script. The show generated a range of spinoff books and comics as well as a festival and various fan clubs. In the UK an animated cartoon series – *Count Duckula* – enjoyed success in the late 1980s and was later shown in America. *Buffy the Vampire Slayer* was a successful film in 1992. The subsequent television series (1997–2003) ran to more than 140 episodes and rapidly achieved cult status on both sides of the Atlantic. The spinoff series *Angel* (1999–2004) ran to over 100 episodes. Among the notable successors to Buffy have been the television series *True Blood* (2008 onwards) and the supernatural drama/comedy series *Being Human* (2009 onwards). This latest generation of vampires has fewer (if any) ties to Transylvania and, although Transylvania remains firmly established in Western popular culture as the home of Dracula, modern vampires can originate from (and be at home in) almost any country.

Vampires have also thrived in print. During the 1970s a diverse and vigorous vampire literature emerged. Horror comics boomed in America following the relaxation of earlier regulation: these included *Vampirella* and *The Tomb of Dracula* among their titles (Melton 2011). In addition a number of influential vampire novels were published including *Salem's Lot* by Stephen King (1975); Anne Rice's *Interview with the Vampire* (1976); and *Hotel Transylvania* by Chelsea Quinn Yarbro (1978). Vampire fiction exploded throughout the 1980s and 1990s and by 1999 more than 1,000 vampire novels had been published, over 80 per cent of which had appeared after 1970 (Melton 1999). Vampire fiction has enjoyed especial popularity among a young adult readership as the commercial and critical success of Stephanie Meyers's *Twilight* series (2005–8) indicates. Moreover, vampires have also been the inspiration for art, musicals, ballets, video games and even opera (Skal 2004).

The growing popular interest in Dracula and vampires was mirrored by an ever increasing number of societies and fan clubs to cater for people with similar interests (Melton 1999). In America, devotees of Bram Stoker's novel established the Count Dracula Society (1962) and the Count Dracula Fan Club (now called the 'Vampire Empire') (1965). In the UK the Dracula Society was established in 1973 and in Ireland the 'Bram Stoker Society' was created in 1980. As interest spread beyond Stoker's *Dracula* a range of broader vampire-orientated organizations were established. These included two Vampyre Societies (1987), the Vampire Guild (1990) and the Whitby Dracula Society in the UK, Vampire Studies Society (1977), Vampire Information Exchange (1978) and Vampire Junction (1991) in America. Other fan clubs were based on particular books or television shows such as 'Anne Rice's Vampire Lestat Fan Club' (1988) and 'The Munsters and the Addams Family Fan Club' (1988). Dracula and vampire scholars founded the 'Lord Ruthvan Assembly' (1988) as a special interest group within the 'International Association for the Fantastic in the Arts'. With the rise of the internet many traditional fan clubs were superseded by a plethora of websites that enabled Dracula/vampire enthusiasts to make contact, chat and share information. By 2007 there were more than 250 English-language fan sites dedicated to *Twilight* alone (Melton 2011).

Various forms of fashion and lifestyle have taken their inspiration directly or indirectly from Dracula. The 'Gothic' movement has its origins in the UK in the late 1970s and reached America in the early 1990s (Melton 2011). Many (although not all) 'Goths' are attracted to the image of the vampire as an outsider, rebel or nonconformist. They typically dress in loose, black clothing with pale make-up and various accessories including chain mail and silver jewellery. Goth music developed from punk and is characterized by a melancholy emphasis on the darker aspects of life (Melton 2011) and in some cases has caused panic and outrage among older generations. Other enthusiasts seek to imitate or adopt the vampire lifestyle to varying degrees (see Karg et al. 2009). Such activities range from simple role playing (such as dressing as Dracula with long black capes and plastic fangs) to more extreme attempts to take on the identity of a vampire (which might involve sleeping in coffins or graveyards, and filing the canine teeth or arranging fang implants). There are also reports of people who believe themselves to be vampires and behave accordingly, avoiding sunlight and engaging in consensual blood drinking (Dresser 1989, Guiley 1991).

More than 100 years after the publication of *Dracula* the popularity of Stoker's vampire-Count shows no sign of waning. Indeed, in a 2010 poll organized by a science fiction magazine Count Dracula was voted the most popular vampire (Anon 2010). Moreover the vampire has become an established and enduring element of contemporary popular culture in a way which Stoker himself could never have imagined. Representing the outsider, alien or Other, the vampire has proved to be an endlessly adaptable figure, able to represent and articulate a range of meanings that are both located in (and at the same time, beyond) culture (Gelder 1994). While Dracula has become a global myth, enthusiasm for the vampire is best developed in America. As Dresser (1989: 200) argues, 'American vampires have adopted to the soil to which they have been transplanted, reflecting the individualism of the American people' (see also Auerbach 1995). As the vampire has increased in popularity its image has evolved: contemporary vampires bear almost no relation to the vampires of folklore and have little in common with the vampires of Gothic literature. Instead, the vampire has changed from Stoker's predator to something more familiar (Guiley 1991). Today the image of the vampire is something with instant recognition and powerful resonance. It is unsurprising that it has been embraced by consumer culture and is now used to sell an increasingly diverse range of products.

The Literary Dracula in Romania

Gothic fiction has not enjoyed much popularity in Romania although the vampire – as a foreign import – makes occasional appearances in Romanian literature. Ion Luca Caragiale's play of 1884, *O scrisoare pierdută* ('A lost letter'), contains the first appearance of the word 'vampire' in Romanian literature (Iulian 2004), transformed for comic effect into 'Bampir'. However, although Stoker's *Dracula* has enjoyed global success the fictional Dracula was almost entirely unknown in Romania until 1990. Parts of the novel seem to have been published in some form during the interwar period (Light 2009b) and Ion Mânzat (see Chapter 4) recalls reading an abridged version of *Dracula* that was serialized in a popular magazine *Realitatea ilustrată*[3] during this period.[4] Those Romanians able to read foreign languages had more opportunities to read the whole novel. Several of Bucharest's libraries contain English-language versions from the early twentieth century. Moreover *Dracula* was translated into French in 1920 and, given that many educated Romanians were enthusiastically Francophile during the interwar period, it is also possible that some may have read the French edition.

---

3   *Realitatea ilustrată* ('Illustrated Reality') was a glossy weekly magazine concerned with celebrity gossip, fawning articles about the royal families of Romania and other European countries and features of general interest. From 1934 it published a supplement that contained an eclectic range of stories with a strong emphasis on horror, crime and the unexplained. These included articles in 1935 and 1939 about vampires. The supplement also contained regular abridged serializations of foreign novels (often with a horror theme). This seems a very likely place for the first translation of *Dracula* to have been published. However, there are few libraries in Romania that include *Realitatea ilustrată* in their collections and in any case these collections are sometimes incomplete or not available for public access. Consequently I have not yet been able locate the issues that contain the serialization of *Dracula* (see Light 2009b).

4   Ion Mânzat, interview, Mânzat (2008).

Following the declaration of the Romanian People's Republic in December 1947 and the imposition of a Soviet totalitarian model, rigorous censorship of all published materials was introduced (Ficeac 1999, Negrici 1999, Troncotă 2006). Any books considered unsuitable by the regime were withdrawn from general circulation and kept in special rooms to which access was strictly controlled. These included almost everything published by writers from capitalist countries (Ficeac 1999). As such, any Western editions of *Dracula* would certainly have been withdrawn from circulation. Given its attention to Romania's royal family *Realitatea ilustrată* would similarly have been withdrawn. At the same time the selling of old or second hand books was forbidden (Troncotă 2006). In these circumstances knowledge of *Dracula* was now confined to the limited number of people who had read the novel (or its abridged translation) before censorship was introduced.

Such rigid censorship continued until the late 1960s when Nicolae Ceauşescu, the new General Secretary of the Romanian Communist Party (RCP) introduced a period of relative liberalization in Romanian cultural life. Censorship was relaxed (but never abandoned) and translations of many novels by foreign writers were published (Troncotă 2006). One example was Jules Verne's *The Castle in the Carpathians* that had been translated into Romanian in the interwar period. Despite the focus on vampires and the supernatural Verne's novel was reissued in 1967. By the early 1970s *Dracula* seems to have been considered sufficiently inoffensive by the censors for a Romanian translation to be prepared and Cioculescu (1971) makes reference to a forthcoming Romanian edition (Light 2009b). There were even articles about the fictional Dracula in *Romania pitorească* (a Romanian-language tourism brochure) suggesting that the state's censors were fairly relaxed about Dracula at this time (for example Păduraru 1972a, 1972b).

During this period Romanians also had other opportunities to encounter *Dracula*. For example, an increasing number were able to travel abroad (according to Petrescu (1971) 365,000 Romanians were permitted such travel in 1969) some of whom were able to purchase copies of the novel during their travels. A few Romanians were able to read copies which were left by Dracula enthusiasts visiting Romania, while some staff working for ONT (the national tourist office) were permitted to read the novel in order to understand better the demands of foreign tourists.[5] Some historians and literary critics who were researching the 'historical' Dracula seem also to have had access to the novel. While Dracula films were never shown in Romanian some Romanians living in border regions were occasionally able to see such films on foreign television (several Romanian friends from southwest Romania have told me of watching Dracula films featuring Bela Lugosi and Christopher Lee on Yugoslav television).

However, this period of liberalization proved to be short lived. In the 'July theses' of 1971 Ceauşescu condemned the liberalization of the late 1960s (Verdery 1991) and called for a return to centralized Party control and an end to autonomy

---

5   Nicolae Păduraru, interview.

in the cultural sphere. Censorship was reasserted and a list of prohibited books and authors was re-established (Verdery 1991, Negrici 1999). In this context, publication of the Romanian edition of *Dracula* was halted (Cioculescu 1990). Nevertheless, many educated Romanians were aware that the novel existed even if they were unaware of its contents. Since the book was forbidden it was assumed by some to be in some way subversive. Outside educational and literary circles the novel was largely unknown. For most Romanians, the name 'Dracula' (if it meant anything at all) was associated with Vlad Țepeș, a fifteenth-century Wallachian ruler (see Chapter 3).

For Romanians, the name 'Dracula' acquired an additional and sinister resonance during the late 1970s and 1980s. Nicolae Ceaușescu's regime became increasingly repressive during the 1980s when his decision to pay off Romania's foreign debt ahead of schedule created unprecedented austerity for ordinary Romanians. Romania experienced increasing international isolation while Ceaușescu, who had become the focus of a grotesque personality cult, was increasingly portrayed in the West as a predatory, vampiric figure who was quite literally sucking the life out of his country. As such, it was hardly surprising that the label 'Dracula' began to be attached more and more often to the figure of Ceaușescu himself. Thus, Ceaușescu's Romania became 'the land of Dracula', and Ceaușescu himself became 'the vampire of the Carpathians' (Iulian 2004: 90). In response, the Romanian authorities seem to have done what they could to discourage use of the word 'Dracula' and especially any association of Dracula with Ceaușescu. However, the vampirization of the dictator proved unstoppable and had apparently reached such an extent that, after the 1989 Revolution, rumours circulated in Bucharest that Ceaușescu had drunk the blood of new born babies to increase his strength (Sweeney 1991).

Following Ceaușescu's overthrow in December 1989, Romania committed itself hesitantly to a new political and economic course. Censorship was ended and a Romanian edition of *Dracula* (Stoker 1990) was published in late 1990. The novel was initially much sought after among educated Romanians who were keen to learn more of this Dracula about which they had heard so much. But among those Romanians who have read the novel the general reaction seems to have been disappointment in discovering that the book was simply a Gothic horror novel partly set in Romania and not a work of subversive samizdat fiction. On the other hand, Romanians were quite simply surprised that something like this could have been set in their country without them having any awareness of it (Boia 2001a). The enthusiasm for the novel was short lived in Romania and it is now easily found in secondhand bookshops. *Dracula* is a novel that most urban Romanians are aware of but (as in the rest of the world!) most have not bothered to read it.[6]

For some time Romanians showed little interest in the wider vampire subculture, despite the enthusiasm among young Romanians for all things American. A

---

6   I have only met two Romanians who have read Stoker's *Dracula* – and both gave up on the novel without finishing it.

Romanian edition of *Interview with the Vampire* was published in 1995 and episodes of *Buffy the Vampire Slayer* were shown on Romanian television. However these did not seem to generate much interest. Perhaps the increasing awareness that much of the Western world associates Romania with vampires was the reason for this initial unwillingness to embrace the vampire. However, the translation of the Harry Potter novels into Romanian and the success of the films have demonstrated that Romanians are increasingly familiar with the Western fantasy genre. In recent years the *Twilight* novels have also been translated into Romanian (the first in 2008) and the films have developed an increasingly enthusiastic following among young urban Romanians (Grecu 2009, Apostol 2010). Cultural globalization has also introduced Halloween to Romania (Caloian 2009) along with other 'global' traditions such as Easter bunnies, English Christmas Carols and St Valentine's Day. In this context it is probably only a matter of time before the vampire of Western popular culture finds a home in Romania.

Chapter 3
The Historical Dracula

The previous chapter introduced the Dracula of fiction. If Stoker's vampire-Count were the only figure to be named Dracula, then the development of Dracula tourism in Romania would be a relatively straightforward form of literary or screen tourism, constructed around a particular (if unwanted) literary myth. However, the situation in Romania is further complicated by the existence of an historic figure – Vlad III, better known as Vlad the Impaler – who was also known as Dracula and who is held in high regard in contemporary Romania. The confusion has been amplified by influential (if somewhat contrived) attempts to promote the Dracula of Romanian history as the inspiration for Stoker's vampire. Therefore, in order to understand fully the development of Dracula tourism in Romania we need to examine the significance of the 'historical' Dracula.

Vlad the Impaler

The life of Vlad III has been the subject of many biographies written by both Romanian historians (Giurescu 1974, Andreescu 1976, Stăvăruş 1978, Ciobanu 1979, Stoicescu 1976, 1979, Stoian 1989, Giurescu 1991, Dogaru 1994, 1995) and those from the West (McNally and Florescu 1972, Florescu and McNally 1973, Treptow 2000). That said, his date and place of birth remain uncertain. He was born sometime between 1428 and 1431 probably in Sighişoara in Transylvania. His father, Vlad II (also known as Vlad Dracul) was a member of the Basarab dynasty that had ruled Wallachia since the fourteenth century and was himself Voievode (or Prince) of Wallachia between 1436 and 1442. There is little except his place of birth that links Vlad the Impaler with Transylvania and most of his life was associated with Wallachia (see Figure 3.1).

In 1442 the Ottomans took Vlad and his brother Radu as hostages in order to ensure their father's loyalty. During his time as a captive Vlad learnt Turkish and developed an understanding of the workings of the Ottomans. After his release in 1448 he briefly occupied the throne of Wallachia (with Ottoman support) in the autumn of 1448 but was soon overthrown. In 1456 he regained the Wallachian throne and remained as ruler (Voievode) until 1462. His reign was characterized by his exceptional cruelty and severity and during this period he gained his reputation as 'The Impaler' (a name initially attributed to him by the Ottomans) from his practice of impaling his enemies (and anyone else who offended him) on wooden stakes. Horrific though it was, impalement was not an uncommon practice at the time (Giurescu 1991) although Vlad's use of it appears to have exceeded anything

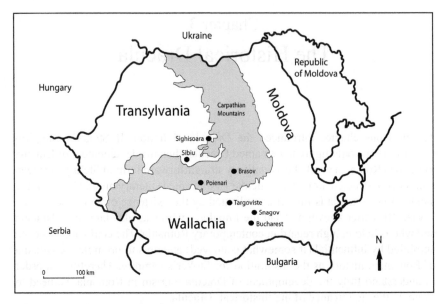

Figure 3.1　　Places in Romania associated with Vlad Tepeş

previously witnessed. His tactics were consistent with an era in which punishment was a public spectacle intended to induce terror and to manifest the power of the sovereign in the body of the executed (Foucault 1977).

On taking the throne, Vlad's first concern was to consolidate his authority and eliminate any internal threats to his position, particularly those posed by the Boyers (the landowning nobility). One famous story tells how, in April 1457, he invited the Boyers (whom he held responsible for the murder of his father and brother) and their families to an Easter feast from where they were captured, marched to Poienari and forced to work on building the Voievode's castle. He also launched punitive attacks on the Saxon communities of Kronstadt (Braşov) and Hermmanstadt (Sibiu) on various occasions since he suspected the Saxons of supporting rival claimants to his throne. During one attack on Kronstad, in August 1460, up to 30,000 Saxons were killed or impaled.

Having secured his throne from internal opposition Vlad turned his attention to the external threat represented by the Ottoman Empire. After several years of refusing to pay the tribute demanded by the Turks he crossed the Danube in 1461 and attacked Turkish fortresses with considerable success. Such provocation could not be ignored and in 1462 the Ottoman Sultan Mehmed II (apparently with an army of 250,000 people) invaded Wallachia with the intention of overthrowing the Impaler and placing his brother Radu on the throne. Vlad and his armies withdrew northwards whilst employing guerrilla tactics to attack the Turks. These included the famous night attack of June 1462 when the Impaler and his army attacked the Ottoman camp and came close to killing the Sultan himself. The Turks marched on to Vlad's capital, Târgovişte, where the Impaler had prepared a 'forest' of impaled bodies. Overawed and shocked the Sultan withdrew. However, the Turks later returned to pursue the Impaler who, abandoned by his Boyers, fled into Transylvania. He was later arrested by the Hungarian king, Matthias Corvinus and imprisoned in Buda. He was released in 1476 and briefly reoccupied the throne of Wallachia for a third time in November of that year before being killed in battle in December. His body was buried at Snagov monastery although his head was reportedly taken to the Sultan himself in Constantinople.

Within Wallachia (and among the Ottomans) Vlad was known as 'the Impaler' (in Romanian, Vlad Ţepeş) (Stoicescu 1976) although this was not a name he used himself. However, Vlad was also known during his lifetime as Drăculea (as well as by variants such as Drakulya, Drakole and Trakel). There are various theories of the derivation of this name (Andreescu 1976, Stoicescu 1976) but the most widely accepted is that it is derived from the Order of the Dragon into which Vlad's father had been invested in 1431 by the German Emperor Sighismund of Luxembourg. Membership of the Order was recognition of gallantry in battle and had no evil connotations (Florescu 1998). Since dragon was translated as *Dracul* in medieval Romanian, Vlad II was known as Vlad Dracul, or Vlad the Dragon. The name 'Dracula' (or Drăculea) was used for Vlad Dracul's son meaning 'son of the Dragon' and was intended to distinguish the father from his son. However, *Dracul* also has another meaning in Romanian: 'the devil'. 'Dracula' in this sense was increasingly adopted by the Voievode's enemies (particularly Transylvanian Saxons) as a form of abuse for a figure considered to be evil (Andreescu 1976). However, on his release from prison, Vlad Ţepeş himself seems to have adopted 'Dracula' and is known to have signed a number of letters this way (Andreescu 1976, Ciobanu 1979, Florescu 1998). Nevertheless, among Romanians he was (and is) remembered as Vlad Ţepeş and it is only relatively recently that Romanians have started to use the name 'Dracula'.

Uniquely among medieval rulers of southeast Europe, Vlad Ţepeş enjoyed notoriety throughout Europe, both during his lifetime and in the years after his death. A wide range of documentary sources written in German, Greek, Turkish and Russian refer to the life and deeds of 'Dracula' (McNally and Florescu 1972, Stăvăruş 1978, Ciobanu 1979, Florescu and McNally 1989, McNally 1991). The most influential were German manuscripts written around 1462 (and apparently based on eyewitness accounts from German monks), which related (often with great exaggeration) the atrocities committed by the Impaler. These German sources portrayed Vlad Ţepes as a brutal and sadistic psychopath – unsurprisingly since the Saxon community of southern Transylvania had frequently suffered at his hands. The recent invention of the printing press enabled these stories to spread rapidly throughout Europe: indeed Florescu and McNally (1989) suggest that these stories represent one of the earliest forms of horror literature. One of the most famous variants is a 1,070 line poem written by Michael Beheim probably in 1463 called *Story of a Bloodthirsty Madman Called Dracula of Wallachia*. A second set of pamphlets written in the late fifteenth and sixteenth centuries circulated in the German-speaking world and featured woodcut images of the

Impaler dining among a forest of impaled bodies. Yet, although German sources portray the Impaler in unremittingly negative terms they did not accuse him of being a vampire.

Another document about Vlad Ţepeş entitled *Tale about Voivode Dracula* was written in Slavic in the 1480s and circulated in Russia. This again related the Impaler's deeds in detail but presented him in a more sympathetic light as cruel but a lover of justice. The document states: 'Dracula so hated evil in his land that if someone stole, lied or committed some injustice he was not likely to stay alive' (cited in McNally and Florescu 1972). Nevertheless, the Slavic source was critical of the Voievode for having abandoned his Orthodox faith and converted to Catholicism whilst a prisoner. Other documents written by Greek and Ottoman historians also recorded the details of Vlad's battles, but since the Impaler was their former enemy they attempted to diminish his military successes.

Given the notoriety he achieved in the rest of Europe, the Romanian documentary sources (the Wallachian chronicles, written in the seventeenth century) are surprisingly sparse in detail about Vlad Ţepes. In these chronicles there is no mention of Dracula, but only of Vlad Ţepes who is portrayed in unexceptional terms as the prince who built the citadel of Poienari and the monastery of Snagov (Boia 2001b). The chronicle also records the Boyers of Târgovişte being forced to work at building Poienari Citadel (McNally 1991). However, the scantiness of the Romanian documentary sources is countered by a rich folklore tradition that preserved the memory of the Impaler, particularly in the area around Poienari (McNally and Florescu 1972, Ene 1976, McNally 1991). These traditions present the Impaler in a sharply different light from the German and Slavic narratives. Vlad Ţepeş is remembered as a 'great warrior and an ideal prince' (Duţu 1991: 210) or alternatively as a 'rational despot' (Florescu and McNally 1989: 216). The folklore narratives portray the Voievode as a strong and just leader who restored order to his country and defended its independence from Ottoman attack. Nothing in the Romanian folklore narratives associates Vlad Ţepeş with vampirism (Ene 1976).

During the nineteenth century many of these oral histories were collected by ethnographers so that the life and deeds of Vlad Ţepeş became more widely known among the Romanians. At the same time, the national idea was taking hold among the Romanian intelligentsia who sought emancipation from the Ottoman and Russian empires. One element of the emerging Romanian national consciousness was the creation of an idealized national history for the Romanian people. In the medieval Voievodes who had fought to defend their country's independence from the Ottomans, nationalist historians found the model heroes for a Romanian national past (Boia 2001b). Thus, in the context of both nationalism and nineteenth-century Romanticism Vlad Ţepes was discovered – and constructed – as a 'national' hero. His excessive cruelty was largely overlooked and he was presented as a valiant figure who had defended his country's independence and restored order and justice.

Some of the earliest evocations of Vlad Ţepes were by Romantic writers and poets for whom the Voievode had a powerful appeal. The Impaler appears in a poem entitled *Ţiganiada* written in 1800 (but published in 1875) by Ion Budai-Deleanu where he is presented as a lawmaker, an educator and the bringer of order to a chaotic society (Stoicescu 1976). In 1863, Dimitrie Bolintineanu published a historic story centred on Vlad Ţepes in which he presented the Voievode as a tyrant but also as someone who fought to protect the Romanian people from the Boyers (Stoicescu 1976). However, the most famous evocation is that of Mihai Eminescu, Romania's most revered poet. In his *Scrisoarea III-a* (*Third Epistle*), written in 1881, Eminescu railed against the immorality and corruption of politicians and called on the Impaler to return and restore order and justice to the country. In lines that many Romanians are able to quote from memory he wrote:

> 'You must come, o dread Impaler, to confide them to your care,[1]
> Split them into two partitions, here the fools, the rascals there,
> Shove them into two enclosures, from the broad daylight enisle'em,
> Then set fire to the prison and the lunatic asylum!'
> (Translation from Leviţchi and Bantaş, 2004)

In the late nineteenth century, nationalist and Romantic approaches to the past gave way to a more analytical approach to the study of history. In this context, historians could no longer overlook the cruelties of Vlad Ţepes. Thus, in the first full history of the Impaler to be published in Romanian, Ioan Bogdan (1896) argued (from an analysis of the German and Slavic sources) that Vlad Ţepeş had been a tyrant and a monster and was not a figure of which the Romanians should be proud. Yet this view did not find widespread acceptance (Boia 2001b). Later historians, while prepared to acknowledge the Impaler's exceptional cruelty, also sought to justify his actions as necessary for the defence of his country from the threat posed by Ottoman expansion. Both of Romania's most eminent twentieth-century historians – Nicolae Iorga and Constantin Giurescu – portrayed the Impaler in favourable terms. Iorga, having initially disapproved of the Impaler's actions (Stoicescu 1976), later described him as 'a cruel hero, for whose toil and desire to defend the country, so much can be forgiven' (Iorga 1937: 193). Giurescu went further, justifying the Impaler's actions as necessary for the defence of the state, whilst arguing that his cruelty was not exceptional:

> Vlad Ţepeş was, in truth, a cruel Voievode who fully justified his nickname. The tortures and executions that he ordered did not originate from a whim, but always had a reason and purpose, very often a *reason of state*. They served as a true example for pretenders to the throne and their supporters who wanted to upset the institutional order, then for doers of evil (who were so numerous as a result of the ceaseless internal struggles), finally even for external enemies who realized that there was a strong leader in the country. As a matter of fact we

---

1   A more direct translation of this first line could be 'Why do you not come Lord Ţepeş'.

should not forget that in the whole of Europe there was an atmosphere of cruelty
at that time. (Giurescu 1937: 41)

By the start of the Second World War this had become the accepted position
regarding Vlad Ţepeş: a cruel leader but one whose actions were justified in the
context of the times in which he lived. While the Impaler was regarded with
considerable esteem (see Iulian 2004), his short reign and short lived success
(along with his exceptional cruelty) meant that he only ever enjoyed a position in
the second tier of the pantheon of Romania's national heroes. On the other hand,
the Impaler's contemporary and cousin, Stephen the Great, enjoyed an exalted
reputation due to his 47 year struggle against the Turks (and it is significant that
both Iorga and Giurescu accorded considerably more attention to the deeds of
Stephen the Great than to Vlad Ţepeş).

In Search of Dracula

Despite his notoriety during his lifetime and the esteem in which he is held in
Romania, Vlad Ţepes would be as little known outside Romania as his cousin
Stephen the Great, were it not for attempts to demonstrate that the Impaler was the
inspiration for Bram Stoker's vampire-Count. A link between the two Draculas
was first suggested in 1958 (Kirtley 1988). Soon afterwards, Ludlam's (1962)
biography of Bram Stoker claimed (although without indicating his source) that
the author had learnt of the deeds of Vlad Ţepeş from Armenius Vambery, a
professor at Budapest University. Nandris (1969) also linked Vlad Ţepeş with the
Dracula of fiction through an analysis of the German and Slavic narratives about
the Impaler. Similarly, in a discussion of the various uses of the 'Dracula myth',
Ronay (1972) argued that Stoker had modelled his vampire-Count on the figure of
Vlad the Impaler.

But by far the most energetic and influential attempt to link the Draculas of
fiction and history was that of two historians working in America, Raymond
McNally and Radu Florescu (who was of Romanian origin). Both had visited
Romania on academic exchanges in the late 1960s (at a time of relative
liberalization in Ceausescu's Romania) and, in collaboration with Romanian
historians, had sought to 'discover' Vlad Ţepes through extensive archive research
and fieldwork. In 1969 they published an article in a popular Romanian history
magazine (McNally and Florescu 1969) explaining their research to a Romanian
audience and in particular their thesis that Vlad Ţepeş had been the inspiration for
Bram Stoker's vampire-Count. For many Romanians, this article was to be the
first occasion when they heard of the fictional Dracula.[2]

In January 1972, after an extensive publicity campaign, McNally and Florescu
launched their book *In Search of Dracula: A True History of Dracula and Vampire*

---

2   Andrei Raiescu, interview.

Legends. Their principal argument was that there was a factual basis for Bram Stoker's Count Dracula. They reasoned that the detailed accounts in *Dracula* of the geography of Transylvania indicated that Bram Stoker had thoroughly researched the region and its history. As such, they argued that Stoker had 'discovered' the figure of Vlad the Impaler (probably from German pamphlets dating from the fifteenth and sixteenth centuries) during research undertaken at the British Museum reading room. They further claimed that, during a meeting with Arminius Vambery, Stoker had been impressed by tales of the historical Dracula and that Vambery had subsequently provided more information on the Impaler, which Stoker had incorporated into *Dracula*.

In Search of Dracula unequivocally presents Vlad Ţepes as a tyrant even likening him to a 'demented psychopath' (47). However, McNally and Florescu did not go as far as claiming that he was a vampire although they were at pains to stress the persistence of vampire legends in Transylvanian folklore. Indeed, after Stoker's novel itself, *In Search of Dracula* has probably played the decisive role in constructing Transylvania as a land of vampires in the Western (especially American) popular imagination. McNally and Florescu appear to have overlooked the fact (or were unaware) that the vampire as a drinker of blood is unknown in Romanian folklore: yet, they were cavalier in translating various Romanian terms for supernatural beings with a single word – vampire[3] – and they sought to present the *strigoi* (ghosts) of Romanian folklore as being vampires.

In Search of Dracula proved to be a minor publishing sensation. It was the first nonfiction work on Dracula to become a best seller.[4] Its appearance was timely: vampires were reaching a new popularity in the 1970s (Auerbach 1995) and *In Search of Dracula* successfully caught the public mood, especially in America (Leatherdale 2000). In 1973 the book was published in England and was subsequently released in French, German, Swedish, Italian and Japanese translations (Giurescu 1977). It was followed in 1973 by a more scholarly biography of Vlad Ţepes, whom the authors invariably name Dracula (Florescu and McNally 1973), and the authors reiterated their arguments in a further book (Florescu and McNally 1989). McNally developed further his research into the possible inspirations for Stoker's Dracula by focusing on the figure of Elizabeth Bathory, a sixteenth-century Hungarian aristocrat who had tortured young peasant women and apparently bathed in their blood (McNally 1983, see also Ronay 1972). The work of McNally and Florescu was the subject of a plethora of press articles and television documentaries, and their argument was made into a documentary film in 1974.[5] Fans and enthusiasts in America championed

---

3   Nicolae Păduraru, interview. See also Florescu and McNally (1973).

4   According to Giurescu (1977) *In Search of Dracula* had sold 270,000 copies by 1975.

5   *In Search of Dracula* (directed by Calvin Floyd). The film starred Christopher Lee playing the roles of both Count Dracula and Vlad Ţepeş. As Miller (2000) notes, using an actor so closely associated with the role of Count Dracula further cemented the supposed

their work and sought to find further links between the historical and the fictional Draculas (Leatherdale 2000).

The importance of *In Search of Dracula* cannot be underestimated. It effectively legitimized Dracula as something to be taken seriously (Skal 2004) and was also a major stimulus to the development of academic Dracula scholarship (Miller 1997; see also Carter 1988b). It brought global recognition to the hitherto obscure Vlad Țepeș who quickly joined the gallery of the 'most evil men in history'. The book was also a direct stimulus to the growth of Dracula tourism (as the following chapter will examine): indeed, following its publication, Romania was 'invaded' by Western journalists, in search of Dracula's castle.[6] But most importantly *In Search of Dracula* created a new orthodoxy: the relationship between Count Dracula and Vlad Țepeș came to be established unequivocally as 'fact'. That Bram Stoker modelled Dracula on Vlad Țepes has been restated repeatedly both in books about Dracula and vampires intended for a popular audience (see for example Brokaw 1976, Varma 1976, Haining 1976, Mackenzie 1977, Dukes 1982, Leatherdale 1993, Barry 1997, Waterfall 1997, Trow 2003) and in some academic analysis (for example, Goldsworthy 1998, Shandley et al. 2006, Tănăsescu 2006, Iordanova 2007, Cazacu 2008). Treating Count Dracula and Vlad Țepeș as essentially the same person is also commonplace in travel guides about Romania and in newspaper accounts of holiday opportunities in the country. The link between the two Dracula is also expressed in popular fiction, most recently in Elizabeth Kostova's absorbing page-turner *The Historian* (2005).

McNally and Florescu were successful in defining a research agenda on their own terms and became the foremost authorities on Vlad Țepeș outside Romania. However, while their work contained much sound scholarship (particularly with regard to the life and deeds of Vlad the Impaler) *In Search of Dracula* also contained much supposition and many of its arguments are not as convincing as they first appeared. In particular, the claim that Vlad Țepeș was the inspiration for Count Dracula has, over the past decade, been the subject of a vigorous critique, led in large part by Elizabeth Miller (1997, 1998, 2000, 2003).

Miller argues that the text of Dracula itself offers little to sustain a relationship between Count Dracula and Vlad Țepes. For example, the fictional Dracula repeatedly describes himself as a Szekler (the Szaklers are a Hungarian-speaking community located in the eastern part of Transylvania) whereas Vlad Țepeș was a Romanian-speaking Wallachian. Similarly Count Dracula describes himself as a Boyer, whereas Vlad Țepes was a Voievode (and continually struggled against the Boyers). At no place in the novel does Count Dracula refer to himself as 'Vlad' or as 'the Impaler'. In addition the geographies of the two Draculas rarely coincide (compare Figure 2.1 and Figure 3.1). The fictional Dracula is firmly set in northeastern Transylvania, particularly in the Borgo Pass where Castle Dracula is

---

link between the fictional and the historical Draculas. Like the book by McNally and Florescu, the film insists that vampires are an integral part of Transylvanian folklore.

6   Nicolae Păduraru, interview; see also Păduraru (1972a).

situated. The historical Dracula had few connections with Transylvania and all the important sites associated with him are in the separate principality of Wallachia, south of the Carpathian Mountains. McNally and Florescu (1972) acknowledge that Stoker set the novel in the 'wrong' place but imply that he did so deliberately.

Miller also demonstrates that a detailed understanding of the sources which Stoker did – and did not – use to write *Dracula* can be found in the author's working notes (now held at Rosenbach Museum in Philadelphia).[7] These notes give an almost unparalleled insight into the process of composition of the novel (Leatherdale 2000). Stoker's key source appears to have been William Wilkinson's *An Account of the Principalities of Wallachia and Moldavia* published in 1820. This book makes three brief mentions of a 'Voivod Dracula' (the only one of Stoker's known sources to use the name) and includes a footnote stating 'Dracula in the Wallachian language means Devil'. Stoker copied this footnote, giving a clear indication of where he found the name of his vampire. Miller demonstrates that the (superficial) account that Count Dracula gives of his own history can all be traced to Wilkinson's book. There is no reference to Arminius Vambery in Stoker's working notes (and no evidence that Vambery gave Stoker any information about Vlad Ţepeş since all the details of Count Dracula's past can be traced to Stoker's source texts). Stoker's notes contain no references to Vlad the Impaler (or, for that matter, Elizabeth Bathory); indeed there is no evidence that Stoker had ever heard of him.

Indeed, Stoker's working notes reveal a lot about his working methods. While he clearly read widely in preparing *Dracula* his research seems to have been far from meticulous. 'Stoker seemed content to combine bits and pieces of information from his sources without any concern for accuracy. After all, Stoker was writing a Gothic novel not a historical treatise' (Miller 1998: 174). Certainly his understanding of Transylvania's geography was patchy at best (Light 2005) and there is no reason to assume that his understanding of the region's convoluted history was any better. Thus, Stoker seems to have been less concerned to discover a historical prototype for his vampire-Count than to glean odd bits and pieces of information to give his novel the semblance of accuracy. As such, he took a name (Dracula), a place (Transylvania) and a few scraps of historical detail and wove them into his novel (Frayling 1991). Thus, over three decades after its publication, the arguments presented by *In Search of Dracula* no longer appear persuasive. Indeed, McNally and Florescu modified some of their claims in a second edition published in 1994, although McNally persisted in his stance that Stoker was well informed about the historical Dracula (see McNally 1999).

---

7   Stoker's complete working notes have been published as a facsimile edition (see Eighteen-Bisang and Miller 2008).

The Response in Romania

To understand fully the Romanian response to *In Search of Dracula* we need to consider the broader context of historiography in socialist Romania and the changing importance attached to Vlad Țepeș. Following the Communist Party takeover of power at the end of 1947 the new regime immediately set about rewriting Romania's history on materialist foundations. Whereas previous historiography had been founded on the idea of the nation (and the national struggle for independence), the new approach to history was reframed in terms of class, and particularly class struggle (King 1980, Deletant 1991). At the same time, the national idea was almost entirely suppressed and replaced by socialist internationalism (Verdery 1991, Boia 2001b). In this context, historians largely ignored Vlad Țepeș in the early socialist period in favour of other medieval figures who had had closer ties with Russia.[8] Later research (for example, Câmpina 1954) sought to present the Impaler as a form of early Marxist, presenting him as a champion of the lower classes and stressing his conflicts with the landowning Boyer class (Treptow 2000).

However, during the 1960s there was a radical shift in the nature of Romania's relationship with the Soviet Union. In 1964, in a so-called 'declaration of independence', Romania started to distance itself from the Soviet Union (whilst still adhering to the Soviet model) and follow its own path of economic and political development. Socialist internationalism was abandoned in favour of a renewed emphasis on national values (Boia 2001b). This policy was to be pursued with particular vigour by Nicolae Ceaușescu (elected General Secretary of the RCP in 1965) who frequently invoked a distinctly Romanian path towards communism. Romania thus presented itself in the curious situation of a state supposedly founded on Marxist-Leninist principles overtly espousing national ideology (something that Tismăneanu (1999) has termed 'national Stalinism'). Verdery (1991) has argued that in Romania the national idea was so entrenched that more than a decade of socialist internationalism had made little headway in eradicating it. Moreover, in a state like Romania where the Communist Party enjoyed little popular support, an appeal to the idea of the nation was one of the few ways in which the leadership could gain any form of popular legitimacy. Thus, the Party – and Ceaușescu in particular – sought to appropriate national ideology for their own ends.

This changing context inevitably affected the way that history was written in socialist Romania. Thus, during the late 1960s, nation displaced class as the dominant theme in Romanian historiography, while the pro-Slavic emphasis of the 1950s was categorically abandoned. The medieval Voievodes who had fought against the Ottomans to preserve the independence of Wallachia and Moldova were swiftly restored to the pantheon of national heroes. In this context, Vlad Țepeș was again evoked as a heroic statesman who had fought to preserve his country's independence. Although this development has sometimes been interpreted as the

---

8   Ștefan Andreescu, interview.

rehabilitation of Vlad Țepeș (Sweeney 1991, Rady 1992) in fact it was simply a return to the discourse about the Impaler that had existed before the Second World War (Light 2007b). By 1970 Romanian historians were describing the Impaler in a way that was almost identical to that of Constantin Giurescu in the interwar period. For example, Oțetea et al. (1970: 144) argued that 'In Vlad Tepes the Romanian people had a remarkable man of state and a leader devoted to the defence of the independence of his country'.

This renewed emphasis on national values was paralleled from 1971 onwards by the construction of an extraordinary personality cult around the figure of Nicolae Ceaușescu. The General Secretary of the RCP attempted to identify himself overtly with the nation's past and was represented as the embodiment of the nation and its historic struggle for unity and national independence. The medieval Voievodes who had similarly fought to preserve the independence of their principalities represented ideal antecedents and archetypes. Hence, Ceausescu was portrayed as the heir of the warrior leaders of Wallachia and Moldova, and as the latest in a long line of Romanian statesmen who had similarly championed Romania's national independence. To reinforce this supposed continuity of strong leaders, Ceaușescu was frequently photographed beside the statues of national heroes (Georgescu 1991, Deletant 1991, Rady 1995). The anniversaries of the deaths of the medieval Voievodes were the occasion for major national commemorations. According to Boia (2001b) Ceaușescu's favourite figures were Mircea the Old (1386–1418), Stephen the Great (1457–1504) and Michael the Brave (1593–1601). However, Vlad Țepeș was also evoked as a strong and progressive leader whose foreign policy and defence of the national interest mirrored that of the RCP under Ceaușescu's leadership (Cioranescu 1976, King 1980)

This, then, was the situation in Romania at the time when *In Search of Dracula* was published. The book was not translated into Romanian and was apparently banned by the socialist authorities (Florescu 1997). However, Romanian medieval historians were familiar with its contents (probably from copies brought to Romania by the authors or from the French translation of 1973). While Romanian scholars were appreciative of the historical research of McNally and Florescu they were – unsurprisingly – dismayed and displeased that an historical figure who was presented in Romania as a national hero should be promoted in the West as the prototype for Stoker's vampire. Romanian historians generally accepted the claim of McNally and Florescu that Stoker had known of Vlad Țepeș and used the Voievode as the inspiration for his vampire-Count. However, they were at pains to refute any relationship between the historical and the literary Draculas. For example, Andreescu (1976) argued it was an obligation of Romanian historiography to re-establish the historical truth regarding the Voievode. As such, Romanian historians sought to counter the negative image of Vlad Țepeș presented by *In Search of Dracula*. The desire to convince Romanians that there was no association between Vlad Țepeș and vampirism may also have contributed to the cancellation of the Romanian translation of *Dracula* (see Chapter 2).

On the occasion of the 500th anniversary of Vlad Țepeș's death in 1976 Romania's socialist regime took the opportunity to promote the Voievode's achievements and defend him from any association with Bram Stoker's vampire. There has been something of a tendency to exaggerate the nature and scale of the 1976 commemorations, implying that Vlad Țepeș enjoyed an especially exalted status in socialist Romania. For example Florescu and McNally (1989: 219–20) claim that 1976 was declared 'Dracula Year'. They continue:

> Panegyrics, commemorative eulogies, discussion panels, lead articles in the press and in scholarly journals (the popular *History Magazine*) dedicated its entire issue of November 1976 to Dracula), radio and television commentaries, and films were devoted to the subject. Even Romania's president Ceaușescu invoked the memory of Vlad. A special commemorative stamp was issued.

In fact, the 1976 commemorations appear to have been much less spectacular than has been previously suggested (Light 2007b) and were little different from those for any other medieval leader.[9] Neither is there much evidence to suggest that Vlad Țepeș enjoyed any exceptional esteem in socialist Romania. Certainly there was an article in the Communist Party newspaper (*Scînteia*) in December 1976 that lauded the Impaler as 'an ardent fighter for freedom and independence, for the independence of the country ... a bringer of justice who used drastic methods so that order and honesty would reign in the country which he ruled' (Căzănișteanu, 1976: 4). Yet this was printed on page four, while the front page was more concerned with commemorating the 375th anniversary of the death of Michael the Brave. One academic history journal (*Revista de Istorie*) did dedicate the November 1976 issue to papers about the Impaler but on the other hand a popular history magazine (*Magazin Istoric*) made only a brief reference to Vlad Țepeș in the December 1976 edition. A commemorative stamp was issued featuring Vlad's image but this was nothing exceptional. The medieval Voievodes were regularly featured on commemorative stamps (Drăgușanu 1997) and the 1976 stamp of Vlad Țepeș was a routine action rather than an indication that the Voievode enjoyed any special esteem (Light 2007b). A film about Vlad Țepeș was released in 1978 but this followed previous films about Michael the Brave (1971), Stephen the Great (1975) and Dimitrie Cantemir (1975) (see Boia 2001b).

One of the few ways in which the 1976 commemorations of Vlad Țepeș differed from commemorations of other medieval rulers was in the publication of two books dedicated to the life and deeds of the Voievode (Andreescu 1976, Stoicescu 1976).[10] Both were addressed to a Romanian audience and, in different ways, sought to counter negative portrayals of Vlad Țepeș. Nicolae Stoicescu, an established historian, sought to recover the image of the Impaler from the various legends that

---

9   Ștefan Andreescu, interview.

10   Usually the commemoration of one of the medieval voievodes was marked by the publication of a single officially approved book (Ștefan Andreescu, interview).

portrayed him as a tyrant. He argued that the Impaler had been an exceptional ruler and that his cruelty was nothing exceptional for its time. Stoicescu could barely hide his disdain for Stoker's fictional vampire and dismissed any relationship between the historical and fictional Draculas. Andreescu, a younger historian, sought to present a balanced account of the Impaler's life and deeds (something which apparently caused him problems with the state's censors).[11] While prepared to acknowledge the literary merits of Stoker's novel, Andreescu rejected the claim that Stoker knew anything of Vlad Țepeș arguing that the author had simply taken the name 'Dracula' and the location of Transylvania in order to add realism to his vampire story. A summary of the key arguments of both Stoicescu and Andreescu was subsequently published in English (Cernovodeanu 1977).

Having sought to safeguard the image of Vlad Țepeș among a Romanian public (which nevertheless knew next to nothing of the fictional Dracula), Romania's socialist regime attempted to restore the Impaler's image (and to negate any connection with the fictional Dracula) among a Western audience. As such, a revised edition of Stoicescu's book was published in both English and Japanese (Stoicescu 1986). In the English edition, the author acerbically argued that the popularity of the vampire Dracula indicated a 'collective psychosis' among a sensation seeking readership. He continued:

> Whoever knows something about Vlad Țepeș may smile on reading such nonsense [the literary Dracula], but this nonsense ascribed to Dracula is highly popular and overshadows the true image of the Prince of Wallachia. That is why we considered it necessary to stress that *there are two different characters: the historical Vlad Țepeș and the Dracula of fiction who has got only the surname of the former ... Those who would like to go on cultivating Dracula the vampire are free to do it without, however, forgetting that he has nothing in common with the Romanian history where the real Vlad Țepeș whom we know by his deeds has a place of honour.* (Stoicescu 1978: 178–9, emphasis in original)

Romania also used other means to project a positive image of Vlad Țepeș to the West, one of which was tourist promotion. For example, an article in *Holidays in Romania* (a monthly English-language tourist magazine published by the Ministry of Tourism) in 1976 was entitled 'The truth about Dracula' (Neagoe 1976). It presented Vlad as a righteous and courageous military leader, with predictably no mention of vampires.

During the late 1970s and 1980s Romanian writers and historians continued to defend the reputation of Vlad Țepeș from any associations with the literary Dracula (for example Stăvăruș 1978, Ciobanu 1979, Leu 1986, Stoicescu 1986, Stoian 1989) although some of them clearly knew almost nothing about the literary Dracula and had not read the novel. Some, indeed, engaged in wild speculation about Bram Stoker's sources: Leu (1986) for example claimed that

---

11 Ștefan Andreescu, interview.

Stoker had written horror plays for a German theatre company and had found material for his novel during a visit to Vienna or Budapest. Meanwhile, during the 1980s reactions to the literary Dracula became increasingly extreme. Within the increasingly isolationist and exceptionalist form of nationalism promoted by Ceauşescu (see Verdery 1991), some writers interpreted the whole Dracula phenomenon as a direct attack on Romania itself. Hence, Adrian Păunescu, one of the socialist regime's ultranationalist 'court poets' claimed: 'This is not the first occasion when questionable interests behind so-called artistic works from abroad combine to tarnish and compromise the national history of the Romanians ... the Dracula film, like the whole Western literature on Dracula is just a page from the great pact of political pornography through which our enemies work against us' (1986: 13). Given that most Romanians were unaware of the novel's contents it is not surprising that language such as this led many to assume that the novel was in some way subversive.

The paranoiac nationalism of Ceauşescu's Romania (which persisted, in some circles, in the post-socialist period) was also notable for its extreme anti-Hungarian rhetoric. In this context, some nationalist writers went so far as to interpret the literary Dracula as a Hungarian plot to smear the image both of Romania and of one of its national heroes (see Florescu and McNally 1989). Such Magyarophobia had its origins in the long dispute between Romania and Hungary over – coincidently – Transylvania. Although the Treaty of Trianon awarded Transylvania to Romania in 1920, nationalist Romanians have accused Hungary of having irredentist claims to the region and engaging in anti-Romanian propaganda to this effect. As such, the supposed contribution of the Hungarian professor Arminius Vambery to the writing of *Dracula*, proposed by McNally and Florescu (1972), was interpreted as evidence that the novel formed part of anti-Romanian propaganda on the part of Hungary. The leading role in the early Dracula films of the Hungarian actor Bela Lugosi further raised suspicions of Hungarian interests behind the Western Dracula myth. This argument was initially raised by Barsan (1975: 44) who took a swipe at the whole Dracula phenomenon, describing it as 'a warped image of escapism and insanity' and was developed most fully by Ungheanu (1992), another of the ultranationalist writers from the Ceauşescu era. Ungheanu argued that Hungarian propaganda in various forms was behind both the defamation of Vlad Ţepeş and the presentation of Transylvania as a land of vampirism and evil forces. Such arguments may appear both farfetched and unfounded (and as Elizabeth Miller has demonstrated, there is no evidence that Arminius Vambery made any contribution to the writing of Dracula). Nevertheless, as the following chapter will examine, one individual's suspicions of Hungarian irredentism played an important role in the development of Dracula tourism in Romania in the 1970s.

Ultimately, Romanian efforts to draw a distinction between Count Dracula and Vlad Ţepeş have had limited success. The dubious conflation of Vlad Ţepeş with Count Dracula that was initiated by McNally and Florescu remains widely accepted outside Romania. It is an argument that has been uncritically restated many times in print[12] and which appears to have gained an unstoppable momentum. Moreover, Coppola's 1993 film *Bram Stoker's Dracula* further reinforced the supposed relationship between the literary and the historical Draculas. Today, despite convincing arguments to the contrary, many people throughout the Western world take it as 'read' that Bram Stoker based Count Dracula on the character of Vlad the Impaler.

Meanwhile, over the past two decades, Vlad Țepeș – under the guise of Vlad the Impaler, or the 'real' Dracula – has found his way into Western popular culture as a pervasive cultural icon in his own right (Miller 2003, Bibeau 2007). The figure of the Impaler has inspired various novels, films, cartoons and comics. The Impaler provides staple fodder for anything themed on 'evil men of history', whether for television documentaries or children's books. The figure of the Voievode even features in Madame Tussauds Waxwork museum in London. As Miller (2003) notes, Vlad is increasingly represented as a vampire: the confusion between the literary and the fictional Draculas seem irreversible. Romania no longer has control over the way in which Vlad Țepeș is represented within global popular culture.

An understanding of the historical Dracula – Vlad Țepeș – and his significance for Romanians is the second element that is necessary for understanding the phenomenon of Dracula tourism. For more than one hundred years (and particularly since the 1970s) Romanian historiography has constructed Vlad Țepeș as an exemplary and heroic figure for his efforts to defend his country's independence from external powers. The Voievode continues to enjoy an esteemed reputation in Romania: I have not met a Romanian with anything but a positive view of the Impaler. But outside Romania, the Voievode's image is rather different: Vlad Țepeș is represented both as a tyrant and as the prototype of evil adopted by Bram Stoker for his vampire-Count. The internal and external representations of the Impaler are therefore in collision: for 40 years Romanian writers and historians have vigorously sought to disassociate the historical and literary Draculas. This was the background against which Dracula tourism developed in socialist Romania in the 1970s.

---

12 A recent example is Trow (2003) who maintains that Count Dracula and Vlad Țepeș are the same person.

Chapter 4
Dracula Tourism in Socialist Romania

In the preceding chapters I introduced the Draculas of fiction and history. As Chapter 2 noted, popular interest in the fictional Dracula grew rapidly from the 1960s onwards, spawning a broader and vigorous vampire subculture, particularly (but not exclusively) in America. Since international tourism was also expanding and diversifying in the 1960s it is not surprising that some Dracula enthusiasts sought to extend their interest to their holidaymaking. This led some people – mostly from Western countries – to Transylvania on their own search for the sites and sights associated with both Stoker's Count Dracula, and Vlad the Impaler. This chapter examines the development of this form of tourism (which hereafter I refer to as 'Dracula tourism').

This chapter starts by examining the broader context in which Dracula tourism developed in Romania from the 1960s up to 1989. Such tourism unfolded in very distinct circumstances since at this time Romania was a socialist (communist) state, and, like its neighbours in Central and Eastern Europe, was following a model of political and economic development that was quite unlike that of the West. As such, the development of tourism took place in a specific context and was intended to accord with wider state objectives. I then examine the development of Dracula tourism in Romania from the 1960s onwards and the responses of the Romanian state (at both central and local levels) to this activity. Throughout the chapter I seek to situate Dracula tourism in its wider political and ideological context.

The Development of Dracula Tourism in Socialist Romania

The Context: Tourism Policy in Socialist Romania

Tourism was not initially an immediate priority for the Romanian People's Republic. An organization entitled *Associatia Turismul Popular* (The People's Tourism Association) was established in 1948 (Hossu-Longin 1980) to promote domestic tourism for the working classes. However, no importance was attached to international tourism and ONT (*Oficial Naţional de Turism*) the national tourist office (established in 1936), was dissolved in 1949 (Marinescu 1986). In the early years of state socialism Romania was effectively closed to foreign tourists: in 1956, the country received just 5,000 foreign visitors (Petrescu 1971), most of whom would have been from other socialist states.

However, in the late 1950s Romania began to turn its attention to the development and promotion of international tourism. As D. Hall (1991) has noted, this trend was mirrored (to varying degrees) by the other state socialist regimes of Central and Eastern Europe. The period after Stalin's death in 1953 was characterized by a (relative) relaxation and reduced hostility towards the West within the Soviet Union and its European satellites. Moreover, having consolidated their rule, socialist regimes came to recognize that tourism (both domestic and international) could contribute to economic and political development in such a way as to achieve specifically socialist priorities (D. Hall 1984, 1990). The countries of Central/Eastern Europe were also increasingly concerned to project a favourable image of themselves and their achievements to the wider world (both socialist and non-socialist) and began to use tourism to this end (D. Hall 1991, Sanchez and Adams 2008). In Romania, ONT was re-established in 1955 under the direction of the Ministry for External Trade (Marinescu 1986). Subsequently, in 1958 – the same year in which Hammer Studios launched its first Dracula film – ONT launched a regular, glossy English-language magazine entitled *Rumania for Tourists* (with similar editions in French and Italian).[1] It was renamed *Holidays in Romania* in 1965.

The 1961–5 Five Year Plan (Partidul Muncitoresc Român 1960) was the first to address tourism specifically, proposing the allocation of funds for tourism/recreation and for hotel construction. Much of the development was intended for domestic tourists, but ONT also worked rapidly to promote Romania as a destination for foreign visitors (from both socialist and non-socialist countries) and international tourism arrivals increased rapidly (see Figure 4.1). As early as 1962, the Black Sea Coast where most tourism investment was initially concentrated (Turnock 1974) received tourists from 36 countries (Anon 1962). By 1963, ONT had established links with travel companies throughout the West, including 11 firms in Canada, 17 in the UK and 48 in America (*Rumania for Tourists* 1963). Further measures were adopted to facilitate travel to Romania and, during a period of relative liberalization in the mid-1960s, Romania quickly became one of the most accessible socialist countries for Western tourists. Border formalities were minimal, visas were cheap and easily obtained, tourists faced no compulsory currency exchange requirements, and there were no restrictions on the accommodation available (Turnock 1974, 1989). Tourism – at least in official rhetoric – was regarded as a means of promoting peaceful and friendly relations between different countries of the world (Bozdog 1968).

The pace of tourism development continued to increase after Nicolae Ceauşescu became General Secretary of the RCP in 1965. For Ceauşescu, tourism was one way for Romania to present its independent face to the West. Indeed, according to Ştefan Andrei, Ceauşescu's foreign minister during the 1970s, tourism was promoted primarily for political and propagandist motives rather than

---

1   It can be no coincidence that *Rumania for Tourists* was launched in June 1958 immediately following the announcement in May of the withdrawal of Soviet troops from Romania.

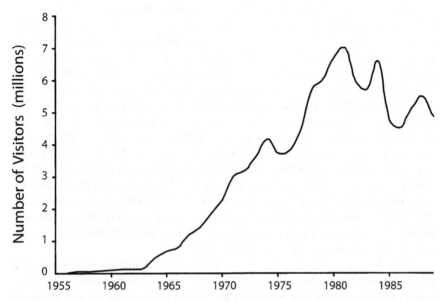

Source: Derived from Petrescu (1971), Snak (1976), Turnock (1991a), Comisia Naţionala pentru Statistică (1995)

Figure 4.1   Number of foreign tourists visiting Romania (1955–89)

as a generator of hard currency.[2] Consequently there was continued investment in tourism development (again largely focused at the Black Sea) and the 1966–70 Five Year Plan allocated 3.5 billion lei (£84 million at the 1972 exchange rate) to tourism (Cosma 1973). By 1970, Romania received over 2.2 million foreign tourists. Most (around 83 per cent) were from other socialist states (Turnock 1989) but there were 366,591 visitors from Western countries, including 169,504 from the Federal Republic of Germany, 19,130 from the UK and 18,893 from America.[3] As Romania embarked on its independent course after 1964, Americans in particular were encouraged to visit Romania in order to sustain the country's independence from the Soviet Union.[4] Thus, a Romanian academic visiting America in 1968 recounted being given a tourist brochure promoting travel to Romania as 'the country that dared to be independent' (Giurescu 1971: 193).

The Romanian state continued to support tourism development during the 1970s and the 1971–5 Five Year Plan allocated around six billion lei (approximately £120 million) for tourism development (Cosma 1973). Ceauşescu apparently issued instructions in the early 1970s that all relevant government departments

---

2   Ştefan Andrei, interview.
3   Source: ONT internal data, provided by Andrei Raiescu.
4   Nicolae Păduraru, interview.

and ministries should contribute to making Romania better known in the West[5] and tourism had an important role to play in the process. One indication of the importance now attached to tourism was the establishment of a new Ministry of Tourism in 1971 (along with ONT offices in each of Romania's 40 counties) in order to develop and coordinate tourism policy in accordance with the Five Year Plan. The Ministry was set the target of attracting four million visitors by 1975 (Sobanu 1971), a target which was reached in 1974 (see Figure 4.1). The new Ministry also sought to achieve a more even spatial distribution of tourism by reducing investment at the Black Sea and encouraging the development of new forms of tourism elsewhere in the country. In particular, there were efforts to promote cultural and heritage tourism in Transylvania and other regions of the country (see Cosma 1973). In 1970, 80 per cent of international tourists had been concentrated at the littoral, but by 1975 this had fallen to below 50 per cent (Enache 1976). During the period of the following Five Year Plan (1976–80) the Ministry continued its efforts to diversity Romania's tourist product and redistribute tourism activity throughout the country (Enache 1978).

This, then, was the environment in which Dracula tourism developed. The claim that socialist Romania was unprepared for tourism, both ideologically and in terms of facilities (Florescu and McNally 1976) is not justified. Instead, Romania was ideologically committed to developing international tourism and considerable investment was undertaken in the provision of hotels and restaurants throughout the country. Although the majority of tourists were always from other socialist states, Romania was open and accessible to Westerners, increasing numbers of whom were interested to see a country which came to be regarded as the maverick in the Soviet bloc.

Conceptualising Dracula Tourism

As Romania opened to international tourism, Dracula enthusiasts from the West were free to visit the country on their own searches. Thus, a distinct form of special interest tourism developed, based in various ways on the Western Dracula myth. From the outset such Dracula tourism was a minority form of tourism in Romania. During the socialist era most of Romania's foreign tourists were nationals of other socialist states and probably knew little, if anything, of the Dracula of literature and cinema. Furthermore, many Westerners who visited Romania went to beach or mountain resorts and Dracula was not an important component of their visit. Nevertheless, there was sufficient interest in Dracula for Dracula tourism to be identified as a distinct form of niche tourism.

From the outset it is important to recognize that Dracula tourism was a diverse phenomenon and that Dracula tourists themselves were not a homogenous group. Instead, Dracula tourism embraces a broad range of interests and motives. One

---

5   Ion Mânzat, interview. It is possible that Mânzat was referring to what Pacepa (1988) describes as 'Operation Horizon'.

group can be identified as literary tourists (see Chapter 1). In searching for the literary roots of *Dracula* such visitors were seeking to experience for themselves the places and landscapes evoked by Stoker, in particular the wild landscape of northeast Romania in which Castle Dracula (a central feature of the beginning and end of the novel) is located (see Chapter 5). Among these literary tourists some were undoubtedly what Herbert (2001) has identified as literary pilgrims, in this case, dedicated fans of Stoker's novel or enthusiasts for Gothic fiction more broadly. The visits to Transylvania of Britain's Dracula Society from 1974 onwards certainly fit into this category. Others, who were more general fans of the novel, were also seeking to experience for themselves the geographic setting of *Dracula*.

However, Dracula tourism was more than simply an example of literary tourism. Many more people had encountered Count Dracula through cinematic and television adaptations of Stoker's novel. As Chapter 2 noted, Universal's film *Dracula* (1931) starring Bela Lugosi established Count Dracula as an enduring popular cultural icon, which was reinvigorated by the Hammer films from the late 1950s onwards. For another group of Dracula enthusiasts it was the encounter with Transylvania as represented through film and television that generated the interest in seeing the region for themselves. Screen tourism began to develop in the 1970s and Dracula tourism in Transylvania was one of the earliest examples. None of the major Dracula films was made in Transylvania (and the Hammer series used the English Home Counties as a substitute) but, as noted in Chapter 1, film tourism is frequently centred on the place that is *represented* in a film rather than the actual location where filming took place (Tooke and Baker 1996, Busby and Klug 2001, Roesch 2009). Hence, film tourists were seeking an encounter with an idea of Transylvania – as a dark, forested, mountainous and sinister place – rather than any specific location. Like many literary tourists, such visitors were seeking Transylvania as a *lieux d'imagination* (Reijnders 2011a, 2011b) and a visit to the region was an opportunity to 'connect' with, and temporarily enter into, the imaginative world of Dracula.

However other tourists were drawn to the supernatural roots of the Dracula myth.[6] Their interest may have been initially sparked by fiction or film but the visit to Romania was more than a search for locations with literary or cinematic connections. Instead, it was an occasion to engage with the broader place myth of Transylvania as the home of the unknown, the mysterious and the ineffable (see also Inglis and Holmes 2003). For such tourists a visit to Transylvania offered the ultimate experience of Otherness: the excitement of a potential encounter with the supernatural. Transylvania was a magical realm that held the possibility of 'enchantment' in a world from which such thrills had supposedly been banished (see Holloway 2010). A visit to Transylvania was an occasion to delight in being frightened. Such was the resonance of the Transylvania place myth that the region came to be known as *the* place to visit in search of vampires. Various guides were

---

6   Nicolae Păduraru, interview.

published to cater for those seeking the supernatural in Transylvania (for example, Brokaw 1976, de Ludes 1981).

Such tourism – based on visiting supposedly haunted places or a search for the supernatural – is not a recent phenomenon, neither is it unique to Transylvania. Since at least the eighteenth century, English travellers have been drawn to Scotland in search of ghosts. Inglis and Holmes (2003) argue that the rise of modernity effectively banished the supernatural to the geographical and imaginative margins. Hence, in order to escape the ordered, prosaic realities of everyday life English travellers were drawn to the peripheries (particularly the Highlands of Scotland) where it was believed that ghosts and phantoms still resided. Thus the Highlands came to be read as a marginal, pre-modern world, where beliefs in the supernatural were still a part of the popular imagination. It was a place that offered 'extraordinary' experiences of the mystical and ineffable that were not available at home. The parallels with Western 'ways of seeing' Transylvania are obvious. But this was not just a nineteenth-century phenomenon: instead ghosts and phantoms continue to be enthusiastically promoted as a core element of Scotland's tourist product (Inglis and Holmes 2003).

Indeed, in recent decades, travel founded on an (imagined) experience of the paranormal has emerged as a discrete form of special interest tourism in its own right, albeit one that has received little detailed scrutiny. This practice has been variously labelled as 'Ghost tourism' (Inglis and Holmes 2003, Gentry 2007, Holloway 2010), 'fright tourism' (Bristow and Newman 2005), 'Spook tourism' (Krebbs 2006) or 'haunting tourism' (D'Harlingue 2010). Some writers (Bristow and Newman 2005, Gentry 2007) argue that this is a form of 'dark tourism', an activity based on visiting places associated with death and/or disaster (Lennon and Foley 2000). There is clearly some overlap with dark tourism – ghosts are, after all, the spirits of the dead – although there are also forms of supernatural based tourism that are not directly associated with death, disaster or tragedy.

One of the most widespread forms of supernatural based tourism is the ghost walk (see Gentry 2007, Holloway 2010). Since at least the 1970s the city of York has offered guided walking tours themed around ghosts and the paranormal. Many other cities in the UK and around the world now offer similar haunted tours. There are also places that draw tourists principally because of their associations with the supernatural and the haunted. A prominent example is Salem, Massachusetts where 19 people accused of witchcraft were executed in 1692. The Salem witch trials have attracted tourists to the town since the second half of the nineteenth century but there was a significant increase in the late 1960s and 1970s (Gencarella 2007) which has continued to the present day. The town now attracts over one million visitors a year (Bristow and Newman 2005) and styles itself as the Halloween capital of the world. Similarly, New Orleans has long appealed to tourists searching for its supernatural and occult associations. The city offers a plethora of guided walking tours themed around ghosts, cemeteries, Voodoo and vampires (Pile 2005). Since the 1970s, Whitby in Yorkshire has drawn tourists on account of its Dracula associations. The town now boasts a 'Dracula experience' attraction and Dracula-themed walking tours. Moreover, since 1994 the town has hosted a popular Gothic festival that now runs twice yearly (in April and at Halloween).

Transylvania, then, is far from unusual in attracting tourists on account of its supernatural associations. As part of the increasing international division of tourism (itself the result of a Western imaginary which projects and attributes particular qualities to particular places) there are locations and countries that are increasingly seen as specializing in particular forms of tourism (Edensor 1998, Urry 2002). In this context, some places have developed a reputation as places to visit for an experience of the 'dark' or the supernatural. While some locations have enthusiastically embraced the supernatural for the creation of unique place identities, others (Romania is the best example) have been extremely reluctant to exploit such associations.

Finally, it was not only the fictional Dracula that drew tourists to Transylvania. As a result of the publication of *In Search of Dracula* (McNally and Florescu 1972) Vlad Ţepeş suddenly enjoyed unprecedented global popularity (see Florescu and McNally 1976). Thus, some tourists visited Romania to search out places associated with the life and deeds of the Impaler. This appears to be a form of heritage tourism but with a considerable degree of overlap with both literary tourism and supernatural based tourism (Hovi 2008b).

Overall, then, it is important to recognize that Dracula tourism was (and remains) a complex and multifaceted activity. While in some cases the motive for visiting Transylvania may have been clearly defined (such as an enthusiasm for Gothic literature) in many other cases tourists will have been drawn to Romania from a diverse and intertwined set of interests in the literary, cinematic, supernatural and historical roots of the Dracula phenomenon. The result is that Dracula tourism defies simple categorization beyond identifying it as a form of special interest tourism.

The Early Search for Dracula

Western tour operators began to offer packages in Romania (and other socialist countries) during the 1960s (Bray and Raitz 2001) and initially some Dracula enthusiasts took the opportunity to visit Transylvania on a cultural tourism package. They usually returned disappointed, not because of any hostility towards Dracula on the part of the socialist authorities but instead because the literary Dracula was almost completely unknown in Romania at this time. As a result there was no awareness of the significance of places mentioned in the novel (particularly Bistriţa and the Borgo Pass) and such places were overlooked in favour of Transylvania's other cultural attractions. ONT guides were bewildered when asked by Westerners for more details about Dracula or vampirism in Romania.[7] However, some tourists

---

7   Nicolae Păduraru, interview.

encountered guides who were happy to talk about Vlad Ţepeş[8] at a time when the Impaler was increasingly being evoked in heroic terms in Romania.

Other Dracula enthusiasts embarked on their own searches for Stoker's vampire. There were no restrictions on independent travel in Romania; indeed, ONT offered considerable logistical support (such as drivers, guides and interpreters) for Western tourists wanting to travel independently. Dracula fans invariably focused their search on the Borgo (Bârgău) Pass where, during the 1960s, increasing numbers of foreign tourists hunted in vain for the ruins of Dracula's castle (Păduraru 1973). Some tourists, in seeking to trace the exact route to the castle described by Stoker, got lost in the mountains and needed the help of local shepherds to find their way back down to the road.[9] Among these visitors was apparently a group of three American journalists seeking out Castle Dracula (Misiuga 1995). By the early 1970s local peasants had become used to tourists asking for directions to the castle (McNally and Florescu 1972).

Despite the absence of any trace of Dracula some of the tourists who were seeking out the supernatural in Transylvania found evidence to support their preconceptions. Stoicescu (1976: 203) sardonically recounts the case of an Italian reporter who visited Romania in 1968. In the Borgo Pass he came across a roadside cross with the inscription '*Doamne, apără-mă de dracul*' ('Lord, defend me from the devil'). Misunderstanding this unexceptional petition, the reporter took it to indicate that popular belief in vampires was widespread in Transylvania.

But while there was no genuine Dracula's castle in Transylvania Western tourists quickly found something else that met their expectations. Bran Castle, a fourteenth-century building in southern Transylvania has no connection with either the fictional or the historical Dracula. However, the building does bear a superficial resemblance to Castle Dracula as depicted in literature and film. Since it is something of an architectural showpiece, and moreover is located close to Transylvania's largest city (Braşov), a visit to Bran was included in many organized tours and excursions to Transylvania. Thus Dracula enthusiasts appear to have been quick to project their fantasies and expectations of Transylvania onto this building. At some stage in the 1960s the building was labelled as 'Dracula's Castle' and by the end of the decade the building was widely known in this way outside Romania. At Bran Castle, Dracula fans found what they wanted in Transylvania (Light 2007a). This process is examined in more detail in the following chapter.

Spotlight on Dracula

The publication of *In Search of Dracula* in 1972 proved to be a major stimulus to the development of Dracula tourism in Romania, although in ways that the authors can hardly have imagined. After the launch of their book, Raymond McNally and Radu Florescu devised the idea of a package tour to Romania, themed around

---

8   Jeanne Keyes Youngson, personal communication.
9   Nicolae Păduraru, interview.

the historical and literary Draculas (Florescu and McNally 1976). It was an appropriate moment for such a tour given the interest their book had aroused; moreover, during the 1970s vampires were increasingly popular in America (Auerbach 1995). The New York based travel company General Tours developed the concept in conjunction with Pan-Am airline. One of America's oldest travel companies, General Tours had been founded by Alexander Harris in 1947 with the intent to use tourism as a means of increasing mutual understanding between citizens of American and those of Eastern Europe and the Soviet Union (Harris 2008). Over the years, the company had developed a number of themed tours to the socialist countries of this region.

General Tours had collaborated with ONT since the early 1960s and so a representative of the company approached the ONT office in New York to ask for their participation in developing the tour. Leading the ONT's New York office was Andrei Raiescu. With a background in economic sciences, Raiescu had been appointed to this position in August 1971 and given annual targets to attract more American visitors to Romania.[10] This was a prestigious posting and Raiescu would have been under pressure to deliver results. Consequently he was open to new ways to attract Americans to Romania. When approached by General Tours he was initially surprised since – like most Romanians – he had not heard of the literary Dracula and knew little about Vlad Țepeș. Nevertheless, he was able to consult Constantin Giurescu, a professor of history from the University of Bucharest who was at that time on a teaching sabbatical at Columbia University (see Giurescu 1977). Raiescu subsequently worked with General Tours on the production of a Dracula tour.[11]

The resulting tour – entitled *Spotlight on Dracula: An Adventure in Transylvania* – was launched in September 1972. At a starting price of $935, the 18 day escorted tour offered the opportunity to 'participate in a re-creation of the Dracula legend, completely immersed in the original environment in which it flourished – the dense forests, quaint villages and craggy moors of Transylvania in Romania' (General Tours 1972: no pagination). The majority of the package was centred on locations associated with Vlad Țepeș but the tour also included a few nights in the part of northeastern Transylvania where Stoker's novel is located. *Spotlight on Dracula* was well received by the American press, which described it as 'the first genuinely new tour concept in 500 years,' (Florescu and McNally 1976: 3).

According to his own account,[12] Andrei Raiescu had his own agenda in contributing to *Spotlight on Dracula* and this went beyond attracting more American tourists to Romania. Raiescu had been born in Transylvania and, like many Transylvanian Romanians, was troubled by what he perceived as irredentist Hungarian claims to the region. I have alluded to the tension between Hungary

---

10   In 1971 Romania received 18,696 American visitors (source: internal ONT data supplied by Andrei Raiescu).

11   Andrei Raiescu, interview.

12   This section is based on interviews with Andrei Raiescu.

and Romania in previous chapters and it is necessary here to discuss the situation in more detail. The dispute between Hungary and Romania over the status of Transylvania has a long history. Both Romanians and Hungarians claim to be the first to settle in Transylvania and both claim the region as the cradle of their history and culture. Romanians claim uninterrupted settlement of the region since Roman (and in some cases, pre-Roman) times. Hungarians, on the other hand, claim that after the Roman withdrawal from the region in AD 271, Transylvania was almost entirely depopulated, so that the Magyar tribes that settled Transylvania in the tenth century found the land uninhabited. As such, Hungarians, claim to be the earliest continuous inhabitants of the region.

Transylvania was under Hungarian rule until after the First World War when the Treaty of Trianon transferred the region to Romania. Although the majority of Transylvania's population were Romanians the region also contained a sizable Hungarian minority which was now isolated from the rest of Hungary. Many in Hungary regarded this decision as a grave injustice; consequently, many Romanians feared that Hungary wished to reclaim Transylvania. This, in fact, was exactly what happened during the Second World War when Hungary, with Hitler's approval, reclaimed much of northern Transylvania. At the end of the War, Transylvania was returned to Romania and since then the Hungarian state has scrupulously recognized the 1920 borders. However, popular Hungarian attachments to Transylvania are deeply rooted and, as Verdery (1991: 352) observed, 'almost any casual conversation with Hungarians, both in Hungary and living abroad, reveals widespread sentiment that Transylvania rightly belongs to them'. Similarly, there were (and are) many Romanians who have genuine (if unfounded) concerns that Hungary intends to 'take Transylvania back'. This issue can arouse strong passions among Romanians so that the country's political leaders from Ceauşescu onwards have had little difficulty in mobilizing popular support by claiming to defend Romanian interests against Hungarian irredentism.[13]

Andrei Raiescu's concerns about Hungarian irredentism were not without foundation. Living and working in America he had encountered a vigorous Hungarian lobby that sought to convince American public opinion that Transylvania was rightly Hungarian territory.[14] Hungarians émigrés who had

---

13   In 1996 Hungary and Romania signed a historic treaty in which Hungary recognized the 1920 frontier with Romania, while Romania offered guaranteed rights for the Hungarian minority in Transylvania. Since then tensions between Hungary and Romania have eased considerably. Since 1996 the political party representing Transylvanian Hungarians (the Democratic Union of Hungarians in Romania) has played a constructive role as a coalition partner in successive Romanian administrations. Both states are now members of NATO and the European Union.

14   America in the 1970s contained a large Hungarian-American community. According to the 1970 census (United States Department of Commerce 1973) there were 603,668 people of Hungarian origin, while the community of Romanian origin was much smaller (216,803 people).

fled the 1956 uprising formed a vocal element of this lobby.[15] Many people in America (and of course elsewhere) were unaware of Transylvania's exact location. Due to the Dracula novel and films the region existed in the popular imagination more as an idea or a metaphor, rather than as a real place (see Chapter 2). This very ambiguity over Transylvania's exact location meant that it was susceptible – even vulnerable – to propagandist attempts (whether by Hungary or Romania) to persuade American public opinion that the region rightly belonged to them: to a certain extent, Transylvania was up for grabs.

Even Count Dracula was implicated in the Hungarian-Romanian dispute over Transylvania. The actor most closely associated with the role of Dracula was, of course, the Hungarian-born Bela Lugosi. Lugosi's biographers (Cremer 1976, Lennig 2003) agree that, after settling in America, the actor remained patriotically devoted to his country of birth and was an active supporter of Hungarian cultural activities in America. At the same time, like many Hungarians of his generation, Lugosi appears to have had little love for Romanians (see Cremer 1976); indeed, according to Barsan (1975) (who is not an impartial source), Lugosi could barely hide his contempt for them.[16] Perhaps it was as a result of Lugosi's influence that, in Universal's 1931 film of *Dracula*, Transylvania has a distinctly Hungarian feel. At the start of the film a coach draws up to a Transylvanian inn which is advertising its wares in Hungarian, while the local peasants are all talking in Hungarian.[17] Thus, for Andrei Raiescu, Bela Lugosi and his portrayal of Dracula was something that reinforced the association between Transylvania and Hungary in the American imagination.

Raiescu's concern, then, was to counter the Hungarian claims to Transylvania that were promoted by the Hungarian lobby in America but also to cement an association between Transylvania and Romania in the American consciousness.[18] Now aware of the popularity of Dracula in America, he realized that Romania could use Dracula to its advantage. His participation in the development of *Spotlight on Dracula* was intended to use tourism as a means to reinforce the status of Transylvania as a part of Romania in the American popular imagination. In promoting *Spotlight on Dracula*, Raiescu could argue that he was acting in

---

15   According to the American Hungarian Federation, 65,000 Hungarian refugees arrived in the USA after the 1956 Hungarian revolution (Source: American-Hungarian Federation [Online, Available at: http://www.americanhungarianfederation.org/about.htm accessed 17 March 2008]).

16   Lugosi was apparently a supporter of the short-lived Hungarian Soviet Republic which was ended by an invading Romanian army in 1919. It was as a result of this invasion that Lugosi had to leave Hungary, never to return. This might have further deepened his animosity towards Romanians.

17   This information is derived from David Skal's authoritative commentary on the 1931 Universal edition of *Dracula* which is included in *Dracula: The Legacy Collection* (released on DVD by Universal in 2004).

18   See also Hainagiu (2008) which also appears to be based on an interview with Andrei Raiescu.

accordance with the RCP's *economic* policy to increase hard currency earnings from international tourism. However, he was following his own *political* agenda to use Dracula tourism to reinforce the territorial status of Transylvania as a part of Romania among the American public. In the absence of a state policy regarding Dracula, Raiescu devised his own which he considered to be in Romania's interests, taking advantage of the geographical distance between New York and the central authorities to pursue his own agenda.

As things turned out *Spotlight on Dracula* did not prove to be a great success. Since the tour included visits to isolated locations that were outside the main tourist circuits it was more expensive than other packages to Romania and beyond the means of many Dracula enthusiasts (see Florescu and McNally 1976). The tour was scheduled to run 16 times between 1972 and 1973 (General Tours 1972) but most of these trips were cancelled due to lack of demand, although the tour did run on a few occasions with low numbers.[19] The Romanian government showed little enthusiasm for the tour but did not actively oppose it.[20] However, the significance of *Spotlight on Dracula* was that it brought Dracula to the attention of the Romanian authorities for the first time, compelling them to respond in some way.

The Romanian Response

The launch of *Spotlight on Dracula* caused consternation among the central authorities in Bucharest in a way that Raiescu had not anticipated.[21] By his own account Raiescu had not obtained prior approval for the tour: instead, he had sent the necessary documentation to the propaganda section of the Central Committee of the Communist Party in Bucharest at the same time as the first group of tourists arrived. Raiescu was recalled to Bucharest to explain his actions. The Ministry of Tourism was similarly perturbed by *Spotlight on Dracula*. In the late 1960s, ONT had developed increasing experience in the development of themed tours (largely based on rural, heritage and cultural tourism) but Dracula tourism was a new form of special interest tourism that tourism planners had not anticipated and did not understand. Consequently, the Ministry of Tourism was completely unprepared for a tour which light-heartedly advised tourists to stock up on garlic to ward off evil and which presented Transylvania as 'the home of vampire lore, ancient superstitions and rituals dating back to pre-Christian times' (General Tours 1972: no pagination). Ioan Cosma, the Minister of Tourism[22] called a meeting of

---

19   Alexander Harris (Chairman of General Tours), interview.

20   Alexander Harris (Chairman of General Tours), interview.

21   Nicolae Păduraru, interview; Andrei Raiescu, interview.

22   Ioan Cosma was Minister of Tourism from December 1970 to March 1978. Originally a railway fitter, he had previously been Minister for Railways and Minister for Agriculture and Forestry. He had been a member of the Central Committee of the RCP since 1955 (Consiliul Naţional pentru Studierea Arhivelor Securităţii 2004). His knowledge and understanding of tourism was probably limited.

various ONT employees and established a working group to look at how Romania should respond to *Spotlight on Dracula*. Among those present were various ONT guides who, through interpreting for foreign tourists, had come to understand the Western interest in the fictional Dracula (at least one guide present had read a copy of *Dracula* donated by a foreign tourist). As a result there were some within the Ministry of Tourism who understood the power of the Western Dracula myth for attracting foreign tourists to Romania.[23] Romania's tourism planners now faced a choice of whether to exploit or discourage this form of tourism.

From the outset Dracula tourism presented socialist Romania with a dilemma. On one hand, Romania had much to gain by promoting this form of tourism. Dracula was a means to attract additional Western tourists to Romania, thus generating further hard currency earnings. Romania was open to new forms of tourism development and Dracula was a means for the country to diversify its tourist product by offering something in addition to the beach holidays and cultural tourism that were currently its main attractions. Moreover, since Romania's association with Dracula was unique, this was not a form of tourism that could be offered (or imitated) by other European countries (including Romania's neighbours). In addition, the promotion of Dracula could potentially contribute to making Romania better known at a time when Ceauşescu was seeking to raise Romania's international profile.[24]

On the other hand, at a time when the Romanian state was seeking to use international tourism to celebrate the agenda and achievements of state socialism and to raise Romania's international profile and standing, Romania had strong reasons for wanting nothing to do with Dracula tourism. In various ways such tourism, based around some form of belief in vampires and the supernatural, was fundamentally discordant with Romania's identity as a socialist state. Socialism was a political project founded on a radical and irreversible break with the past (Boia 1999, 2000). Its aim was the creation of a completely new society and a 'new man'. The ideology of Marxist-Leninism was resolutely scientific and materialist in its foundations. Thus anything associated with the supernatural was regarded as the remnant of a discredited past that socialism was busily sweeping away.[25] Socialist regimes tended to treat rural areas – where superstition and beliefs in the supernatural lingered longest – with particular distrust. Marx and Engels had famously spoken of the 'idiocy of rural life' (1998: 7) and socialist regimes pursued a policy of modernization that was intended to eliminate the divide between town and country and turn rural peasants into an urban proletariat (see Turnock 1991b).

---

23   Nicolae Păduraru, interview.

24   According to Ion Pacepa, one of Ceauşescu's senior intelligence officers who defected in 1978, Ceauşescu launched 'Operation Horizon' in 1972, a campaign to raise Romania's profile as an independent minded state within the socialist bloc (Pacepa 1988). However, Pacepa's book may not be entirely reliable (Deletant 1995).

25   An indication of the Romanian government's position regarding rural superstitions can be found in Hillyer (1988: 64).

In the course of this social transformation rural superstitions were expected to disappear entirely. Therefore socialist Romania had no desire to encourage tourists in their search for something – the supernatural – that was the very antithesis of the socialist project (see also Yan and Bramwell 2008).

Dracula tourism was additionally problematic for Romania's socialist regime in that it was inseparable from long established ways of representing Transylvania that were unwelcome in Romania but over which the country had little influence. In particular, the Balkanist discourse of *Dracula* insists on the Otherness of Transylvania (and by extension, Romania) by portraying it as part of a backward, marginal and undeveloped periphery that lags behind Western Europe in terms of economic and social development. Yet such a portrayal starkly collided with Romania's image of itself (and the identity it sought to project to the wider world) as a rapidly modernizing, industrialized state, engaged on building a new society to rival that of the capitalist West. Similarly, at a time when Nicolae Ceauşescu was seeking to raise his country's profile and present himself as an international statesman he had no wish for his country to be regarded by the rest of the world as a vampire-stalked netherworld.

Thus, Dracula tourism presented Romania with a dilemma that Tunbridge (1994: 127) has described (in a related context) as 'identity versus economy' (see also Light 2000). The exploitation of Dracula for tourism offered considerable economic benefits but at the same time would compromise Romania's sense of its own identity and the image it was seeking to project to the rest of the world. Acting as the arbiter and protector of the cultural and political identity presented to tourists (Wood 1984, Cano and Mysyk 2004) and protector of the country's interests (see C.M. Hall 2005) the Romanian state appears to have given priority at this time to safeguarding the image of socialist Romania itself, and of Vlad Ţepeş, one of its prominent national figures. It was hardly surprising, then, that Ioan Cosma's working group decided that the promotion of tourism based on the Western Dracula myth was not an appropriate development for socialist Romania.[26]

Nevertheless, Cosma seems to have accepted that Dracula could attract tourists to Romania. His response was to ask ONT to develop a Romanian-led themed programme based on the historical Dracula.[27] ONT's Programme Development Department seems to have approached this task with considerable enthusiasm,[28] treating it as a new opportunity to showcase socialist Romania for Western tourists who might not otherwise visit.[29] The tour – entitled *Dracula: Legend and Truth* – was launched in mid-1973 (and continued to operate throughout the socialist

---

26   Nicolae Păduraru, interview.

27   Nicolae Păduraru, interview.

28   ONT also invited academic historians to participate in writing the script for the tour guides (Cazacu 2008).

29   Nicolae Păduraru, interview. See also Păduraru (1972b).

period). It was offered in four, eight and 14 day versions[30] (the second week of the latter was often spent at the Black Sea). The tour was centred on the life of Vlad Ţepeş, and included visits to places associated with the Voievode in Bucharest, Snagov, Poienari, Târgovişte, Braşov, Sibiu and Sighisoara (see Chapter 3). However, visits to places associated with the fictional Dracula were not included and the tour made no mention of vampirism.[31] The state also developed souvenirs tied in with the tour including Vlad Ţepeş dolls and woodcuts that were sold in hard currency shops (Brokow 1976, Haining 1976).

Dracula: Legend and Truth was more than just a themed tourist package intended to accommodate Western interest in Dracula. Like any presentation of a nation-state's history to foreign visitors, the tour was underpinned by an ideological agenda (Horne 1984, Allcock 1995). *Dracula: Legend and Truth* had a clearly propagandist scope: it was a rhetorical presentation of Vlad Ţepeş as a national hero and was intended to refute the image of the Voievode as a cruel tyrant that was prevalent in the West following the publication of *In Search of Dracula*.[32] Furthermore, in presenting Vlad as a figure who had fought to defend Romania's national independence, *Dracula: Legend and Truth* contained echoes of Ceauşescu's attempts to pursue an independent foreign policy. On another level, in rejecting the association between Vlad Ţepeş and vampirism the tour sought to counter the Western place myth of Transylvania as the home of the supernatural. There were also other dimensions. By including visits to sites (such as the Princely Court at Târgovişte) that had been recently restored, socialist Romania was able to demonstrate to tourists its concern for the historic environment. Through the inclusion of a Transylvanian leg (even if some of the locations included were only marginally connected with the life of Vlad Ţepeş) the tour affirmed Transylvania's status as a part of Romania (in accordance with Andrei Raiescu's activities in America). Overall, *Dracula: Legend and Truth* was socialist Romania's attempt to challenge and contest Western representations of the country's history and identity and to try to manage Dracula tourism on Romania's own terms (Light 2007a, Hainagiu 2008).

At around the same time as the launch of *Dracula: Legend and Truth*, a special edition (May 1973) of *Holidays in Romania* was dedicated to the theme of Dracula. This was the first occasion that Dracula had been mentioned in Romania's foreign-language tourist promotion. The issue was written by a team who clearly had some understanding of the Dracula novel and films[33] and even included quotes from

---

30   Source: *Holidays in Romania;* Mackenzie (1983); information supplied by Andrei Raiescu.

31   According to Ştefan Andrei (Romania's foreign minister, 1978–1985) ONT guides were specifically instructed not make any reference to vampires.

32   Nicolae Păduraru, interview.

33   According to Nicolae Păduraru, during the preparation of *Dracula: Legend and Truth*, Ioan Cosma arranged for a limited number of Romanians (mainly historians, literary critics and those working in foreign tourism promotion) to read Stoker's novel and to see

Stoker's novel.[34] The magazine contained articles about the global popularity of Count Dracula (sometimes written in a faintly incredulous tone); features on some of the Romanian locations in the novel; and articles about Vlad Ţepeş (including a piece by Constantin Giurescu), along with suggestions for visits to places associated with the historical Dracula. In its way this edition of *Holidays in Romania* had the same propagandist agenda as the *Dracula: Legend and Truth* tour, seeking to present a favourable image of Vlad Ţepeş and using Dracula as the starting point for promoting Transylvania more generally. Nevertheless, by using 'Dracula' for both the literary and historical figures it did little to resolve the confusion between them.

   Dracula: Legend and Truth proved to be a popular offer, attracting tourists from Spain, America, West Germany, France and Sweden in its first year (Anon 1973). However, for many visitors the tour did not live up to their expectations. Some turned up in capes and plastic fangs clearly expecting an experience based on Stoker's vampire. Consequently, many were perplexed to be following the trail of a fifteenth-century Voievode in whom they had little interest. Thus, while *Dracula: Legend and Truth* was intended to communicate a particular message, tourists 'read' the tour in different ways than intended, and many may have misunderstood it. Unwittingly, the tour did exactly the opposite of what it was intended to achieve: rather than clearly differentiating between Stoker's vampire and Vlad Ţepeş, it ended up furthering the confusion between the two.[35]

Local Initiatives in Northeast Romania

While the Ministry of Tourism attempted to confine its involvement with Dracula tourism to the promotion of a Vlad Ţepeş trail, it was unable to contain the enthusiasm of Dracula fans and literary tourists who continued to seek out the locations mentioned in Stoker's novel. The search led them to northeast Transylvania where Stoker's novel opens. In what is probably the most inspired and evocative part of *Dracula,* Stoker paints a vivid picture of an Englishman journeying into an unknown and sinister land. Jonathan Harker's journey takes him from Budapest, through Klausenberg (Cluj in Romanian) to Bistritz (Bistriţa) where he spends a night at the Golden Crown hotel before leaving for Castle Dracula in the Borgo Pass. In this remote part of Romania, a form of Dracula

---

some of the Dracula films, in order that they might better understand the Western Dracula phenomenon.

   34   The quotations from *Dracula* in this edition of *Holidays in Romania* are not taken directly from the English-language version of the novel. Instead, they appear to be translations *into* English from a Romanian edition. This further suggests that a Romanian translation of Stoker's novel was in existence at this time (see Light 2009b) even if it was not on general release.

   35   Nicolae Păduraru, interview.

tourism based on Stoker's novel was discretely developed in the 1970s, through local initiatives that were largely unknown to the central authorities in Bucharest.[36]

In 1968 a group of three American journalists had visited the Borgo Pass (*Pasul Bârgăului*) in an unsuccessful search for Dracula's castle (see Păduraru 1973). They had sought help from Alexandru Misiuga, then director of the local *Casa de Creația Populară* (an organization concerned with folk culture and traditions). Like most Romanians, Misiuga knew nothing of *Dracula* and tried to convince the journalists that there was no castle in the Borgo Pass. Nevertheless, he noted the name and author of the book that had inspired their search.

In May 1971 Misiuga – who was a charismatic, energetic and creative individual – was named director of the newly created *Oficiul Județean de Turism* (County Tourist Office) for the county of Bistrița-Năsăud. Although this was not among the most prestigious positions within the local socialist hierarchy it was nonetheless an important promotion for Misiuga and in order to achieve the position he would have needed to be in good standing with the county committee of the RCP. Since the post of director would have involved contact with foreign tourists as well as access to Western currencies Misiuga's promotion would also need the clearance of the county division (*Inspectorat*) of the state security service (the *Securitate*[37]). By coincidence, Ion Mânzat,[38] the deputy head of the *Inspectorat* and head of the counter-espionage service for the county of Bistrița-Năsăud was a long-time friend of Misiuga's: the latter had appointed Mânzat to his first job in a Cultural Centre in the Bârgău valley in 1955. Mânzat, in turn, was close friends with the Deputy

---

36   The following section is based on interviews in 2004 with Alexandru Misiuga and Ion Mânzat, supplemented by material from Mânzat's memoirs (Mânzat 2008). Each told a broadly similar story although there were some significant differences between their accounts (and I suspect that the flamboyant Misiuga may have exaggerated his own role in affairs). The narrative that follows is my interpretation of how events unfolded, based on Misiuga's and Mânzat's stories. Wherever possible I have triangulated this narrative against external events or published information.

37   The *Securitate* (*Departamentul Securității Statului* or Department of State Security) was the state body concerned with national security in Romania throughout the communist period. It has gained a notorious reputation, particularly for the terror and repression it instituted during the 1950s and again for the surveillance, repression and harassment employed during the 1980s (see Deletant 1995). It should be noted that the particular time discussed here (the early 1970s) was one of relative relaxation in Ceaușescu's Romania. Furthermore, in the remote rural county of Bistrița-Năsăud the activities of the *Securitate* are likely to have been less draconian and intrusive during the early 1970s than in earlier decades (I am grateful to Dennis Deletant for this observation).

38   Such is the reputation of the *Securitate* that a county head of this organization might be expected to be a severe, single-minded and even amoral individual. Mânzat, who is an educated and dignified man, does not fit this stereotype. According to his own account he was disgraced and forced to take early retirement in 1985 for failing to implement an order from Ceaușescu to arm the police in rural areas to enable them to open fire on anyone caught stealing food before the harvest (see also Mânzat 2008).

First Secretary of the local Communist Party, Lazăr Tănase. Among Tănase's roles was overseeing the development of tourism in Bistrița-Năsăud, but he was prepared to give Misiuga a free hand to pursue his own projects. Thus, Misiuga had plentiful social capital – defined as 'an individual's knowledge of and ability to utilize social networks and spheres of influence' (Ghodsee 2005: 13). Indeed, in socialist Romania, personal contacts, connections and 'who you knew' were crucial in being able to get something done or to secure access to scarce resources (Verdery 1991, 2004). Misiuga's personal contacts and good standing with both the local Party, *Securitate* and State institutions allowed him the freedom to be creative in his plans to develop tourism in the county.

Nevertheless, Misiuga's options in Bistrița-Năsăud were limited. This remote and predominantly rural county was far removed from the main tourist circuits in Romania and contained few tourist attractions. Consequently the county contained little tourist infrastructure and attracted few foreign tourists (Mânzat 2008). However, the national Five Year Plan (1971–5) aimed for a greater redistribution of tourism throughout Romania, in addition to increasing hard currency earnings from tourism. As such, Misiuga was required to increase the level of tourism activity in Bistrița-Năsăud. Indeed, he recounted that his guiding principle at this time was '*noua ne trebuie valuta'* ('we must bring in hard currency').

Since the town of Bistrița had no hotel, Misiuga's first action was to bid to the Ministry of Tourism for the investment necessary to build a new hotel in the town. He argued that he would be unable to fulfil his requirement to attract foreign tourists and hard currency to Bistrița-Nasăud without being able to offer adequate accommodation. Misiuga had a strong case and both Mânzat and Tănase supported the project with the higher authorities in Bucharest.[39] Funding for the hotel was quickly granted and a site was selected on an empty plot of land on the edge of the town centre. Misiuga was able to persuade the architects to build something that differed from the standardized rectangular concrete block that was the usual form for hotels in socialist Romania. Instead, the Bistrița hotel was more individualized in its design and sympathetic to its surroundings.

Misiuga had succeeded to secure accommodation for foreign tourists but he was now also aware that Western tourists were increasingly drawn to his county in the search for the literary Dracula. This was confirmed when he received a promotional brochure for the General Tours *Spotlight on Dracula* package which included a visit to Bistrița. As a matter of course he would have been required to inform the local *Securitate* and Communist Party of the fact. Coincidentally, Ion Mânzat was one of the few people in the county (and country) who knew something about the literary Dracula. Mânzat had been born in the Borgo (Bârgău) Pass and, as a teenager he had read the abridged version of *Dracula* that had been serialized in *Realitatea ilustrată* which he had discovered in a neighbour's house. Mânzat was able to give Misiuga more information about the literary Dracula and was even able to find a copy of the *Realitatea ilustrată* serialization of *Dracula*

---

39   According to Mânzat, Tănase had good political connections in the capital.

(although Misiuga was only able to keep it for a few days). Misiuga subsequently became an enthusiastic fan of the novel.[40]

Thus, both Mânzat and Misiuga recognized that Dracula could play a key role in putting Bistriţa-Năsăud on the tourism trail. As head of the local *Securitate,* information was Mânzat's job and he was in a position to find out more on the popularity of the fictional Dracula in the West. He contacted a former school colleague now working at the British Embassy in London who supplied more details. Mânzat passed his findings on to Misiuga who now had all the information he needed to make Bistriţa the centre of Dracula tourism in Romania. Mânzat also sounded out his superiors in Bucharest about the use of Dracula to promote tourism in the Bistriţa region.[41] They raised no objection (although how much they understood of what was planned in Bistriţa is uncertain) and advised him to proceed 'intelligently'.

Bistrita's planned hotel, now under construction, had yet to be allocated a name. Misiuga was, by now, well aware of the potential of Dracula to attract tourists to Bistriţa-Năsăud and he determined to name Bistriţa's hotel after the Golden Crown Hotel in Stoker's novel. However, this was not Misiuga's decision to make: the act of attributing names was an important manifestation of authority in socialist Romania (see Light et al. 2002) and the name for the hotel would have to be approved by the county committee of the RCP. Although the local Party had supported the building of the hotel, Misiuga was aware that he would have trouble persuading the Party to accept the name *Coroana de Aur* (Golden Crown) since any evocation of royalty was anathema in a socialist state. Misiuga was also aware that he would have difficulties persuading the Party to approve a name linked to a form of tourism based on vampires and the supernatural.

After two unsuccessful attempts Misiuga succeeded in persuading the local Party to accept *Coroana de Aur,* although only after inventing a story that the eponymous crown was that of a local Voievode, Petru Rareş. Misiuga took a copy of the *Spotlight on Dracula* brochure to a meeting with the First Secretary of the Bistriţa-Năsăud Party, Adalbert Crisan. He explained the story of the fictional Dracula, presenting it as a story about the triumph of good over evil (and almost certainly avoiding any reference to vampires), and that it had the potential to attract

---

40　Misiuga himself often told the story of how he used personal contacts in Bucharest to gain access to a Romanian translation of *Dracula* dating from 1923 which was kept 'under index' (that is, restricted access) in a Bucharest library. Since there is no record in any of Bucharest's deposit libraries of a Romanian translation of *Dracula* before 1990 I think it is more likely that Misiuga read the *Realitatea ilustrată* serialization of Dracula that was provided by Mânzat.

41　According to Mânzat, among those he consulted were Nicolae Doicaru (then head of the *Departamentul de Informaţii Externe,* the foreign intelligence service) and Ion Pacepa, Doicaru's deputy. Perhaps anything involving attracting foreign tourists to Bistriţa needed some form of clearance from the branch of the *Securitate* that dealt with external matters. Doicaru died in 1991 while Pacepa defected to the USA in 1978.

large numbers of foreign tourists (and foreign currency) to Bistriţa. Since Crisan was an ethnic Hungarian, Misiuga also appealed to national sentiment by arguing that had *Dracula* been set in Hungary, the Hungarians would have exploited it for tourism. He was also aware that under the Five Year Plan each county was expected to attract hard currency through any appropriate means, and that the First Secretary of the local Party was responsible for achieving the demands of the Plan. Moreover, as a Hungarian in Ceauşescu's Romania, Crisan's position was potentially uncertain if he failed to fulfil the Plan.[42] Crisan knew nothing about the fictional Dracula, but since Misiuga had a solid reputation with the local Party and *Securitate* he was prepared to back Misiuga's initiative.

The 216 bed *Coroana de Aur* hotel opened on 30 April 1974 (see Figure 4.2) and received its first guest two weeks later (Anon 1974). There was little other than the name to link the hotel with Dracula (for example, before 1989 there was no Dracula or vampire theme in the hotel's internal décor) but it nevertheless quickly became one of the most important sites for Western tourists on the Count Dracula trail. Misiuga continued to cater for Dracula fans, devising a menu based on that eaten by Jonathan Harker at the fictional Golden Crown and a series of souvenirs for Dracula enthusiasts, including a Dracula 'elixir' (Mackenzie 1977, 1983). Any foreign tourist familiar with the Dracula phenomenon would have little doubt of the hotel's significance. On the other hand, beyond the hotel's employees, the local Party and *Securitate* and some of those who wrote for Romania's foreign-language tourism promotion, there were few people in Romania who would have recognized the significance of the *Coroana de Aur* for Western Dracula enthusiasts.

The building of *Coroana de Aur* hotel illustrates the interplay between central power and local initiative in socialist Romania as well as the importance of individual agency in a state which worked on the basis of centralized decision-making and which distrusted individualism. There is a widespread assumption that socialist party-states such as Romania were all-seeing and all-powerful entities. They were believed to work on the basis of total and perfect control from the 'centre': the decisions taken in the centre were consistently implemented at all levels of society and throughout the state's territory. Moreover, the supremacy of centralized decision-making was ensured through a complex surveillance apparatus. However, in reality, this was far from the case. For example, Nelson's study of local political elites in socialist Romania (1980) revealed that such groups did not always share the agenda or priorities of the 'centre' and sometimes disagreed in their interpretations of what should be given priority. This opens up the possibility that localized decision-making was not simply passive obedience to the dictates of the centre. Similarly, Turnock (1991b, 1991c) has highlighted how local authorities in the northern county of Maramureş sought to circumvent the planning regulations issued from the centre about the restructuring of rural settlement. As Verdery (1991: 84) argues: 'Policies may be made at the centre, but they are *implemented* in local settings, where those entrusted with them may

---

42   I am grateful to Daniela Dumbrăveanu for this observation.

Figure 4.2 **The *Coroana de Aur* hotel**

ignore, corrupt, over-execute, or otherwise adulterate them'. Hence, outside the centre, the power of the state progressively diminished and could be compromised, negotiated and even resisted in all sorts of ways at the local level. As such, Verdery (1991, 1996, 2004) has argued that socialist states were much weaker than is frequently supposed.

This seems to be the framework for understanding what happened in Bistriţa. The central tourism authorities had no policy to develop tourism based on the fictional Dracula. Had such a policy existed, the Dracula connection could have been exploited (with far more vigour) at other locations associated with Stoker's novel – Cluj, the Borgo Pass, Galaţi and even Vereşti. Instead, the Ministry of Tourism had made a decision in 1972 not to encourage tourism based on the vampire Dracula. As such, the decision to theme Bistriţa's hotel to cater for Dracula tourists was a local initiative, resulting from Misiuga's personal enthusiasm for the fictional Dracula and his effective partnership with Ion Mânzat. Like Andrei Raiescu in New York, Misiuga was able to use the geographical distance between himself and the 'centre' to pursue his own agenda. He could take advantage of being one of the few people in Romania to have read *Dracula* and to have recognized its significance for tourism. He was then able to put his personal enthusiasm for the novel to work in order to achieve the state's economic plan for his county. Through a combination of his personal charisma and determination, his extensive social capital, and his ability to ensure that nobody knew anything more about his plans than they needed to, Misiuga was able to achieve his desire of building a Golden Crown Hotel in Bistriţa. This is not to say that Misiuga's actions were entirely altruistic. By attracting foreign tourists and foreign currency to Bistriţa-Năsăud

Misiuga would have gained prestige and influence with the local Communist Party in addition to consolidating his personal position as head of the local OJT.[43]

However, while Misiuga was the driving force behind the *Coroana de Aur* he would have been unable to proceed without the support of the local Communist Party and *Securitate*. For the Party, Dracula tourism was simply a means to attract hard currency to Bistriţa. It is unlikely that any of the local Party officials shared Misiuga's understanding of the Western Dracula. For the local *Securitate* Misiuga's project was something that achieved the state's economic policy without posing any threat to national security. Indeed, Ion Mânzat's discreet support (and apparently the absence of any objections among his superiors within the *Securitate* at this time) was crucial to enabling Misiuga to turn Bistriţa into the centre for Dracula tourism in Romania. Buoyed by his success with the *Coroana de Aur* Misiuga went on (once again, with Mânzat's support) to develop a hotel-castle in the Borgo Pass, specifically to cater for Dracula enthusiasts who were searching for Castle Dracula (see Chapter 5).

The Reluctant Acceptance of Count Dracula

In the early 1970s the Romanian Ministry of Tourism had been unwilling to promote a form of tourism based on the literary Dracula. Its priorities were to reject any association between Romania and the supernatural and also to safeguard the reputation of Vlad Ţepeş from any associations with vampires. However, during the mid-1970s the Ministry appears to have adopted a more pragmatic position. While there were few Ministry officials with enthusiasm for (or understanding of) Stoker's vampire, they appear to have recognized that the popularity of the Western Dracula was something that attracted tourists to Romania. Undoubtedly, a crucial consideration was the target of the 1971–5 Five Year Plan (Partidul Comunist Român 1969) which called for a 40–45 per cent increase in external trade (and identified international tourism as a key component of Romania's external trade). At the same time the Romanian economy was starting to face difficulties. In 1971 Romania had a trade deficit with the industrial West of $1.8 billion (Braun 1978) which had risen to £3.6 billion by 1977 and $10.2 billion by 1981 (Deletant 1999). The 1973 oil crisis had a major impact by raising the price of Western imports (Braun 1978) and in 1974 a compulsory foreign exchange requirement of $10 per day was introduced for foreign tourists.

In these circumstances, much as it might have wanted to continue safeguarding Romania's international image from any association with vampires and the supernatural, the Ministry of Tourism could not ignore the potential of Dracula to attract Western tourists and their hard currency spending. Thus, during the mid

---

43   The heads of the County Tourism Offices (OJTs) were influential people in that they were responsible for managing the hard currency exchanged by foreign tourists within their county as well as the sale of goods to foreign tourists within hard currency shops. I am grateful to Daniela Dumbrăveanu for this observation.

and late 1970s the Ministry seems to have adopted a position of accepting and reluctantly tolerating tourism based on the Western Dracula myth, but without doing anything to encourage it.[44] Renato Iliescu, a Ministry of Tourism official expressed Romania's position as follows:

> Vampirism never existed in Romanian folklore and this character depicted by Stoker was purely the product of his imagination. We reject his position completely. What we want to do now is show the people the real Dracula, our hero. We are, of course, always pleased to earn money, but not at the expense of our history. (cited in Tyler 1978: 4)

The Ministry of Tourism's stance on Dracula tourism is reflected in its foreign-language tourism promotion, particularly *Holidays in Romania*. No attempt was made to promote Romania as the land of the literary Dracula and there was obviously no emphasis on the strange and supernatural in Romania. Instead, the magazine stressed the wide range of other attractions the country offered. Nevertheless, *Holidays in Romania* acknowledged that Western tourists were interested in Dracula and during the 1970s and 1980s there were usually a few features each year which mentioned Stoker's vampire. However, the writers often adopted a mocking tone, suggesting little enthusiasm for the vampire Dracula. For example:

> We did not try to look for vampire stories along Valea Bîrgăului [Borgo Pass] ... for people are busy with more simple and more important problems ... In the village of Rusu Bîrgăului ... we drank sweet flavoured plum brandy which would have made any Dracula forget his vampire duties and drink the health of ordinary beings. Dracula might have become a perfectly well-disposed person if he could have visited with us the village of Josenii Bîrgăului. (Raicu 1978: 19)

In addition, *Holidays in Romania* continued to play a role in the propagandist effort to counter the confusion between the literary and historical Draculas. Like Romanian historians, the writers for *Holidays in Romania* had accepted the argument of McNally and Florescu (1972) that Stoker had used Vlad Ţepeş as the model for Count Dracula. However they frequently stressed that the two were entirely different characters and that Vlad Ţepeş had no links with vampirism. A two page article in 1976 lauded the Voievode in language identical to that used by Romanian historians for an internal audience. The Impaler was evoked as 'a hero who devoted his life to defending his country's independence, as well as European civilisation ... he made all this because he loved justice more than any other thing' (Neagoe 1976: 9).

---

44   Ştefan Andrei, Ion Mânzat and Andrei Raiescu each independently described the stance of the Romanian state regarding Dracula tourism in these terms.

However, while the Ministry of Tourism was unwilling to promote directly a form of tourism based on Stoker's vampire, Dracula enthusiasts were undeterred and some started to devise their own themed holidays in Romania. One of the first such visits was that of Britain's Dracula Society in September/October 1974. Two Gothic literature enthusiasts had founded the Society in the previous year after one had returned from a visit to Romania disappointed that the tour had not included any of the locations mentioned in Stoker's novel (Davies 1997). The Society was founded purposely to undertake travel to Romania for Dracula enthusiasts who wanted to see for themselves the places described by Stoker. The then Secretary, Bernard Davies, devised a detailed itinerary for the 12 day tour that followed the locations described in the novel. ONT participated in arranging a tour based on this itinerary: it seems to have been prepared to accommodate a special interest group which was searching for the literary rather than the supernatural roots of the novel (see Anon 1975). The tour included a stay at the recently opened *Coroana de Aur* hotel in Bistriţa. The ONT guide who accompanied the group noted that it was an eye-opening experience to observe the seriousness with which enthusiasts took the literary Dracula.[45] The Dracula Society returned to Romania again a number of times in the following years.

Subsequently, Western tour operators began to recognize that there was a demand for Dracula tours to Romania. During the 1970s an increasing number of holiday companies developed their own packages themed (to varying extents) on the Western Dracula myth[46] (see Cioranescu 1977, Davies 1997). These also included themed 'Halloween in Transylvania' tours. These packages ran in parallel with ONT's *Dracula: Legend and Truth*.

Furthermore, some ONT guides, recognizing the interest in the fictional Dracula began to promote Dracula tourism on their own initiative. They were able to take advantage of the widespread ignorance of the fictional Dracula in Romania to offer their own excursions to the part of Transylvania where Stoker set Dracula. This was an acceptable practice since guides were encouraged to offer extra visits and excursions to Western tourists as a way of encouraging them to spend more money in Romania.[47] At least one ONT guide, recognizing that many who had taken the *Dracula: Legend and Truth* tour were disappointed with their experience, offered tourists the opportunity to forego a part of their second week at the Black Sea and spend three days in northeast Transylvania

---

45   Nicolas Păduraru, interview.

46   Daniel Farson's 1974 BBC documentary *The Dracula Business* (Directed by Anthony de Lotbiniere) includes footage of a 'Sovereign Holidays Dracula Tour'. Farson argues that the Romanian authorities were enthusiastic about developing Dracula tourism although his main source for this claim was Alexandru Misiuga whose agenda (as I have argued earlier) did not mirror that of the central authorities in Bucharest.

47   See Brokaw (1976, 33–34).

visiting locations associated with the fictional Dracula. In most cases around half the group took up his offer.[48]

Romanian tourism experienced a healthy expansion during the 1970s. By 1975 Romania received 3.7 million foreign visitors (see Figure 4.1). Although the proportion of visitors from non-socialist countries did not change greatly (17 per cent in 1975) the absolute numbers of visitors from such countries continued to increase. In 1975 Romania received 630,706 Western tourists, a 48 per cent increase on 1970, while over the 1970–75 period the number of visitors from the UK, America and France increased by 96 per cent, 86 per cent and 73 per cent respectively.[49] By now Dracula tourism had established itself as an important (if still a minority) market segment. Although there is little data to indicate the extent of such tourism there are isolated indications of the significance of Dracula to Romanian tourism. For example, Daniel Farson claims that 6,000 Spanish Dracula enthusiasts were booked to visit Romania in 1974.[50] By 1977 Bran Castle – widely known outside Romania as 'Dracula's Castle' – attracted over 200,000 visitors. In Bistriţa, the *Coroana de Aur* hotel apparently had an 80 per cent occupancy rate, with around half of all visitors being from outside Romania.[51]

Although the Ministry of Tourism was unwilling to use the literary Dracula in its tourism promotion, Andrei Raiescu in New York was more enthusiastic (see Agniel 1975). Recognising the appeal of Dracula in America Raiescu's promotion for an American audience evoked the image of Transylvania that was associated with Gothic horror films. One widely used advertisement featured a full moon and stormy sky, in front of which stood the spires and turrets of a medieval castle surrounded by forests. Superimposed on the moon was the text 'Yes there is a TRANSYLVANIA and Wallachia and Moldovia and they're all in ROMANIA'.[52] Similar allusions to Dracula (without ever mentioning the character by name) were used in radio advertisements featuring the sound of a howling wolf and an impersonation of Bela Lugosi declaiming 'Welcome to the Carpathians'. Once again, Raiescu was following his own agenda, taking advantage of his distance from the central authorities. In a competitive market to attract American tourists Raiescu was prepared to use whatever was mostly likely to be recognized by the American public to promote Romania.[53]

48　Nicolae Păduraru, interview (see also Hainagiu 2008).

49　These figures are derived from internal ONT data concerning the number of visitors from selected non-socialist countries during the 1970s. These data were supplied by Andrei Raiescu.

50　Daniel Farson, *The Dracula Business* (Directed by Anthony de Lotbiniere).

51　Alexandru Misiuga, interview. Despite repeated searches I have not been able to obtain any figures for visitor numbers at the hotel before 1989 and it is unlikely that such data still exists.

52　Andrei Raiescu showed me a copy of this advertisement which was in his personal collection. By his own account, Raiescu did not clear it with the central authorities in Bucharest.

53　Andrei Raiescu, interview.

Romania's uneasy compromise with Dracula tourism continued through the 1970s but during the 1980s attitudes hardened. Ceauşescu pursued an increasingly isolationist course, pushing ahead with a series of draconian policies that caused unprecedented austerity and hardship for most Romanians. As I noted in Chapter 2 the label 'Dracula' came to be increasingly applied to the president himself. Ceauşescu almost certainly had some awareness of this since he had been barracked by protesters chanting 'Dracula', during a visit to the USA in 1978 (Pacepa 1988).[54] Evidently, this was not a reputation that the regime wished to encourage and in response Ceauşescu's Romania became increasingly hostile towards the Western Dracula, the best example being Adrian Păunescu's bitter attack on the whole Dracula phenomenon (see Chapter 3).

Thus, in the 1980s Romania appeared to disassociate itself from Dracula tourism as much as possible (see Ionescu 1986). Tourists visiting Romania for Dracula were still tolerated and indeed ONT arranged its first Halloween tour in 1986 (Păduraru 1986). However, references to Dracula in *Holidays in Romania* all but disappeared and those few articles that do mention Dracula tourism do so very briefly. In any case, international tourism in Romania experienced a sharp decline during the 1980s (see Figure 4.1) and visitor numbers fell from seven million in 1981 to 4.85 million by 1989.[55] Ceauşescu's debt repayment policy resulted in rationing of food and energy while, due to a lack of investment, the quality of tourism infrastructure declined to a level below that expected by Western tourists. The regime's paranoia meant that foreigners (including tourists) were the objects of suspicion and subject to careful surveillance[56]. In these circumstances Romania rapidly ceased to be an attractive destination for Western tourists (Light and Dumbrăveanu 1999). By all accounts Romania had become the 'land of Dracula' in more ways than one, and visiting was a horror experience in its own right.

Conclusion

This chapter has traced the development of Dracula tourism in Romania during the socialist period. Demand for this tourism was something generated entirely outside Romania. As Dracula emerged as an increasingly popular global cultural icon during the 1960s and 1970s, fans and enthusiasts began to visit Romania in

---

54   Ceauşescu would have certainly known that Dracula was a name used by Vlad Ţepeş but he was also aware of the Western vampire Dracula, having been briefed on the subject before a press conference during a visit to the USA (Ştefan Andrei, interview).

55   These figures are derived from Comisia Naţională pentru Statistică (1995).

56   Since ONT guides working with foreign tourists were routinely required to report to the *Securitate* on the activities of their groups (see Turnock 1991a, Elliott 1993) there would have been some awareness of Dracula tourism at the lower levels within the *Securitate*. How detailed these reports were and how high up the hierarchy they reached is not clear.

increasing numbers in search of the literary, cinematic and supernatural roots of the Western Dracula myth. This was a form of tourism for which Romania was initially unprepared since the fictional Dracula – and the wider vampire subculture – were almost unknown in Romania. It was also a form of tourism that was politically problematic for the Romanian authorities and its impact was disproportionate to the number of actual tourists involved. Romania's dilemma rested on whether or not to exploit the revenue-generating possibilities of Dracula. The whole notion of tourism based on vampires and the supernatural was unwelcome in Romania since it collided with the country's cultural and political identity as a progressive, modernizing, socialist state (and this was the face that Romania wished to present to the wider world). It was also a form of tourism that risked promoting the unwanted confusion between Count Dracula and Vlad Țepeș.

Romania, then, faced the problem of reconciling what (some) foreign tourists wanted from the country and what it was prepared to offer them. The Romanian state adopted a position of seeking to safeguard Romanian identity and history from associations with vampirism and the supernatural. The only centrally approved attempt to cater for Dracula enthusiasts was the provision of the *Dracula: Legend and Truth* package. This tour, firmly themed on the life of Vlad Țepeș, represented the state's attempt to negotiate and manage Dracula tourism on Romania's own terms but also to counter Western representations of Romania's cultural identity and history. The provision of *Dracula: Legend and Truth* seems to have been the only formal response of the Ministry of Tourism to cater for the demand for Dracula tourism. But, while many tourists took the tour, it failed to satisfy true fans of Stoker's vampire who persisted in their search for the locations mentioned in the novel. Romania's need for hard currency and the success of Dracula in generating it led the state into a position of reluctantly tolerating Dracula tourism whilst making virtually no effort to encourage it. During the 1980s Romania became increasingly hostile to Dracula tourism, but by this time Western tourists were shunning the country anyway.

While there was no central policy to encourage Dracula tourism, there were discrete local initiatives intended to cater for Western Dracula enthusiasts. However, these were the results of individuals who had the confidence and determination to pursue their own agendas without the central authorities fully understanding what they were doing. In New York, Andrei Raiescu played an influential role in the development of Dracula tourism through his participation in the production of *Spotlight on Dracula*. His motives were as much personal and political – to counter what he regarded as a strong Hungarian lobby in America – as they were to implement the state's economic policy to develop international tourism. However, his actions led indirectly to the Ministry of Tourism adopting a policy of using the historical Dracula to attract tourists to Romania. In Bistrița, Alexandru Misiuga used the state's economic policy as a justification to pursue his own enthusiasm for Dracula. The *Coroana de Aur* hotel (and later Hotel Tihuta) was a local initiative, which was only possible because of Misiuga's extensive social capital (his personal friendships with local Party and *Securitate* officials).

Misiuga was able to take advantage of the widespread ignorance of the literary Dracula within Romania to provide Dracula enthusiasts with the experiences (in the right locations) they sought in Transylvania, consolidating his position and reputation at the same time. Yet, there were few outside Bistriţa who understood the significance of what Misiuga had developed. Both Raiescu and Misiuga were operating at the limits of state authority and each was able to exploit their geographical distance from the centre. In any case, despite popular beliefs in the West about the omnipotence of socialist states (Verdery 2004), the authority of such states was much weaker than is widely supposed, and there was plenty of scope at the margins of state power for creative and determined individuals to do their own thing.

Chapter 5

Fiction, History and Myth
at Dracula's Castles

The previous chapter focussed on the development of Dracula tourism in socialist Romania. In this chapter I examine in more detail one of the most significant aspects of Dracula tourism during the socialist period: the search for Castle Dracula. This castle is a key element of Bram Stoker's novel. Jonathan Harker's journey to Transylvania ends at the castle where he is received by Count Dracula. It is from here that Dracula departs for England, leaving Harker to his fate. At the end of the novel, Dracula flees from London to his castle, pursued by Van Helsing and his committee where, in the story's climax, he is finally killed.

Stoker provides an evocative and fairly detailed description of Dracula's castle and one thing is clear: the castle is a ruin. On his arrival, Jonathan Harker describes it as: 'a vast ruined castle, from whose tall black windows came no ray of light, and whose broken battlements showed a jagged line against the moonlit sky' (Stoker 1997: 20). Dracula himself reflects that 'the walls of my castle are broken; the shadows are many, and the wind breathes cold through the broken battlements and casements' (29). In terms of the castle's position, Harker notes that the 'castle is on the very edge of a terrible precipice. A stone falling from the window would fall a thousand feet without touching anything!' (31).

However, Stoker is vague on the exact location of Dracula's castle. Harker notes that he was 'not able to light on any map or work giving the exact locality of the Castle Dracula' (Stoker 1997: 10). A common (but mistaken) assumption is that the castle is located in the Borgo (Bârgău) Pass, although careful attention to the novel reveals that the castle is not in the Pass itself. Harker travels by coach from Bistritz to the Borgo Pass where he is met by Dracula's calèche. From there his journey apparently takes him either south or east along an unmade road that leads into the mountains to Castle Dracula. The journey takes several hours: Harker arrives at the castle at some hour in the middle of the night and has time to eat a meal before dawn arrives (Melton 2011). At the end of the novel, the same journey by Van Helsing and Mina Harker takes two days. From this limited evidence it would seem that Castle Dracula is maybe 20 miles (32 km) from the Borgo Pass. The configuration of the border between Transylvania, Bucovina and Moldova in this area raises the intriguing possibility that (the imaginary) Castle Dracula might not even be located in Transylvania!

Various buildings have been suggested as the inspiration for Stoker's Castle Dracula. In accordance with their thesis that Stoker undertook extensive research into Transylvanian history and geography, McNally and Florescu propose that

Stoker had a specific Transylvanian castle in mind. One contender is Bran Castle in southern Transylvania (McNally and Florescu 1972, MacKenzie 1977, Crisan 2008), while other ruined castles in northeast Transylvania have also been suggested (McNally and Florescu 1994). Others have claimed a source of inspiration outside Transylvania. Haining and Tremayne (1997) suggest Slains Castle in Cruden Bay in Scotland – where Stoker is known to have holidayed – as a model, while others have suggested a combination of Whitby Abbey and Slains Castle (Dukes 1982). Some have even suggested that Stoker was inspired by Elizabeth Bathory's castle at Csejthe (Marigny 1994 cited in Miller 2000). But, while it is possible that Stoker had a real place in mind when he wrote about Castle Dracula it is equally likely that the castle was simply the work of his imagination (Miller 2000). The ruined castle was, after all, a well-established motif in Gothic fiction.

But while Castle Dracula has never existed beyond Stoker's imagination it has, as a result of its repeated portrayal in books and films, become the focus of a powerful and enduring cultural myth. Castle Dracula has become an exemplar of the isolated, crumbling, spectre-ridden ruin that recurs in Gothic literature and film. It is an archetype of Otherness, a sinister and unworldly place where the ineffable and the supernatural have full reign. It is also a distillation of the wider Transylvania place myth and a metonym for Transylvania itself. Castle Dracula represents a liminal space, a 'borderland between the mundane and extraordinary' (Pritchard and Morgan 2006: 764). To visit the castle is to cross (temporarily) a threshold and experience something extraordinary and magical. For some Western tourists such places are irresistible, offering the promise of thrill and enchantment that they could not expect to find at home (see Inglis and Holmes 2003).

Consequently Castle Dracula has long enticed people to Transylvania. Reasoning that Stoker wrote about real places, many tourists have assumed that Dracula's dilapidated castle is a real building and have set out to find it for themselves. However, what they were searching for was arguably an idea or myth of Castle Dracula – a castle of the imagination – rather than a 'real', material location. For those interested in the literary or cinematic roots of *Dracula*, the Castle was a place of discovery, fun, play and escapism. It was an opportunity to give full reign to the imagination and visualize what had previously been seen only in print or on the screen. But for those in search of the supernatural roots of *Dracula* a visit to Castle Dracula promised the ultimate *frisson* of an encounter with the supernatural and numinous (Light 2009a, see also Inglis and Holmes 2003).

Such was the demand among Western tourists for Castle Dracula that, from the 1960s onwards, three places in Romania – Bran Castle, Poienari Citadel and Hotel Tihuţa - have come to be known by this name (see Figure 5.1). In two cases, the name of 'Castle Dracula' was attributed outside Romania to a Romanian fortress, without the support or encouragement of Romania's socialist authorities. However, the third case was a deliberate attempt to construct a building to match the expectations of Western tourists seeking Castle Dracula, although this again was a local initiative that was almost unknown to the central authorities in Bucharest.

This chapter examiners the three Castle Draculas in Romania and considers how the myth of Dracula came to be associated with each of them.

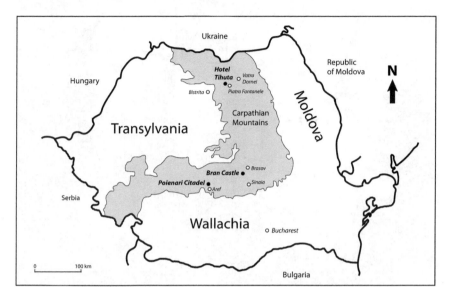

Figure 5.1   The three places in Romania known as Dracula's Castle

Bran Castle

The best known and longest established contender for the role of Castle Dracula is Bran Castle (see Figure 5.2). Located in the very south of Transylvania (and only 100 m from the border with Wallachia), 20 miles (32 km) south of Braşov, the castle stands on a rocky outcrop in the narrowest part of the Bran Pass (see Figure 5.1). The castle – first mentioned in 1377 – was built by the Saxons of nearby Braşov and its principal role was the administration and defence of the border crossing and the collection of customs taxes. Bran Castle was occupied by the Austro-Hungarian army in 1878, and returned to Braşov in 1886 after which it became the headquarters of the Forestry Administration (Prahoveanu 1999). The castle ceased to function as a border point following the union of Transylvania with Wallachia and Moldova in 1918. The city of Braşov subsequently donated the castle to Romania's Queen Marie who used it as a summer residence. Following the proclamation of the People's Republic at the end of 1947 the castle was nationalized. It was subsequently looted by both Soviet troops and Romania's Communist Party authorities and its remaining contents were transferred to the Ministry of Construction and Industry (Anon 2001a). It remained the property of the Romanian state until 2006.

Bran Castle is today in excellent condition. This is partly because its isolated location (and the fact that the Bran valley was easily bypassed) meant that the

Figure 5.2   Bran Castle

castle saw little military action. But, in addition, Bran has undergone repeated and extensive restoration. It was first renovated in 1723 and later extensively restored by the Austro-Hungarian authorities between 1883 and 1886 (Prahoveanu 1999). However, the most extensive restorations and additions took place after 1920 when the castle was transformed into a royal palace. Bran was remodelled in a Romantic, neo-Gothic style which was partly drawn from the castle's original form but which also reflected the flamboyant neo-Gothic royal palace at nearby Peleş. Thus, what visitors see today is less a medieval castle than an early twentieth-century reconstruction of what such a castle might look like.

Bran Castle has no association with the fictional Dracula. It is not mentioned in the novel and Stoker clearly places the fictional Castle Dracula 150 miles (240 km) to the north in the Borgo Pass. Unlike Stoker's fictional castle, Bran is not a ruin. Yet, this has not deterred some writers from seeking to present Bran as the archetype for Castle Dracula. McNally and Florescu (1972: 86) assert that the 'analogies between Stoker's mythical Castle Dracula and the real Castle Bran are simply too close to be coincidental' and even speculate whether Queen Marie chose Bran because of its similarities with the fictional Castle Dracula. MacKenzie (1977) suggests that Stoker may have come across a reproduction of Bran during research at the British Museum and used the castle as the inspiration for Castle Dracula. Yet, such claims exaggerate Stoker's knowledge of Transylvania since there is no mention of Bran in any of Stoker's known sources and no evidence that the author ever knew of the castle (Miller 2000).

Similarly, there is little evidence to connect Bran Castle with Vlad Țepeș. The Impaler certainly did not build Bran. He is recorded by customs documents as travelling through the pass on several occasions (Stoian 1980).[1] He may have stayed as a guest at the castle (Henegariu 1963) although firm evidence is lacking. In 1462 the Impaler was arrested at nearby Piatra Craiului (Andreescu and McNally 1989) on the orders of the Hungarian king and may have subsequently been imprisoned at Bran for a short time before being transferred to Buda (Stoian 1980). Yet from these unpromising foundations, Bran has come to be inseparable from the myth of Dracula. For many Western tourists Bran *is* Dracula's castle. In order to understand how this has happened we need to look at both the production (or presentation) of the site by the Romanian tourist authorities and the way in which it was consumed by Western tourists.

With the growth of both domestic and international tourism during the 1950s and 1960s the Romanian state began to develop various locations as visitor attractions. Despite the rewriting of the national past and the agenda of building a new society, socialist Romania did not initially neglect its legacy of historic buildings and monuments. Many such places were promoted for tourism although they were reinterpreted so as to accord with Marxist (and later, nationalist) narratives of national history. In this context, Bran opened as a visitor attraction in 1957. The socialist authorities sought to reconfigure the formal royal palace by presenting it as a museum of history and feudal art. The interior of the castle contained an eclectic collection of items including furniture from the seventeenth to nineteenth centuries; acts and documents testifying to its administrative and legal function during feudal times; decorative furnishings and tapestries; exhibitions of medieval armour; displays of porcelain and musical instruments; and displays of Romanian and Oriental art and craftsmanship (Prahoveanu and Coşuleţ 1985). An open air ethnographic museum opened beside the castle in 1961 to interpret the rural heritage of the Bran area (Henegariu 1963). A further museum interpreting the history of the border crossing was opened in 1987.

From the late 1950s onwards Bran was actively promoted as a sightseeing attraction for foreign tourists and it featured regularly in foreign-language tourist promotional materials (*Holidays in Romania*). It was only ever promoted as a fine medieval building and never as Dracula's Castle (unsurprisingly, since almost nobody in Romania knew of the fictional Dracula, and the building had very few associations with the historical Dracula). As one of Transylvania's finest monuments (which, furthermore, is easily accessible by road) a visit to Bran Castle featured in many of the organized coach tours of Transylvania introduced by Western holiday operators during the late 1960s and 1970s. In addition, the close proximity of Bran to the nearby Prahova valley meant that it was extensively

---

1   Ioan Prahoveanu, interview.

promoted as a destination for day excursions for tourists staying at the ski resorts of Sinaia, Predeal and Poiana Braşov

The 'official' presentation of Bran Castle was intended to present the castle as an important historical monument and a showpiece of medieval architecture. This was the dominant meaning of the building for domestic tourists. But tourists from non-socialist (Western) countries appropriated or consumed Bran in a completely different way from that intended by the Romanian authorities. To understand the meanings of Bran Castle for Western tourists we need to consider what they brought with them to the site (see Craik 1997, Light 2012). I examined in Chapter 2 the pervasiveness of the Transylvania place myth in Western popular culture and by the 1960s Transylvania had come to be inseparable from Dracula in the Western popular imagination. There were probably few Western tourists (particularly those from English-speaking countries) who had no knowledge of the Dracula of popular culture. Instead, many were drawn to Romania specifically to search for Dracula and some were clearly expecting to find Castle Dracula (see for example, Păduraru 1970). For the tourist, the encounter with Bran will have been framed by a wide range of intertextual representations of Castle Dracula from books, films and other media. Bran Castle is in Transylvania and perhaps most importantly it looks *right*. Its combination of turrets, jagged towers, battlements, narrow stairways and winding passages, suggests (superficially at least) an archetype for Castle Dracula.

In these circumstances it is not surprising that Western tourists quickly projected all their fantasies and expectations of Castle Dracula on to Bran Castle.[2] As such, despite bearing little resemblance to the castle described by Stoker, Bran swiftly became 'Dracula's Castle' for Western tourists. It may have only needed one tourist or journalist to describe Bran in this way for the name to catch on and spread rapidly in the travel press in America.[3] What is noteworthy is just how rapidly the association with Dracula was attached to Bran.[4] During a visit to America in 1968 the Romanian historian Constantin Giurescu recounted being given a tourist brochure in which Bran is described as the 'unvanquished castle of Dracula' (Giurescu 1971: 193). Within a decade of opening up to international tourism, Romania's foremost tourist attraction had become 'Dracula's Castle'.

Rojek (1997) argues that places become tourist sights through some sort of distinction that sets them apart in the minds of tourists as being different or extraordinary (see also Urry 2002). While Bran Castle is impressive in its own right it is only one of many impressive medieval castles in Europe. But once the

---

2   Ioan Prahoveanu, Nicolae Păduraru, interviews; Light (2007a).

3   Nicolae Păduraru, interview.

4   Nicolae Păduraru and Ioan Prahoveanu both identify an early package tour for American tourists as having played an important role in turning Bran into Dracula's Castle. Organized by a Yugoslav company (Kompass Travel) the tour included three-day stays in Yugoslavia, Bulgaria, Romania and Hungary. The Romanian leg of the tour included a stay in the Prahova Valley and an excursion to Bran which was the only castle included in the Romanian part of the visit.

Dracula myth was attached to Bran, the castle became somewhere extraordinary. It was a distinct *lieux d'imagination* (Reijnders 2011a), a place that offered the possibility to connect with the imaginary world of Dracula. It was also an opportunity to engage directly with the place myth of Transylvania (Light 2012). A visit to Bran offered thrills that were not available elsewhere, particularly the prospect of a slightly scary (but ultimately safe) encounter with the supernatural (see Inglis and Holmes 2003, Holloway 2010). In the absence of a real 'Castle Dracula', Bran became an appropriate substitute for those tourists who wanted (and maybe needed) to find Dracula in Transylvania. Thus, the renaming of Bran as 'Dracula's Castle' can be interpreted as an act of appropriation to ensure that the experience of visiting Transylvania accorded with the Western stereotype of Romania as the land of Dracula.

Once Bran had been transformed into Dracula's Castle both the Western travel press and popular writing which catered for the growing Dracula craze further promoted the myth. McNally and Florescu (1972) were clearly aware that Bran was not Castle Dracula but seem to have been reluctant to disappoint their readers and *In Search of Dracula* hinted that it might have been the model for the fictional Castle Dracula. Other writers were less restrained. In a book intended for a popular audience which is notable for its enthusiastic efforts to present Transylvania as a vampire-stalked netherworld, Brokaw (1976: 52–3) had no reticence in labelling Bran as Castle Dracula and described it as everything a Dracula fan would expect it to be: 'It [Bran] is every castle that has ever sent a chill up and down your spine in the horror movies all wrapped into one. Ugly and scaly, pitted and ripped, satanic, devastating – Transylvania's *masterpiece*'. The front cover of the book featured an image of Bran Castle at night behind which were fluttering bats and a full moon.

This reading of Bran as Dracula's Castle by Western tourists collided with the official presentation of the site as a splendid medieval edifice, and the creation (and property) of the Romanian people. As I argued in Chapter 4, socialist Romania had no desire to encourage a form of tourism based on a literary myth which portrayed Romania as a backwards and superstitious place. Yet, during the 1960s, the Romanian tourist authorities seem to have been entirely unaware of the new meanings being attached to Bran by Western tourists. However, some travel agencies and hotels in the Prahova Valley recognized that foreign tourists were more willing to take a day excursion to Bran if the castle was advertised as Dracula's Castle.[5] But if there was any recognition that Bran was becoming known as Dracula's Castle the Romanian authorities probably assumed that the Dracula in question was Vlad Țepeș.

However, during the early 1970s, as Romania started reluctantly to recognize Dracula tourism, the tourist authorities and the castle's managers seem to have acknowledged that Bran Castle meant Castle Dracula in the minds of many Western tourists. Yet nothing was done to encourage this association. The castle

---

5   Nicolae Păduraru, interview; see also Ciobanu et al. (1984).

was always presented and interpreted as a museum of history and art and there was no attempt to cater for those Western tourists who were expecting to find Castle Dracula. However, despite only tenuous connections with Vlad Țepeș, Bran Castle was included in the *Dracula: Legend and Truth* tours (it had earlier been included in *Spotlight on Dracula*). This may have been an attempt to negate the association between Bran and the fictional Dracula by directing the attention of tourists towards the historical Dracula, or may simply have been intended to showcase one of Romania's finest castles. Nevertheless, the inclusion of the castle in *Dracula: Legend and Truth* inadvertently furthered the association between Bran and Dracula, as well as amplifying the confusion between the historical and literary Draculas.

Despite some claims (for example McNally and Florescu 1994, Florescu cited in Wingrove 1997, Miller 2000, Melton 2011) that Romania's tourist authorities actively promoted Bran as Dracula's Castle I do not believe this was the case. In Romania's pre-1989 tourist promotional materials, both in English (*Holidays in Romania*) and Romanian (*România pitorească*) Bran is never labelled as Dracula's Castle. Similarly, none of the English-language guide books published in Romania before 1989 make any association of Bran with Dracula.[6] Instead, Bran is only presented as a fine medieval castle, worthy of a visit in its own right. However, some articles in *Holidays in Romania* acknowledged that, in the minds of Western tourists, Bran was inseparable from Dracula (Raicu 1975, Trofin 1979, Basarab 1980). The Romanian authorities seem to have been prepared to allow foreign tourists to assume that Bran was Dracula's Castle without doing anything to encourage this association. This accords with what I identified in the previous chapter as a practice (if not a formal policy) of tolerating (but not directly promoting) Dracula tourism. Western tour operators faced no such restraints and vigorously promoted Bran as Dracula's Castle.

What, then, did those Western visitors who had travelled to Bran in the expectation of finding Castle Dracula make of the place? The first reaction can only have been one of disappointment.[7] Indeed, disappointment may be a far more common component of the tourist encounter than is sometimes recognized

---

6   Socialist Romania published a large number of guidebooks in English (and other languages) for foreign tourists. The state also published more general books that were intended as a presentation of the country to foreigners. The following sources were consulted, all of which mention Bran Castle but make no mention of Dracula: Anon (1966), Anon (1971), Anon (1979) Anon (1984a) Anon (undated), Bonifaciu et al. (1974), Bonifaciu (1985), Cioculescu et al. (1967), Cruceru (1986), Epuran and Bonifaciu (1966), Istrate (1986). Needless to say there is nothing about Dracula in any of the Romanian guidebooks to Bran Castle (for example, Henegariu 1963, Prahoveanu and Coșuleț 1985) or Brașov County (Catrina and Lupu 1981).

7   This continues to be a common response to the castle. I have taken many student groups to the building over the years and the initial reaction of many is disappointment that the building did not live up to what was expected (see also Muresan and Smith 1998 and Banyai 2010).

(Rojek 1997, Shackley 2001, Light 2009c) and it certainly seems to be a common experience of screen tourists (see, for example, Carl et al. 2007, Connell and Meyer 2009). Faced with a castle from which Dracula was conspicuously absent, tourists had little choice but to draw on their own resources and improvise if they wanted their visit to live up to their expectations of Castle Dracula. Their visit became an opportunity to engage in a little fantasy and escapism, to play at being scared, and to act out scenes from the Dracula films (see Banyai 2010, Light 2012). In this way visitors were able to re-enchant the castle and open up all sorts of new possibilities for the building (see Holloway 2010). They were fortunate in that the towers and narrow staircases of the building itself and the medieval furnishings of the history museum bore some similarities to cinematic representations of Dracula's Castle and were therefore an appropriate backdrop. There is abundant evidence that many tourists performed Bran as Castle Dracula. This is apparent in some of the (often slightly bemused) articles in *Holidays in Romania*. According to one report:

> Americans have often called Bran Castle Dracula's place. When they get there they test the walls by knocking, carefully inspect the winding staircase that leads to the tower, and look into the 500m deep well in the castle's inner courtyard which is said to have had secret galleries and caves. (Raicu 1975: 3)

Similarly:

> We visit the Castle [Bran]. People keep quiet. Words turn into whispers. Everybody is watching his steps. The narrow polished wooden stairs creak loudly while the sparsely lit walls, illuminated by some torches seem to draw closer to each other, and the group of people moves with hushed steps, holding their breaths. The Dracula Vampire! Dracula! He is here, he must be here and everybody feels his presence! In a corner a window with shutters is shattered by the wind and just behind our backs a sinister voice sounding as if coming out of a grave bursts into an awful peal of laugher, then says: "I'm Dracula, who are you?". (Trofin 1979: 17)

And:

> Visitors like to take pictures everywhere. They prefer the darkest corners of the rooms, or the wall of the princes who once inhabited the Bran castle. They think Dracula, the invisible vampire, is upon their traces, ready to jump upon them; is he? (Diana 1979: 22)

Another popular form of play at Bran was for visitors to hide behind doorways or furnishings and then to leap out to scare their companions (such behaviour remains popular today if my experience of taking student groups there is anything to go by!). Even ONT guides sometimes joined in, hiding in chests and opening the doors menacingly as tourists approached.[8] One wonders what Romanians (and visitors from other socialist countries) made of all this.

Bran Castle illustrates the dilemma Romania faced with Dracula tourism, particularly the tensions between the production and consumption of sites on the Dracula trail. On one hand the Romanian tourist authorities sought to present the castle as a fine medieval building and to avoid any association with the Western vampire Dracula. However, many Western tourists produced entirely different meanings for the building based on what they brought with them to the site from their home culture (Light 2012). For them, Bran offered an experience of Castle Dracula that resembled the classic Dracula films. Hence, many visitors performed the building as Castle Dracula in an attempt to create meaningful experiences and memories that accorded with their expectations of Transylvania. Through such performances visitors were active participants in recreating and reproducing the symbolic meanings of the castle (see Edensor 2001), reinforcing the association of Castle Dracula with Bran Castle.

By the late 1970s Bran Castle had established itself as one of the most popular attractions in Romania for both Romanian and foreign tourists. In 1977 it attracted over 220,000 visitors (Anon 1978). In response to this level of tourism demand, the car park outside the castle developed as a space for informal trading. A tradition of enterprise was better developed in the Bran area than in many other parts of Romania, partly due to a long history of cross-border trading in the area but also because the mountainous land around Bran was deemed unsuitable for agricultural collectivization during the 1950s. As a result, the people of the Bran area retained an attachment to private property and gained a reputation as being more resourceful and independent than elsewhere in the country where collectivization had been applied (see Roberts 1996). Consequently they were quick to identify the opportunities presented by the popularity of Bran Castle.

The first kiosk opened beside the castle in 1972 and sold books, postcards and local handicrafts[9]. It was administered by CENTROCOOP, the state organization responsible for agricultural products and handcrafts produced by the small agricultural private sector. The state's tourism policy at this time required CENTROCOOP to assure that the private sector in rural areas provided food and traditional handicrafts/souvenirs for tourist sites and routes (Snak 1976). The following year a further group of local people obtained permission from the Bran *Primărie* (town hall) to sell their products privately from tables in the car park. In return they were required to rear animals on behalf of the state. For the entrepreneurial peasants of Bran, trading at the castle was a lucrative (if seasonal)

---

8   Ioan Prăhoveanu interview; Richardson and Denton 1988). However the story of an American tourist who died of a heart attack during one such encounter (see Richardson and Denton 1988) seems to be just another myth attached to Bran. No one I have spoken to has any recollection of the event.

9   The following section is based on conversations with local traders at Bran undertaken in 2004.

business and more and more local people were granted the right to sell their products. Their tables were gradually replaced by kiosks which, by 1989, ringed the entire car park.

Before obtaining permission to trade at Bran, local people had to present samples of their goods to the 'Culture Committee' of the local authority for Braşov County. This process of verification effectively controlled what could be sold at the castle. The market at Bran offered a range of locally produced handicrafts including ceramics, baskets and textiles. Especially popular were knitted pullovers in grey and white wool and local traders were quick to recognize that those which featured the words 'Transylvania', 'Castelul Bran' or 'Vlad Ţepeş' were the most popular. Once the castle was included on the *Dracula: Legend and Truth* tour, souvenirs featuring the image of Vlad Ţepeş also appeared at the site. A 1974 documentary[10] focuses on a bottle of *ţuica* (plum brandy) on sale that featured the word 'Dracula' (but with no other image) on the label. The local authorities would have approved such a souvenir since the name Dracula was an acceptable label for Vlad Ţepeş. However, the existence of such souvenirs does not indicate that the authorities supported the association with the Western Dracula at Bran Castle and there is no evidence that any souvenirs featuring images of the Western vampire Dracula were sold at Bran during the socialist era.

Poienari Castle

Poienari Castle (see Figure 5.3) is the second place in Romania that has been labelled as Dracula's Castle and came to be described as such after the name had already been attached to Bran. Poienari is situated in the Carpathian Mountains in the narrow valley of the River Argeş, 15 miles (24 km) north of Curtea de Argeş. The castle stands at 850 m altitude on a rocky crag some 366 m above the road (see Figure 5.1). Poienari bears a (very) superficial resemblance to Castle Dracula as described by Stoker in that (unlike Bran) it is a ruin. But it is a very small ruin and hardly the 'vast ruined castle' described by Stoker. Like the fictional Castle Dracula, it stands on the edge of a precipice with a sharp drop on three sides. Unlike Castle Dracula, it is in Wallachia and not Transylvania. Some have claimed that this is indeed the castle used by Stoker as the model for Castle Dracula, although again Miller (2000) argues that it is almost impossible that the author had any knowledge of Poienari.

However, Poienari has direct associations with the historical Dracula since it was rebuilt by Vlad Ţepeş during his second reign. The earliest part of the castle dates from the thirteenth century but it was already a ruin by the mid-fourteenth century (Ciobanu et al. 1984). The Impaler's decision to rebuild the castle seems to have stemmed from his campaign to subdue the landowning Boyer class. Thus,

---

10   The Dracula Business (directed by Anthony de Lotbiniere, presented by Daniel Farson).

Figure 5.3   Poienari Citadel

according to the Wallachian Chronicles, on 17 April 1457, Vlad Ţepeş invited
the Boyers to an Easter feast at Târgovişte. The entire company was arrested,
many were impaled, and those remaining were marched to Poienari where they
were put to work building Poienari until, as the Chronicles state, 'the clothes fell
off their backs' (McNally and Florescu 1972, Andreescu 1976). Poienari Castle

seems to have been built as a mountain refuge since its location had little strategic or military value. The mountains to the north of the castle (the Făgăraş) are the highest in Romania and there was no pass through the mountains at this time (the modern road which leads northwards across the mountains to Transylvania – the 'Transfăgăraş highway' – opened only in 1974).

Poienari castle is the focus of many legends and folklore narratives linked with the name of Vlad Ţepeş that are preserved in the nearby village of Aref (see Ene 1976, McNally 1991). According to the legends, after the aborted attack on Târgovişte in 1462 the Ottomans returned and pursued the Voievode to Poienari. According to one story (a modified version of which featured in the 1992 film *Bram Stoker's Dracula*) the Ottomans shot an arrow into the castle with a message warning the Voievode to escape while there was still time. The Impaler's wife threw herself from the castle into the river below rather than be captured by the Ottomans. Vlad Ţepeş himself escaped with the help of peasants from Aref and fled across the Făgăraş mountains on a horse which had been shod backwards to deceive his pursuers (McNally and Florescu 1972).

After the death of Vlad Ţepeş, Poienari Castle remained in use for another century until being abandoned at some stage in the 1670s. It was recorded as being a complete ruin by 1747 (Ciobanu et al. 1984). During the nineteenth century the castle (which was still known as the castle of Vlad Ţepeş) became a popular site among Romantic writers and painters. Part of the castle collapsed and fell down the hillside in 1888 and an earthquake further damaged the structure in 1916 (Florescu and McNally 1973, MacKenzie 1977). Poienari Castle, by now almost covered in vegetation, was rediscovered by Radu Florescu and Raymond McNally during fieldwork in 1969. The Romanian government subsequently sponsored archaeological excavations at the site in 1969 and 1970 (Cantacuzino 1971).

The rediscovery of Poienari in the late 1960s took place during a context in which Nicolae Ceauşescu was pushing national ideology to the forefront of political and cultural life in Romania (see Chapter 3). In championing a national and independent form of socialism Ceauşescu increasingly evoked the Voievodes who had fought for Romanian independence in the medieval era. In consequence, places throughout Romania associated with the medieval rulers were restored and promoted as places of national significance. Many countries promote domestic tourism as a means of reinforcing and affirming senses of national history and identity (Franklin 2003) and in this context Romanians were encouraged to visit places associated with the Voievodes. Thus, as Vlad Ţepeş reappeared in Romanian historiography during the late 1960s the most important locations associated with the Impaler were developed as visitor attractions. The Impaler's former Princely Court at Târgovişte was excavated and restored between 1961 and 1973 (Moisescu 1979) while another of the Voievode's palaces, Curtea Veche (the Old Court) in Bucharest, was excavated in 1967 and opened as a museum in April 1972 (Panait and Ştefănescu 1973).

Poienari Castle was similarly restored between 1969 and 1972 (Ciobanu et al. 1984). The two remaining towers and the curtain walls were partially rebuilt in order to give the castle a more impressive appearance from the road. A new path to the castle was built in 1971 along with handrails and a new wooden bridge. Floodlights were also added to highlight the castle at night. Poienari was promoted as a place of national importance for the Romanians (see Florescu and McNally 1976), a status which Bran Castle (built and administered by Transylvanian Saxons) never achieved. The stories attached to the castle accorded well with the values of Ceauşescu's Romania: Poienari represented Vlad Ţepeş's struggle with (and, according to the legends, successful evasion of) the 'national' enemy (the Ottomans). Moreover, built by the forced labour of the Boyers, Poienari embodied the defeat of the class enemy. Poienari was also promoted (although less often than Bran) to foreign tourists as a place associated with a national hero and was an important destination within the *Dracula: Legend and Truth* tour.

While Poienari may have been constructed as a national site for Romanians, its significance (like that of Bran) for Western tourists diverged sharply from the Romanian interpretation. Outside Romania, Poienari Castle came to be known as the 'real' Castle Dracula. McNally and Florescu (in *In Search of Dracula*) were the first to describe Poienari in this way. There was a certain logic in their argument: Vlad Ţepeş was known as Dracula, Poienari was built by Vlad Ţepeş, therefore Poienari could be described as 'Dracula's Castle'. However, McNally and Florescu chose not to label Poienari in this way but instead as 'Castle Dracula'. In so doing, they transferred the meanings of the Castle Dracula of Stoker's novel and the Dracula films onto Poienari. As Azaryahu (1996) argues, attributing a name to something is not always a value free strategy but instead can represent an act of appropriation and a manifestation of authority. The labelling of Poienari as Castle Dracula was such an act in which a Romanian castle was transformed into something that accorded with the expectations and fantasies of Western Dracula enthusiasts. Needless to say, the name of the building is contested by Romanians who never describe Poienari as either Dracula's Castle or Castle Dracula but only ever as *Cetatea Poienari* (Poienari Fortress) (Miller 2000).

McNally and Florescu (1972) went further in promoting the confusion between Poienari and Stoker's Castle Dracula. On the flimsiest of foundations (but perhaps motivated by the desire to appeal to their readership of Dracula enthusiasts in America) *In Search of Dracula* mapped the supernatural and occult associations of the fictional Castle Dracula onto Poienari. In doing so, McNally and Florescu created an entirely new mythology of Poienari Castle (or, in their conception, Castle Dracula) as a wolf-infested, sinister, haunted place. For example, in recounting their 'discovery' of Poienari, McNally and Florescu speculated that some sort of curse hung over the ruins. Their story is related with gusto by Brokaw (1976: 67): 'Professor Florescu's uncle fell down a ravine and was seriously injured … McNally, 'was briefly stricken with fright at the threshold to the castle and for minutes could not enter its grounds'. Florescu himself was very shaken at the experience of finally setting foot in an authenticated Dracula site unknown to modern man'. McNally and Florescu (1972: 190) speculated that these experiences were 'Dracula's way of saying that despite the ruins of his castle, he still rules in some other, unearthly domain'.

Similarly, like the Castle Dracula of Stoker's fiction, McNally and Florescu claimed that local people had a profound fear of Poienari Castle and did not dare to visit it. For example: 'In the eyes of the superstitious, the spirit of Stoker's "undead hero" still dominates the place' (1972: 102). Similarly, for them, Poienari is a place where 'none dare trespass at night' (190). Yet, writing a few years later, MacKenzie (1977) who had visited Romania in search of folklore and the supernatural found no evidence of a superstitious fear of Poienari Castle among local people (and reasonably asks why, since Vlad Ţepeş is regarded as a local benefactor, the ruins of his castle should be feared).[11]

However, the myth of Poienari as a haunted, unworldly place rapidly established itself. Poienari gained a new significance for Dracula enthusiasts who were apparently unable (or unwilling) to distinguish between the fictional and the historical Draculas. In Poienari they found everything they expected from a 'real' Castle Dracula. One of the most extraordinary accounts is that of Varma (1976) whose conflation of the literary and the historical Draculas seems to have been total. His account of the visit to the ruins is as follows:

> In the spirit-haunted wild Carpathian mountains still stand, gaunt and lonely, the ruins of Castle Dracula ... The climb begins from the village Capatineni where one encounters the horrified looks and also blessings of the superstitious local people ... There could not possibly be a more apt setting for fearful crimes or mysterious haunting ... Perhaps no other castle is filled with such awful memories. They say that evil spirits still haunt these ruins and the peasants of the valley speak of strange flickers, as of candlelight, being visible from a distance on dark nights ... A curious unease pervaded my soul as I gazed at the relic ... This mood of foreboding was created by an intolerable gloom which engulfed my spirit ... a dense and impenetrable silence fell with an oppressive hush. There was something unutterably overpowering and disquieting about the place so weird and awesome. A dreadful fear overwhelmed me ... We felt as if we were being watched all the time ... we could sense an unearthly presence of evil. (Varma 1976: 46–7)

Such was the power of Poienari's reputation as a haunted place that some took up the challenge of spending a night at the castle. McNally and Florescu (1972:103) had thrown down the gauntlet contending that spending a night at Poienari had 'become a sport commanding a high fee ... only one person of our acquaintance has survived the ordeal'. Vincent Hillyer, an American writer and adventurer took up the challenge in 1977 in a much publicized attempt to be the

---

11   During one visit to Poienari and Aref I also asked local people if Poienari Castle was something of which they were afraid. None of them had any knowledge of such superstitions. One local man described the castle as something '*obişnuit*' (ordinary).

first Westerner to spend a night at Poienari. The Deputy Minister of Tourism did his best to dissuade Hillyer, not on the grounds of any danger from the supernatural, but because of the potential for attack by wolves or bears. Nevertheless Hillyer persisted and the Romanian authorities eventually backed down. Hillyer spent a restless night at Poienari but returned with puncture marks on his neck which a local doctor attributed to a spider bite. His published account of his adventures (1988) reinforced the earlier claims of McNally and Florescu that Poienari Castle really was haunted by the ghost of Vlad Țepeș.

At Poienari, then, those who had visited Romania in search of Castle Dracula (or the supernatural and unworldly more generally) found what they were looking for. Framed by the place myth of Transylvania as the home of the supernatural, Poienari came to be constructed and represented outside Romania as a haunted castle on the top of a mountain. Unlike Bran, which was perhaps slightly too tidy to be really frightening (if anything, it resembles a film set of Castle Dracula), Poienari gained a reputation as a genuinely sinister place. This reading of Poienari Castle again illustrates the role of tourists themselves in constructing the meanings of tourist sites (see Wallace 2001), according to the values of their home cultures. But, as at Bran, the meanings attached by foreign tourists to Poienari were unacceptable to the Romanian authorities. Not only was Poienari a place associated with a national hero, but also the myth of Poienari as a haunted place again collided with Romania's self-image as a modern and progressive socialist state. Yet, the Romanian tourist authorities were unable to control the production and diffusion of this myth. Guides on the *Dracula: Legend and Truth* tours sought to negate Poienari's reputation as Dracula's Castle by discouraging tourists from confusing the literary Dracula with the historical Dracula.[12] But such was the influence of *In Search of Dracula* (and its followers such as Hillyer) that Poienari was firmly established among Dracula enthusiasts as the 'real' Castle Dracula.

While McNally and Florescu (1972) claimed that Poienari could become the most important tourist attraction in Romania, Poienari has never experienced the popularity among Western tourists that is enjoyed by Bran. The castle's remote location meant that it was less often included in 'general' tours of Romania since Bran Castle was far more easily reached from the main tourist circuits in the country. Those foreign tourists who simply wanted a short stop at Dracula's Castle found everything they expected at Bran. Once at Poienari, tourists were confronted with a climb of 1,480 steps to reach the castle itself and this was enough to deter many casual visitors. For this reason no souvenir industry developed around Poienari Castle before 1989.[13] Instead, the popularity of Poienari Castle was largely restricted to the most committed Dracula enthusiasts (whether those in search of Vlad Țepeș or those in search of the 'real' Castle Dracula).

---

12   Nicolae Păduraru, interview.
13   Nicolae Păduraru, interview.

Hotel Tihuţa

The third of Dracula's Castles in Romania is, in fact, a hotel. Unlike Bran and Poienari Castles, Hotel Tihuţa (as it was called until 1991) was purposely built to cater for tourists on the Dracula trail. It is situated in the village of Piatra Fântânele at the top of the Borgo (Bârgău) Pass at an altitude of 1,116 m. There are enough features in the hotel's design for it to resemble a castle (see Figure 5.4): it includes a tower, an inner courtyard, crenellated battlements, labyrinthine winding stairways and wooden panelled interiors, filled with stuffed animals. This said, it bears little resemblance to the ruined castle of Stoker's novel.

Figure 5.4   Hotel Tihuţa

The story of Hotel Tihuţa is the second part of Alexandru Misiuga's project to attract Western Dracula enthusiasts to the county of Bistriţa-Năsăud.[14] By 1972 Misiuga had succeeded in obtaining central funding for a hotel in Bistriţa which he planned to name *Coroana de Aur*. But he was also well aware of the especial resonance of the Bârgău Pass for Dracula fans and of the unique appeal

---

14   Once again, the narrative that follows is my interpretation of events based on interviews with Ion Mânzat and Alexandru Misiuga and triangulated wherever possible with other published sources.

of Castle Dracula. Misiuga was unusual in communist Romania in that he had an understanding of the demands of foreign tourists and knew what he needed to do to cater for that demand.[15] He therefore set out to build a hotel in the style of a castle in the Borgo Pass specifically to cater for Western Dracula fans. He was fuelled by his personal enthusiasm for the novel, but also well aware of the additional prestige he would enjoy through attracting more Western tourists to his remote and isolated county.

Indeed, Misiuga seems to have embarked on his own search for the ruins of Castle Dracula in the Bârgău Pass. In 1972 he reported the discovery of the remains of a castle at Răchiţele and claimed that the remains were known to locals as the ruins of a castle built by Vlad Ţepeş (Păduraru 1973). Remarkably, *Scînteia,* the RCP's daily newspaper, also reported the discovery of the remains of a castle known to locals as Ţepeş's Citadel and speculated that this could have been the inspiration for Castle Dracula in Bram Stokers novel (Anon 1972).[16] In fact, a Transylvanian archaeologist suggested that the remains were those of an eighteenth-century building associated with the Austrians who built the road through the Bârgău Pass (Păduraru 1973).

For all his enthusiasm, Misiuga's options were limited. Coming soon after the *Coroana de Aur* the request for central funding for a second large hotel was highly ambitious for a small county such as Bistriţa-Năsăud. The hotel was not included in the Five Year Plan for the county. Moreover, the proposal to build a hotel at an altitude of more than 1000 m required additional expense, while the proposed location was not close to any major tourist attractions. Furthermore, any hotel with an overtly Dracula theme was unlikely to get the support of the Ministry of Tourism in Bucharest at a time when the Ministry was reluctant to encourage Dracula tourism. Misiuga arranged a number of meetings with Ioan Cosma, the Minister for Tourism but his requests for central funding were repeatedly refused (see Misiuga 1995).

---

15   In 1968 Misiuga had taken a Transylvanian folklore ensemble on a visit to France for 5 weeks. During this visit he encountered Western practices of tourism development and operations which gave him ideas that he could later implement in Bistriţa-Năsăud (Mânzat 2008).

16   This extraordinary article demands further comment. Knowledge of Bram Stoker's novel would have been fairly limited at this time and it is probable that many readers of *Scînteia* would not have understood the reference. Nevertheless, it suggests that at this time (September 1972) the socialist regime was not overtly hostile towards Stoker's novel. *Scînteia* was preoccupied with state propaganda and reports of the activities of the RCP and its General Secretary. It included little in the way of broader news. So how did the newspaper come to include an article about Dracula? An obvious source would be Alexandru Misiuga himself. Indeed the timing of the article (just before the first *Spotlight on Dracula* tour) may not have been coincidental. However, when I asked him about this Misiuga denied all knowledge of the article. Nevertheless, it seems that Misiuga had good contacts with the writers of *Scînteia* since the opening of the *Coroana de Aur* was also reported in the newspaper in 1974 (Anon 1974).

Misiuga therefore needed a way to circumvent the usual processes of central planning and decision-making. Taking advantage of his good standing with the local state institutions, Misiuga enlisted the support of the local Party Secretary (Adalbert Crisan) and *Securitate* (Ion Mânzat). Once again, Mânzat was supportive of Misiuga's efforts to attract Western tourists to Bistriţa and he consulted his superiors to determine a strategy for approving a hotel in the Borgo (Bârgău) Pass. Among those he consulted was Nicolae Doicaru, the head of the external intelligence service and Ceauşescu's national security advisor (see Deletant 1995). Ceauşescu was an enthusiastic hunter (Behr 1991) and regularly visited Bistriţa-Năsăud for hunting sessions in the Bârgău woods (sessions that Mânzat and Crisan were expected to arrange). Mânzat was advised to use the opportunity of such visits to win the General Secretary's support for the hotel project. Indeed, the evening gatherings that followed a day's hunting were well established occasions for local politicians to lobby Ceauşescu for his support for their particular projects.[17] At one of these gatherings Crisan, Mânzat and Lazăr Tănase (Deputy First Secretary of the local Party) raised the idea of a new hotel with Ceauşescu. They also presented Ceauşescu with a model (constructed by Misiuga) of the proposed hotel. Eventually, Ceauşescu gave the idea his support, apparently saying to Crisan 'who's stopping you from building it?' (Anon 2004a, see also Mânzat 2008). Ceauşescu would not have known that he was approving a castle-hotel for Western Dracula tourists: he had simply approved the construction of an unusual hotel at Piatra Fântânele. Nevertheless, indirectly, Misiuga's personal project to promote Dracula tourism in Bistriţa-Năsăud had the approval of the head of state.

Mânzat and Crisan subsequently advised Misiuga to arrange a meeting with Ioan Cosma to request funding for the new hotel. Given that the head of state had approved the project Cosma had little choice but to support it. However, Misiuga was once again adept in ensuring that the higher authorities knew no more than was necessary about the project. Thus, he made no mention of Hotel Tihuţa as an attraction for Western Dracula tourists.[18] Instead, he presented the hotel to Cosma as a new development midway between Bistriţa in Transylvania and the spa resort of Vatra Dornei in Bucovina. The road through the Bârgău Pass which linked Transylvania and Bucovina was regularly used by both Romanian and international tourists visiting the famous painted monasteries of Bucovina. Misiuga argued that there was no tourist 'objective' between the two towns and no place at which coaches could stop for restaurant facilities. Cosma was unimpressed with Misiuga's initial design (which, from the outside, partly resembled a ruin[19]) and

---

17   Attempts to influence or manipulate Ceauşescu's decision-making do not appear to have been uncommon. See for example M. Popa (2007) in the case of urban planning in Bucharest.

18   Both Misiuga and Mânzat expressed doubts that Cosma was ever aware that the hotel was intended to cater for Dracula enthusiasts.

19   Daniel Farson's 1974 BBC documentary *The Dracula Business* includes footage of Misiuga's model for the hotel-castle, something which Farson describes as 'a mixture of

demanded something that more conventionally resembled a hotel (Anon 2004a). Misiuga was also told that the hotel had to be complete within a year and a half.

Once funding for the hotel was approved, Misiuga worked closely with a Bucharest architect, Codrea Marinescu, on its design. Marinescu, like most Romanians, knew almost nothing about the fictional Dracula. However, Misiuga explained to him the plot of the novel and his requirement that the hotel should resemble the fictional Castle Dracula (Codrea Marinescu, interview). Marinescu's design for the hotel included the features required by Misiuga (a tower), and also incorporated elements adapted from another Gothic castle in Transylvania at Hunedoara.[20] However, the Ministry of Tourism demanded changes to the design in order to reduce costs and to make the building look less like a castle.[21] In particular, the original design had included a drawbridge and a grand flight of stairs leading to a reception on the first floor. These features were subsequently abandoned (although the first floor reception, the only one of its kind in Romania) was retained.

With the help of Crisan and Mânzat, Misiuga selected a suitable location at Piatra Fântânele, near to the top of the Bârgau Pass with fine views of Transylvania. Building work started in April 1976. However, despite Misiuga's original projections, construction was repeatedly delayed by bad weather and poor winters[22] and at one stage was close to being abandoned. However, once again Misiuga's social capital proved crucial. In 1978 one of Mânzat's superiors, Nicolae Doicaru, replaced Ioan Cosma as Minister for Tourism. Doicaru had apparently taken an active interest in the project (Mânzat 2008) and, as Minister of Tourism, was able to support the hotel at a key moment, securing the assistance of the army in construction work, particularly the provision of water and electricity supplies.[23] Building work was finally completed in 1983 and the 140 bed hotel opened in August of that year. According to one source (Petru and Năstase 2004) the construction work cost 25 million lei which equates to approximately £1.25 million or $1.85 million.

Misiuga wanted to name the structure after Dracula.[24] However, by the 1980s any association with Dracula was unacceptable since the central authorities were aware that the name of Dracula was increasingly being attached to Ceauşescu. Moreover, Adalbert Crisan had retired as First Secretary of the local Party in 1979 and his successor was both unaware of the fictional Dracula and much less

---

Disney and Diaghilev'.

20   Codrea Marinescu, interview.
21   Codrea Marinescu, interview. See also Anon (2004a).
22   Codrea Marinescu, Alexandru Misiuga, interviews.
23   Ion Mânzat, interview.
24   According to one of the hotel's employees whose parents live in the Bârgău Valley, local people in Piatra Fântânele were apparently aware that Misiuga was building a Dracula hotel and were expecting the building to be named after Dracula. MacKenzie (1983) also commented that the expected name for the hotel was the 'Dracula Inn'.

sympathetic to Misiuga's new hotel. Recognizing that he was unlikely to get the approval of the local Party for any name containing the word Dracula Misiuga opted instead for Hotel Tihuţa after the nearby mountain pass.

Once the hotel had opened it came to mean very different things to domestic and international tourists. Unsurprisingly, within Romania, the promotion of the castle made no reference to Dracula. Hotel Tihuţa was presented as a 'Castle of the Carpathians' (see Anon 1984b) and was promoted as a base for skiing and walking holidays in the mountains, as well as a stopping point on the Bistriţa-Vatra Dornei road. The opportunities for health tourism (due to the high quantity of iodine locally in the atmosphere) were also stressed (Caraciuc 1983, Anon 1985). There does not appear to have been any attempt to promote the building to Western tourists: there is not a single mention of the hotel in *Holidays in Romania* before 1989, perhaps in an attempt to disclaim the Dracula connection.[25] Nevertheless, the building was quickly absorbed into the Dracula tours organized by Western Dracula societies and tour operators (in addition to fulfilling its role as a transit hotel along the Bistriţa-Vatra Dornei road). For Western Dracula enthusiasts, the hotel was the long desired embodiment of the fictional Castle Dracula: it resembled a castle in appearance, it was situated in the Borgo Pass and it was surrounded by the Carpathian Mountains (Miller 2003). At Piatra Fântânele an entirely imaginary place had taken physical form. High in the Carpathian Mountains, Misiuga had succeeded in creating that which Dracula enthusiasts had long sought.

Although Misiuga had been unable to give the hotel the name of his choice he devised other ways to attach a Dracula theme to the building. A small cemetery in front of the hotel (formerly attached to a peasant household) was retained to add extra atmosphere for horror fans. The public spaces of the interior were decorated with animal skulls. Moreover, from the outset an underground crypt was incorporated into the design for the hotel.[26] Without the knowledge of the local Party authorities (although with Mânzat's tacit approval), Misiuga arranged for the walls of the crypt to be decorated with horror themes and added a coffin[27] from which the hotel's cook would leap to scare tourists (Urma 1985). Visitors were also offered the chance to lie in the coffin for $1 or to spend a night in it for $25.[28] Like Bran Castle (perhaps more so), the hotel was a place of play and fantasy where Dracula fans could give full reign to their imagination in a way

---

25   Some of the writers of *Holidays in Romania* (among them Nicolae Păduraru) were fairly well aware of the Dracula phenomenon and would have recognized the significance of a castle-hotel in the Bârgău Pass for Western Dracula enthusiasts.

26   Codrea Marinescu, interview.

27   In Stoker's novel Count Dracula sleeps in a coffin in an old chapel within Castle Dracula.

28   Such an initiative is not as bizarre as it may sound. In 2004 I accompanied a group of tourists on a Dracula tour, that included a visit to the hotel and many of them enthusiastically took up the opportunity to lie in the coffin (see Light 2009a). Misiuga clearly had a good understanding of Western Dracula fans.

that was not possible at Bran or Poienari. Nevertheless, the experience proved too much for some: a Swiss tourist fainted in the coffin and required hospitalization. Misiuga retired in 1984 and his successor as head of the Bistriţa-Năsăud OJT quickly closed the crypt.

Hotel Tihuţa has become the focus of an entirely different sort of myth than at Bran or Poienari. It is frequently interpreted as a crass and overtly commercial attempt by socialist Romania to cash in on the Dracula phenomena. Florescu and McNally (1989: 220) speak of an 'artificial Disneyland-style vampire scenario centred in Stoker's Borgo Pass region'. Similarly, Florescu claimed: 'Later Ceausescu [sic] himself rediscovered Dracula. He built a ghastly artificial castle in the Borgo Pass, where Stoker set his novel' (cited in Wingrove 1997: 45). I do not agree with these assessments. Socialist Romania's engagement with Dracula went little further than tolerating an unwanted form of tourism because it brought hard currency into the country. Moreover, it is almost inconceivable that socialist Romania would open a castle-hotel intended for Dracula enthusiasts during the 1980s when the head of state (ever conscious of his image both domestically and internationally) was increasingly portrayed as a contemporary Dracula.

Instead, Hotel Tihuta, like the *Coroana de Aur* in Bistriţa, was a local initiative, led by Alexandru Misiuga with the support of the local Party and *Securitate*. Misiuga was a creative and entrepreneurial thinker, working within a system that operated on the basis of top-down decision-making and which encouraged acceptance of, and conformity with, such decisions. Misiuga was able to combine his personal determination and enthusiasm with his abundant social capital. In particular, through Adalbert Crisan and Ion Mânzat he had access to the highest levels of the state bureaucracy and this enabled him to circumvent the normal central planning procedures of the Ministry of Tourism and secure approval for his project directly from the head of state. But at the same time neither Ceauşescu nor the other central authorities fully understood what was happening at Piatra Fântânele. Misiuga exploited the lack of knowledge of *Dracula* in Romania so that few people would understand the significance of a castle-hotel in the Bârgău Pass for Western Dracula enthusiasts. Moreover, Misiuga took full advantage of the geographical distance between Bistriţa county (and Piatra Fântânele in particular) and the centre of power in Bucharest. He was able to operate in way that was not illegal, but in the interstices of state power, to push forward a project that did not accord with the state's tourism policy or with the desire of the central authorities to discourage any reference to the literary Dracula. Once again this calls into question the notion of the all-powerful and all-seeing socialist state and suggests that such states were much weaker than is often believed (Verdery 2004).

The charge of 'kitschness' is frequently levelled against Hotel Tihuţa. In the second edition of *In Search of Dracula* McNally and Florescu dismiss the building as an example of 'bastard Gothic' (1994: 299). One newspaper article describes it as 'iron-curtain kitsch' (Pozzi 2003). Tourist guidebooks are equally dismissive. One describes the building as 'a complete commercial con that somehow manages to persuade guests otherwise despite its theme-park tackiness' (Kokker and Kemp

2004: 163). Another argues that 'the Tihuţa (or Dracula) hotel really does go over the top in its attempts to milk dollars from the story' (Burford (1996: 141). However I am not persuaded by such claims. For a start, recent academic analysis of so-called kitsch (for example, Binkley 2000, Atkinson 2007) seeks to move beyond the simple judgements of 'bad taste' that surround it and explore the ways in which kitsch has far more meaning and significance to its consumers than has been previously acknowledged. In addition, describing Hotel Tihuţa as 'kitsch' is a lazy judgement made on the basis of Western aesthetics but which fails to take account of the context in which it was constructed. The hotel was conceived and designed within a society in which the Dracula of Western popular culture was almost unknown. Neither Misiuga nor Marinescu had seen a Western Dracula (or horror) film, still less a Western-style theme park. In seeking to design a representation of Castle Dracula that would appeal to Western tourists Misiuga and Marinescu had little more to work on than their imaginations. At the same time, the constraints imposed by the socialist authorities limited their scope to design a building that more closely resembled the Castle Dracula of Stoker's novel. Hotel Tihuţa was a courageous – even radical – building for socialist Romania, a considerable departure from the standard, concrete blocks that were typical of socialist-era hotels in Romania. Thus, although the tower, battlements and courtyard of Hotel Tihuţa may appear unconvincing (even tasteless) to Western visitors, the building was remarkable by the architectural standards of socialist Romania. It may not be pleasing to the Western eye but the hotel is, in its way, truly extraordinary.

Conclusions

The case of Dracula's Castle demonstrates the power of the imaginary, and of myth and fantasy in the construction of tourist places. Castle Dracula has never existed except in Bram Stoker's imagination and there is certainly no building in Romania known by this name. However, because of the way that it is represented in Stoker's novel (and the numerous subsequent Dracula films) the myth of Castle Dracula has developed a particular and enduring resonance. As a result, many Western Dracula enthusiasts visited Romania in search of Castle Dracula in perhaps the same way that they have visited Whitby since the 1970s in search of Dracula's grave. For such visitors the distinction between the 'real' and the imaginary does not seem to have mattered very much. Dracula enthusiasts were pursuing more a culturally constructed 'idea' of Castle Dracula than any specific location or building. What was important was to see for themselves something which resembled the Castle Dracula of popular culture. It was a way of validating a visit to Romania and, moreover, affirming the Western place myth of Transylvania as a haunted, supernatural Other.

Consequently, three places in Romania have come to be known as Dracula's Castle. At Bran Castle – an impressive medieval edifice, but one which bears little relationship to the castle portrayed by Stoker – Western tourists seem to have projected onto the castle their existing ideas and fantasies of Castle Dracula. On the other hand, Poienari Citadel has become the focus of a different myth as the castle has been portrayed as the 'real' Castle Dracula, a lonely haunted mountaintop ruin where those searching for the supernatural could find what they wanted. In both cases, the meanings of these places – for Western visitors – was constructed by visitors themselves according to the values of their home cultures. Moreover Bran and Poienari illustrate the tensions between the meanings ascribed to a tourist site by the 'producers' of the site (the Romanian tourist authorities) and those attributed to it by the 'consumers' of the site (the tourists themselves). The Romanian authorities did nothing to encourage the association of Bran or Poienari with Castle Dracula but they were powerless to control (let alone stop) such associations and had little choice but to tolerate – reluctantly – foreign tourists consuming the fortresses in this way. Hotel Tihuţa is a different case in that it was a deliberate attempt to engage with Dracula tourists through providing a castle-hotel in approximately the same location as the archetype of Stoker's novel. Unlike at Bran and Poienari where the imaginary has been mapped onto 'real' historic places, at Piatra Fântânele, the imaginary has taken physical form. Although the constraints of the 1980s meant that Hotel Tihuţa could not be named after Dracula, it rapidly came to assume the role of Castle Dracula for Western Dracula enthusiasts. It is extraordinary because it was developed as a result of local initiative but the central authorities were largely unaware of its significance for Dracula tourists – and yet the head of state himself approved its construction.

In the previous two chapters I have examined how Dracula tourism developed in Romania during the socialist era. In particular I have argued that an understanding of the workings of state socialism is essential for understanding the evolution of Dracula tourism and the response of the Romanian state to this activity. After the socialist regime collapsed in December 1989 Dracula tourism has operated and developed in an entirely different political, economic and cultural context. The nature of Dracula tourism in *post*-socialist Romania is examined in the following chapter.

Chapter 6
Dracula and Tourism in Post-socialist Romania

The two previous chapters examined the development of Dracula tourism in Romania from the 1960s until 1989. At this time Romania was a socialist state (which, by the late 1980s, had given way to an extreme form of totalitarian dictatorship) and this political context was a major constraint on the nature and form of Dracula tourism. Nicolae Ceaușescu's regime came to a bloody end during the 'revolution' of December 1989, which culminated in the capture and execution of the dictator and his wife. Following these events, Romania turned its back on state socialism and committed itself – erratically – to new forms of political and economic development based on Western European models.

The post-socialist period has been characterized by vast transformations in the nature of political, economic and social life in Romania (Turnock 2007). Political reform has centred on replacing centralized single-party rule with a multiparty democracy and a commitment to the rule of law. In the domain of economics, the post-socialist period is underpinned by the dismantling of a centrally planned economy and its replacement by a fully functioning market economy (in which privatization of state owned enterprises and the establishment of a private sector are key components). Much of the academic analysis of post-socialism has tended to concentrate on the 'technical' processes of reform (such as establishing political parties or privatizing state owned enterprises). However there is also an important cultural dimension to post-socialist transformations (Verdery 1999). In particular, a key element of the cultural politics of post-socialism is the redefining of identities in all sorts of ways (Young and Hörschelmann 2007). Since 1989 post-socialist states have sought to redefine senses of national and cultural identity, both for their own citizens but also in the eyes of others, particularly the West. Romania is no exception: the country has striven to convince the West that it is no longer a Cold War Other, but instead a modern, democratic, capitalist state that fully subscribes to the values of the European Union. However, this project is hampered by Balkanist 'ways of seeing' Romania in the West that have considerable resilience. In this sense the association with Dracula and vampires represents an unwelcome stereotype that Romania would rather throw off.

This chapter examines Romania's uneasy relationship with Dracula in the post-socialist period. It begins with an overview of Romania's progress in political and economic restructuring, charting Romania's erratic 'return' to Europe. It then looks at the changing significance attached to both the literary and the historical Draculas in the post-socialist era with particular reference to the enduring popularity of Vlad Ţepeş. The chapter then considers Dracula tourism, an activity that, in the post-socialist period, has taken place in an entirely new context and has been able to develop in completely new ways. In particular, the discussion seeks to situate the evolution of Dracula tourism within wider processes of political and economic transformation.

The Context: Romania after Socialism

Following Ceauşescu's overthrow a group declaring itself the National Salvation Front (NSF) assumed power. The Front immediately renounced communism and declared its commitment to political pluralism, economic restructuring and the process of building a united Europe. Romania enjoyed considerable international sympathy and goodwill at this time and hopes were high that Romanians could put the ordeal of Ceauşescu's tyranny behind them and build a peaceful and democratic future. However subsequent events in Romania led to a rapid deterioration of the country's international standing. It quickly became apparent that the NSF was dominated by former Communist Party officials, intent on retaining as much political and economic power in their own hands. The Front convincingly won elections in May 1990 and Ion Iliescu (a former second rank Communist official) was elected president with a large majority. For both Romanians and the wider world it was apparent that the country had failed to make a decisive break with the Ceauşescu era. Indeed, Iliescu proved to have much in common with this predecessor. For example, in June 1990 student demonstrations against the new regime were brutally repressed resulting in the death of six people and scores of injuries. Romania continued to experience intermittent civil unrest throughout the 1990s.

During 1990 Romania set out hesitantly on a course of economic reform. The NSF government favoured a gradualist course of reform that avoided radical structural reorganization but nevertheless resulted in economic decline and the first 'transformation recession' (A. Smith 2001: 129). The liberalization of formerly state controlled prices in 1990, 1991 and 1993 resulted in dramatic increases in inflation, while wages failed to keep pace with prices so that the purchasing power and living standards of the population plummeted. The reduction in state subsidies to unprofitable socialist-era industries resulted in closures and significant increases in unemployment. The effect for ordinary Romanians was traumatic as many struggled to survive in an increasingly hostile economic environment. But at the same time, the country's resources were widely plundered for personal gain by the former socialist *nomenclatura* and Romania became a byword for corruption and economic mismanagement (Gallagher 1995).

Moreover, the extreme and xenophobic form of nationalism that had characterized the later years of Ceauşescu's rule remained a dominant feature of Romanian political life after 1989 (Gallagher 1995, 2005). Iliescu (along with many other Romanian politicians) proved adept at appealing to national sentiments among Romanians as a means of retaining popular support. Much of the leadership's rhetoric was (as in Ceauşescu's era) directed against the ethnic Hungarian minority in Transylvania. In May 1990 there were violent clashes between Romanians and Hungarians in the Transylvanian city of Târgu Mureş and there were widespread suspicions that various state institutions had manipulated events (Gallagher 2005). In 1992 the Democratic National Salvation Front (the successor of the NSF) won elections but without a clear majority and was forced to govern in coalition with two extreme nationalist parties. The prevalence of xenophobic nationalism in political discourse led to fears in the West that Romania could follow Yugoslavia into a violent civil war.

This, however, proved not to be the case. Instead, during the mid-1990s Romania slowly turned its attention towards greater integration with Western Europe and the adoption of European norms (Papadimitriou and Phinnemore 2008). It concluded a Europe Agreement with the European Union in 1993 and applied for membership in June 1995. In September of the following year Romania and Hungary signed a Treaty of Friendship which recognized the existing border between the two states and guaranteed minority rights for Transylvania's Hungarian population. This was a considerable move in reducing fears of Hungarian irredentism among Romanians. In the elections of 1996 the former socialists – by now rebranded as the Party of Social Democracy of Romania (PSDR) – were defeated by the Romanian Democratic Convention (RDC). A broad centre-right governing coalition was formed which included, for the first time, the Democratic Union of Hungarians in Romania (DUHR). In an attempt to address the need for macroeconomic reform, the new government attempted to introduce a form of neoliberal shock therapy, bringing about the second transformation recession (A. Smith 2001) causing further economic distress for the majority of the population. The new government also placed a priority on improved relations with Hungary and made Euro-Atlantic integration its central foreign policy objective (Papadimitriou and Phinnemore 2008).

For all its good intentions the RDC coalition proved highly fractious, while the failure to improve living standards led to a dramatic loss of popular support. Thus, in the elections of 2000 the PSDR (still strongly favoured by former socialists) returned to power. However, by now the party's leadership had renounced nationalism and, in the clearest indication of the extent to which ethnic tensions had subsided, the Social Democrats governed for a full term with the support of the DUHR. This administration made membership of the European Union a policy priority (Papadimitriou and Phinnemore 2008) and introduced reforms that succeeded in bringing about economic stability and growth (A. Smith 2006). Thus, in October 2004 the European Commission finally declared Romanian to be a functioning market economy. Romania's progress in Euro-Atlantic integration was also recognized in 2004 when the country joined NATO. Yet corruption among the ruling elite (still dominated by members of the former RCP) remained rife (Gallagher 2005) causing concern in the European Commission and generating widespread disenchantment with the whole political process among ordinary Romanians. In the parliamentary elections of November 2004 there was another change of government. The PSDR (now renamed the Social Democratic Party (SDP)) failed to win a majority and the opposition 'Justice and Truth' alliance formed a minority government, once again in coalition with the DUHR. Traian Băsescu, the opposition candidate for president narrowly defeated the SDP's candidate, Adrian Năstase. It was during the mandate of this government that Romania finally joined the European Union in January 2007. Since the elections of November 2008 Romania has been ruled by a series of uneasy coalition governments.

Overall, despite various setbacks, Romania has undergone comprehensive political and economic restructuring since 1989 and has largely succeeded in dismantling the structures of state socialism and replacing them with a functioning democracy and a market economy. Romania has also succeeded in its 'return' to Europe as is demonstrated by its membership of the EU. But for all Romania's efforts since the mid-1990s to present itself as a modern, democratic, European state, it has yet to be fully accepted on such terms by the West. Instead, after 1989, the West has continued to treat Romania as a country that is not 'fully' European. The West has long insisted (and continues to insist) on a division of Europe into West and East (Wolff 1994, Todorova 2009) and, in the Western imagination, Romania is firmly located on the eastern side of this boundary. As a perceptive Romanian historian has recognized, while 'the West defines itself as an ordered and predictable world, Romanian belongs, on the contrary, to a vague and unpredictable space' (Boia 2001b: 185). Since 1989, Romania – along with much of the rest of southeast Europe – has continued to be constructed as an 'irredeemable Other of Western civilization' (Hammond 2004: xi). In other words, Balkanist (Todorova 2009) 'ways of seeing' Romania remain very much alive in the West.

Various events since 1989 have caused the West to question post-socialist Romania's 'Europeanness'. For a start, during much of the 1990s Romania remained inextricably linked in the Western imagination with the absurdity of Nicolae Ceauşescu's dictatorship (Gallagher 1995). Some of Ceauşescu's more monumental building projects – particularly the construction of the 'House of the People' in Bucharest – appeared to demonstrate that in Romania things happened differently from in the West (Light 2001). Among Western policymakers, inter-ethnic tension and state-sponsored violence in the early 1990s, political corruption and economic misadministration raised concerns about Romania's post-socialist orientation and priorities (Gallagher 1997). Moreover, the repeated delays in implementing economic reforms and slow progress towards European integration resulted in Romania being treated as a 'laggard' (Phinnemore 2001). Indeed the whole notion of Eastern Europe somehow 'lagging behind' the West in terms of economic and social development is central to the Balkanist discourse (Wolff 1994, Todorova 2009, Dittmer 2002/3).

But in the Western popular consciousness Romania became synonymous in the 1990s with one issue: orphans. When the dire state of Romania's underfunded and poorly managed orphanages came to light in the early 1990s the issue was widely reported in the Western mass media. The West acted with incredulity and disbelief and many Westerners arrived in Romania to assist in dealing with the problem. In the Western mass media Romania was portrayed as a country that was unable or unwilling to deal with the problem itself and which was in need of Western compassion and expertise to address the issue (Light 2001). Although other former socialist countries had similar (if not as severe) problems with state-run orphanages it was the situation in Romania that received the most coverage. Underpinning the whole issue was a persistent belief that Romania did not share the values of Western Europe.

When, during the mid to late 1990s, the coverage of Romania's orphan problem subsided in the Western press, another issue rose to prominence in which the Balkanist discourse was again central: migration from Eastern Europe to the EU. The right-wing press in Britain produced alarmist predictions about waves of impoverished Eastern Europeans – Romanians in particular – intent on colonizing the UK. Such people (frequently branded as bogus or fraudulent 'asylum seekers') were portrayed as aliens who did not share Western European values. Instead, they were portrayed as single-minded 'parasites' (often with criminal intentions), intent on exploiting Britain's health system and social services to the detriment of British citizens. This hysteria reached a peak as Romania's accession to the EU drew closer. For example, one headline in the Daily Express (a populist tabloid) screamed 'Get ready for the Romanian invasion' (Anon 2006). A month later the same newspaper's front page warned readers to 'Get ready for a huge new invasion' (Fagge and Whitehead 2006). Such language – with its talk of invasion – directly recalls Bram Stoker's *Dracula* with its central character being the predator from the East who is intent on invading and colonizing Britain (see Arata 1990). For the British press, Romanian migrants represented a threat, and this group were evoked in terms that can be unequivocally traced back to *Dracula* (Light and Young 2009).

In the eyes of Western Europe, Romania has continued to have an image problem in the post-socialist era. Without question much of this is of the country's own making. But Romania is also the subject of wider historical and cultural discourses over which it has little control. Uniquely among the former socialist countries of Central and Eastern Europe, Romania is saddled with a pervasive cultural stereotype initiated by a single work of nineteenth-century fiction. Stoker's novel is insistent on the Otherness of Transylvania (and, by extension, Romania). *Dracula* is therefore just one element of a wider political project in the West about the nature and boundaries of Europe itself. The continued association with Dracula and vampires is something that frustrates Romania's post-socialist identity-building, particularly its efforts to represent itself as a modern European state.

Count Dracula and Vlad Țepeș in Post-socialist Romania

After 1989, 'Dracula' ceased to be a proscribed word among Romanians. The state quickly withdrew from any direct attempt to control cultural production. State censorship ceased (and was later forbidden by the 1991 Constitution) and a lively independent press was quickly established. These developments in tandem with the increasing influence of cultural globalization, led to the Dracula of Western popular culture making its first appearance in Romania. A Romanian translation of the novel was published (in a limited print run) in late 1990 (Light 2009b). However, it was just one among a flood of new or previously suppressed books published in 1990 and seems to have generated little interest in the literary press. A Romanian edition of *In Search of Dracula* (McNally and Florescu 1972) was also published in 1992. However, like the novel itself, it seems to have stirred little interest among Romanians (and again is not difficult to find in second hand bookshops).

During the early 1990s Dracula films started to appear in Romanian cinemas and these reached a wider audience than the novel. The best known was Francis Ford Coppola's *Bram Stoker's Dracula*, originally released in 1992 but which did not open in Romania until July 1993. Whilst widely considered to be the most faithful cinematic adaptation of Stoker's novel (see Melton 2011), the film explicitly merged the characters of Count Dracula and Vlad Țepeș (the Voievode even appears at the start of the film). As such, nationalist historians in Romania predictably objected. However, the mainstream press seems to have been more amused than offended by the film regarding it as simply a piece of entertainment and not an attempt to denigrate the reputation of Vlad Țepeș. Most reviewers were appreciative of the film's merits (for example Barbu 1993, Stănescu 1993, Hurezean 1993) but could not avoid drawing attention to what (from a Romanian perspective) are historical or geographical errors in the film. Thus some reviewers wondered how the castle of Vlad Țepeș came to be located in Transylvania or how Vlad Țepeș had become a descendent of Attila. That some of the actors speak in Romanian at various points in the film was a source of amusement for some reviewers! (for example, Florescu, 1993). The preview of the film on 13 July 1993 was followed by a press conference at which a second edition of the Romanian translation of *Dracula* was launched.[1]

Meanwhile, as a private sector began to develop in post-socialist Romania, 'Dracula' was quickly adopted as a brand name attached to a wide variety of products. In other cases, the word was incorporated into the name of newly founded businesses, particularly those trading with Western companies (see Figure 6.1). An alcoholic drink entitled 'Dracula's Spirits' was launched in 1993 to coincide with the opening of Coppola's *Bram Stoker's Dracula* (Melton 2011). In the same year a weekly newspaper entitled 'Dracula' was established which features an eclectic range of articles on paranormal and supernatural themes. It caters for Romanians who have felt disorientated by the pace of post-socialist change and who are searching for meaning or solace in the metaphysical. Brands of wine entitled 'Vampir' and 'Dracula' appeared, targeted at foreign tourists, while brands of beer (see Figure 6.2) and cigarettes (intended for the domestic market) were also named after Dracula. Various hotels and guesthouses (particularly in locations on the Dracula trail) adopted the name Dracula (see Figure 6.3). A 'Count Dracula

---

1   Shortly afterwards, another publisher released a pirated version of the Romanian translation of *Dracula* in a print run of 30,000 copies (Pruteanu 1993) evidently anticipating high sales as a result of Coppola's film.

Club' restaurant opened in Bucharest in 1997. By 2004 there were 123 registered trademarks containing the word Dracula and 14 containing the word Vampire (all of which had appeared after 1989[2]). Even the Romanian postal service issued a set of four stamps featuring various original images of Count Dracula based on the classic films. Overall, the word 'Dracula' has enjoyed an unprecedented circulation in the two post-socialist decades. By 2010 Romanians had become sufficiently familiar with Dracula for the National Museum of Art to host a major exhibition entitled *Dracula – Voievode and Vampire*. This considered the significance of Vlad Ţepeş but also examined the role of the vampire Dracula within popular culture.

Figure 6.1   'Dracula Travel', Bucharest

At a time when Romanians have become increasingly aware of the Western vampire Dracula, the historical Dracula (Vlad Ţepeş) has continued to enjoy an exalted reputation in post-socialist Romania. As Boia (2001b) notes, much of the discourse about history in Romania after 1989 has continued to adopt the themes of socialist-era historiography. As such Romanian historians have continued to

---

2   This figure was obtained from *Oficiul de stat pentru invenţii şi mărci* (State Office for Inventions and Trademarks), Bucharest.

Figure 6.2   'Dracula' beer

Figure 6.3   'Pensuinea Dracula', Aref

evoke Vlad Ţepeş as a heroic and just leader who fought to defend Romanian independence (Ungheanu 1992, Dogaru 1994). In this context, one nationalist historian (Dogaru 1995) even elevated Vlad Ţepeş (whose main reign lasted just six years) to the status of 'Emperor of the East' (Boia 2001b). An eight volume synthesis of Romanian history published by the Romanian Academy portrays Vlad Ţepeş in terms which echo Giurescu: the Voievode's cruelty is acknowledged, but is attributed to a reason of state and the desire to restore order and honesty to his country (Ştefănescu 2001). Even books intended for children have continued to praise the Voievode in this way (for example Djuvaru and Oltean 2003). In this context, any deviation from the orthodox view about Vlad Ţepeş has the potential to cause uproar. This was exactly what happened in 1999 with the publication of an iconoclastic school textbook that challenged many of the long established tenets of Romanian history (Pavel 2000). One of the criticisms directed against this book was the representation of Vlad Ţepeş as a prototype of the vampire Dracula (Boia 2001b). The textbook was eventually withdrawn and reissued in a revised version.

But it is not just historians who continue to hold Vlad Ţepeş in high esteem: the Voievode also enjoys considerable popularity among the Romanian public. Boia (2001b) reports an opinion poll of 1999 in which the Voievode came sixth in a list of Romania's most important historical personalities. More recently, in 2006 a state owned television channel launched a series of programmes called *Mari români* (Great Romanians) where the Romanian public were invited to vote for their favourite historical or contemporary figures. Vlad Ţepeş finished in 12th place (one place after Nicolae Ceauşescu!).[3] One family in southern Romania even gave their child the name *Vlad Ţepeş Dracula* (Anon 2004b). The current popularity of the Voievode seems to be related to the upheaval of the post-socialist era where many Romanians are deeply troubled both by the disorder and uncertainty of the 'transition' period and also by the immorality of much of the country's political elite. In these circumstances many dream of a strong leader such as Vlad Ţepeş who will punish the corrupt and restore order and justice (see Boia 2001a). Mihai Eminescu's famous line – 'Why do you not come Lord Ţepeş?' – has acquired an entirely new resonance in the post-socialist period. This notion of Vlad Ţepeş as a bringer of justice was exploited to the full during the 2004 parliamentary and presidential election campaigns. Standing for president on a firm anti-corruption platform, Traian Băsescu lauded Vlad Ţepeş as one of his heroes (Gruia 2005). Moreover, the image of the stake has taken on a new role in recent years as a symbol for the failings and mismanagement of Romania's politicians. In 2007 the SDP, now in opposition, sought (ultimately unsuccessfully) to impeach President Băsescu. In response, the president's supporters erected 322 cardboard stakes in a Bucharest park, one for each parliamentarian who had voted for impeachment (Vulpe and Chilianu 2007).

However, the esteem reserved for Vlad Ţepeş is not something confined to older people who were educated during the socialist era. On the contrary, young

---

3   www.mariromani.ro [accessed: 16 June 2008].

people also hold Vlad Ţepeş in high regard, and many seem to be resentful of the confusion between the Voievode and the vampire. During a focus group discussion with students from the University of Bucharest[4] Vlad Ţepeş was variously evoked as 'an ideal leader', 'a model leader for the Romanian people', 'a law maker', 'someone who sought to be just' and 'someone the majority of people wish for'. One student remarked: 'I would be pleased if a Vlad Ţepeş were to come again to us'. Another said: 'we deserve a Vlad Ţepeş'. The students were unanimous that Romania needed a new Vlad Ţepeş and believed that the majority of Romanians felt the same way. They hastened to point out that they were not envisaging a tyrant who would rule through capital punishment, but instead, a firm leader who could restore order and honesty to a troubled country. Responses such as this give an indication of why, up to now, Romanians have been unwilling to give up 'their' Dracula in favour of the vampire Dracula of Western popular culture (Boia 2001a).

As the vampire Dracula started to become better known in Romania after 1989, a former ONT guide, Nicolae Păduraru, identified the need for an organization to address the whole Dracula phenomenon from a Romanian perspective. Păduraru had over 25 years' experience working with Western tourists who had come to Romania in search of Dracula. Consequently, he had an exceptional understanding of both the significance of the vampire Dracula for Western tourists and also the widespread misconceptions among Westerners regarding Vlad Tepes. Since there was no sign that the Romanian state had the inclination, expertise or resources to address the Dracula myth, Păduraru decided to take the initiative himself. He gathered together a group of historians and ethnographers who were prepared to engage critically with the Western myth of Dracula and, in 1991, founded the Transylvanian Society of Dracula (TSD).[5]

The TSD was established as a non-political, non-profit cultural-historical non-Governmental organization. It acknowledged the power and popularity of the literary Dracula in the West whilst seeking to distinguish Stoker's vampire from the figure of Vlad Tepes. The aims of the Society were twofold: first, to analyse and understand the Dracula of Western popular culture from a Romanian perspective; second, to establish the significance of the historical Dracula – Vlad Ţepeş – for Romania and to clarify Western misconceptions regarding the figure of the Voievode.[6] Membership of the Society was open to both Romanian and foreign citizens who shared its aims and respected its non-political status. A network of local chapters of the TSD was established in locations (such as Sighişoara and Bistriţa) associated with the fictional or historical Draculas. The statute of the TSD allowed for the establishment of chapters outside Romania, and in the following years chapters were established in Canada, Italy, Japan, Spain and Germany.

---

4   I discussed Vlad Tepes in a focus group of ten students from the University of Bucharest. The students were in the second and third year of their Geography degrees.

5   Nicolae Păduraru, interview.

6   Derived from the Statute of the Transylvanian Society of Dracula.

As Pǎduraru had realized, the TSD was addressing a need for a Romanian perspective on the Dracula phenomenon and the Society rapidly established itself as an information point (a 'lighthouse' in Pǎduraru's words) for Western tourists, journalists and television crews wanting more information on both the literary and historical Draculas. The Society's first major event was the 1995 World Dracula Congress. This was the fulfilment of one of Pǎduraru's long-term projects. In 1986 he had proposed an international conference to be held in Romania at which Romanian and foreign scholars could debate the Dracula phenomenon and where Romania could present its position regarding Vlad Ţepeş. The idea was supported by Romanian historians and ethnographers, but rejected by the higher socialist authorities.[7]

After 1989 Pǎduraru once again had the opportunity to organize such a conference. The World Dracula Congress took place in May 1995 with the title *Dracula: Myth, Legend and History*. It was attended by over 200 people (both academics and Dracula enthusiasts) and included contributions from Dracula scholars around the world. A number of Romanian historians and ethnographers also presented papers (Miller 1997). Unsurprisingly, the Congress generated considerable interest among the international media and more than 100 journalists and television crews (the majority from outside Romania) covered the event. Nevertheless, as Miller (1997) has observed, much of the reportage of the Congress overlooked the academic dimension of the Congress and instead took refuge in a series of Dracula clichés.

The Romanian press (much of it resolutely opposed to the PSDR government which had participated in the organization of the Congress) was largely sceptical – even hostile – about the event (see Miller 1997). Some journalists questioned whether the state should spend its money on promoting Dracula (Stanca 1995) or whether it was appropriate for Romania to be known as the 'land of Dracula' (Paler 1995). Some writers were predictably critical of the confusion between the vampire Dracula and Vlad Ţepeş, which they felt the Congress had perpetuated (Canciovici 1995), despite a number of papers that had directly addressed this issue. Others remarked that the organization of the Congress was unlikely to have impressed foreign visitors (Munteanu and Rusu 1995a). However, there were more pragmatic voices and one journalist argued that 'whether we want it or not, whether we like it or not, we must adopt Dracula' (Gheorghiu 1995: 3).

For all its critics, the Congress had demonstrated the international interest in Dracula and the Transylvanian Society of Dracula subsequently introduced a series of annual colloquia (focused alternately on the fictional and historical Draculas) that provided a forum for an exchange of ideas between Romanian and Western researchers on issues related to the Dracula myth. Even these events did not find universal acceptance. Some historians who regard the Western vampire Dracula as a deliberate slur on the name of a Romanian hero have refused to have anything to do with the TSD. On the other hand an increasing number of Romanian ethnographers

---

7   Nicolae Pǎduraru, interview.

and folklorists were eager to engage with the Western myth of Dracula in order to better understand its implications for Romania (Miller 1997).

Dracula and Tourism in the Post-socialist Period

The Context: Developments in Romanian Tourism

After 1989, Romanian tourism experienced an extended period of uncertainty and decline. Figure 6.4 presents arrivals of foreign visitors during the period 1989–2007. There was a sharp increase in visitor arrivals (35 per cent) in 1990 although this was due to visits by journalists, charity workers, 'revolution tourists' as well as returning Romanian émigrés and cross-border traders from neighbouring countries. Thereafter, the trend in arrivals was more erratic. After an increase in 1992 the number of foreign visitors experienced a sustained decline. Over the period 1990–2002 visitor arrivals declined by 27 per cent and in 2002 Romania received fewer foreign visitors (4.79 million) than in 1989. However since 2003 there has been a clear recovery and in 2008 visitor arrivals reached 8.9 million (Institutul Naţional de Statistică 2011) the highest figure ever recorded (although the impacts of the global economic crisis subsequently caused a decline in arrivals). In 2011 tourism in Romania contributed to 4.5 per cent of Gross Domestic Product (World Travel and Tourism Council 2011).

The erratic performance of Romanian tourism since 1989 can be attributed to both internal and external factors (Light and Dumbrăveanu 1999). First, for much of the post-socialist period there was limited political interest in, or support for, tourism. Faced with the challenges of transforming the obsolete centrally planned economy bequeathed by Ceauşescu, while at the same time avoiding major social upheaval and hardship, successive post-socialist administrations have put tourism low on their lists of priorities.[8] Although there was abundant rhetoric about the economic importance of tourism, Romania's politicians did little to encourage or support tourism development (Pop et al. 2007). For example, there was little strategic planning or policymaking in the tourism sector. It was not until the mid-

---

8   This is demonstrated in the changing fortunes of the Ministry of Tourism itself. Originally established in 1971, it was combined with the Ministry of Commerce in 1990, and later re-established as a separate entity in 1992. In 1998 the Ministry of Tourism disappeared and was replaced by a National Authority for Tourism. The Ministry was re-established in 2000 and later merged with the Ministry of Transport and Construction in 2003. In 2007 responsibility for tourism passed to a newly created 'Ministry of Small and Medium Enterprises, Commerce, Tourism and Liberal Professions'. A separate Ministry of Tourism was re-established in December 2008 and then combined with another Ministry in December 2009 to form a Ministry of Regional Development and Tourism. The continually changing administrative structure with which tourism policymakers have to contend has hampered the development of consistent and long term tourism plans (see Light 2006).

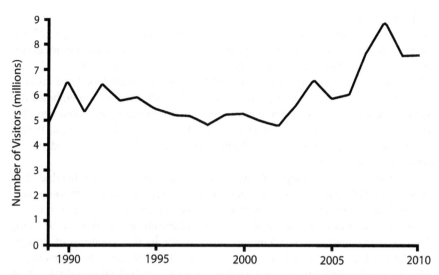

Source: Comisia Naţională pentru Statistică (1995), Institutul Naţional de Statistică (2003a, 2006, 2008, 2011)

Figure 6.4   Arrivals of foreign tourists in Romania, 1989–2010

1990s that the Ministry of Tourism produced a strategy for tourism development but this seems to have been little more than a paper exercise and was never implemented. As a result Romanian tourism – which entered the post-socialist period in an already disadvantaged position – quickly lost the markets on which it had been dependent before 1989 (mostly citizens of other socialist states) but without successfully repositioning itself as a destination. Moreover, the absence of strong political support has been exacerbated by the failure of the tourism industry itself to develop an effective lobby (Pop et al. 2007).

Second, there have been protracted delays in the privatization of tourism accommodation. Romania's hotels suffered from sustained underinvestment during the austerity of the 1980s and many declined below the standards expected by international tourists (Dumbrăveanu 2001). While privatization was widely regarded as necessary for regenerating Romania's hotel infrastructure, such reform was repeatedly stalled. For example, although tourism privatization was launched in 1993 only 53 per cent of hotels were in majority private ownership by 2002 (Institutul Naţional de Statistică 2003b). As a result, many hotels continued to experience neglect and underinvestment in the post-socialist era, hampering Romania's efforts to attract Western tourists. Similarly, the training and education of tourism employees was slow to develop so that socialist-era indifference to the needs of customers lingered long in parts of the hotel sector. As a result Romania lost its former share of the mass tourism market, particularly compared with neighbouring Bulgaria which privatized its Black Sea hotels much more rapidly.

However, a far greater problem for Romanian tourism has been the country's international image after 1989 (Light and Dumbrăveanu 1999, Light 2006). Tourists are highly sensitive to the image of potential destinations and are easily deterred from visiting places that are perceived to be unstable or unsafe (C.M. Hall 2005). Romania's reputation during the 1990s as an underdeveloped and instable country that was struggling to escape from a grim socialist past and embrace the West was enough to deter many Western tourists from visiting. Romania was also known for poor quality facilities and services for tourists, a legacy of the 1980s. Furthermore, its proximity to the former Yugoslavia further depressed tourist demand during the early 1990s.

In addition, this image of Romania as a strange, unpredictable and underdeveloped country was reproduced and reinforced by Western travel guides in which the familiar Balkanist stereotypes are present. For example, the first edition of the Rough Guide to Romania (Richardson and Burford 1995: viii) describes the country as 'challenging ... one of the hardest countries of Eastern and Central Europe to travel in'.[9] Similarly, *Let's Go 1995* describes Romania as 'still untamed and unexplored' (Chwiałkowska 1995: 468). Again, the first edition of the Lonely Planet guide (Williams 1998: 11) claims that Romania is 'the Wild West of eastern Europe'. A later edition describes Romania as the 'final frontier' of Europe (Kokker and Kemp 2004: back cover). Even after Romania joined the EU such representations persisted. For example, one newspaper claimed: 'Romania might be one of the newest stars on the EU flag but this country still retains an exhilarating final-frontier vibe for the adventurous Euro-tourist' (Moore 2007). Such representations reinforce Balkanist notions of Romania as somewhere different and not 'fully' European. The emphasis on the challenging and uncertain nature of travel in Romania will have deterred many potential visitors (particularly those seeking a conventional package holiday in a stable destination). On the other hand, during the late 1990s Romania became a popular destination for independent travellers and adventure tourists.

Romania has attempted to counter such Balkanist stereotypes through its tourism promotion. As I noted in Chapter 1, such promotion (particularly when undertaken by National Tourist Offices) is more than simply assembling attractive images of a destination in order to persuade would-be tourists to holiday there. Instead, the images presented in 'official' promotional materials are intended to project a particular message about a nation-state and its sense of national identity to the international community (Morgan and Pritchard 1998, D. Hall 1999, Light 2006). In a post-socialist context, Romania and other CEE states have used their tourism promotion to underline their rejection of state socialism and their adherence to the political and economic models of Western Europe. In particular, they have sought to overcome negative stereotypes and create new national brands

---

9   The same statement appears in the second edition of 1998 and the third edition of 2001.

that emphasize their modernity and 'Europeanness' (D. Hall 1999, 2010, Light 2006, Szondi 2007).

However, for all its efforts, Romania has had limited success in creating a distinct national brand (Dumbrăveanu 2009). In the early 1990s there were limited central funds for tourism promotion. The problem was compounded by a lack of expertise in place branding among a marketing team who had been trained for techniques of 'external propaganda' during the socialist era. In this context, Romania received assistance from the EU's PHARE project in 1993 and 1995 for the production of promotional materials and the country sought to create a new brand through the use of the slogan *Come as a tourist, leave as a friend*. However, there was little subsequent maintenance of this brand and the state was unwilling to allocate sufficient funds for marketing and promotion. As a result, tourism promotion was able to do little to counter Romania's increasingly negative international image during the 1990s. In 2003 the original slogan was dropped in favour of *Romania: Simply Surprising*. This campaign was intended to re-launch Romania as a tourist destination and to change perceptions of the country (Dolea and Țăruș 2009) but again it had limited success in creating a distinctive national brand (Pop et al. 2007). Another brand – *Fabulospirit* – was launched and swiftly abandoned in 2007 (Dolea and Țăruș 2009). The latest campaign – *Explore the Carpathian Garden* – was launched in July 2010 but has yet to make a significant impact. However, unlike the earlier campaigns which were constrained by a sustained lack of funding, the latest project is allocated a budget of €75 million up to 2013 (Bunea and Rădulescu 2010).

After more than a decade of stagnation and decline in the Romanian tourism industry, there have been early signs of revival in recent years. The privatization process was accelerated in 2003–4 (A. Smith 2006) so that an increasing number of hotels were privatized, while entirely new ones have been constructed by private entrepreneurs (Pop et al. 2007). By 2010, 91 per cent of tourist accommodation was in private ownership (Institutul Național de Statistică 2011). A comprehensive Master Plan for tourism development was drawn up in 2006[10] (Pop et al. 2007). Romania is increasingly promoting new forms of tourism and promotional materials have moved away from the socialist-era emphasis on the Black Sea coast and mountain resorts to focus instead on cultural tourism (particularly in Transylvania) and ecotourism. Romania's accession to the EU has further stimulated business tourism, and in 2007 cultural tourism received a significant boost when the Transylvanian city of Sibiu hosted European Capital of Culture. However, the 'recovery' of Romanian tourism is still at an early stage and a World Travel and Tourism Council report (2011) put Romania in 160th position (out of 181) in terms of the contribution of tourism to Gross Domestic Product.

---

10   Master Planul pentru turism național al României 2007–2026 [Online]. Available at: http://www.turism.gov.ro/turism/studii---strategii [accessed: 21 June 2011].

Dracula Tourism in Post-socialist Romania

After 1989 Dracula tourism unfolded in an entirely new context. However, like many other aspects of post-socialist Romania, the situation was characterized more by continuity with the socialist period than a decisive break from it. Although Romania had renounced state socialism, in many ways the socialist-era dilemma with Dracula had not changed. In particular, the tension between exploiting the Western Dracula myth or trying to deny it altogether was still unresolved. This was linked to the wider issue of how Romania wanted to represent itself to the wider world and the desire to avoid the Balkanist stereotypes associated with the literary Dracula. Furthermore, as the state continued to adopt an ambivalent position regarding Dracula tourism, it was again individual actors who took the initiative although such individuals were now operating within the freedom afforded by the private sector.

In the early 1990s Western tourists continued to visit Romania in search of both the fictional and historical Draculas, although their numbers were much reduced.[11] Although precise data are not available, one indication is the number of visitors to Bran Castle, which in 1991 stood at 40,000 (Adam 1997). In the following years, Dracula tourism started to increase again as Western companies began to develop packages to Romania, partly or exclusively themed around Dracula. Arrivals of visitors from America increased by 25 per cent in 1993 on the previous years, which may, in part, be attributable to the success of Coppola's *Bram Stoker's Dracula* in 1992.[12] By 1994, visitor numbers at Bran Castle had risen to 180,000 (Adam 1997).

In the early 1990s the Romanian state disengaged entirely from its (always limited) involvement in Dracula tourism and its role was taken over by the emerging private sector. The National Tourist Office (ONT) was privatized and transformed itself into a private travel agency. It continued to offer a version of the *Dracula: Legend and Truth* tour, now extended to include Bistriţa (Anon 1990). Many other private travel companies were founded after 1989 (a number by former ONT employees) and some of these also developed Dracula packages for Western tourists.[13] However, since there was still little understanding within Romania of the Western vampire Dracula most of the tours operated by Romanian travel agencies continued to be themed around the life of Vlad Ţepeş and indeed many of them were variants on the former *Dracula: Legend and Truth* package.[14] Western tour operators, facing fewer restrictions on the ways in which they could

---

11   Nicolae Păduraru, Valer Sîmihaian, interviews.

12   These figures derived from Comisia Naţională pentru Statistică (1995).

13   By 2004 there were 20–30 Romanian firms offering tours based on Dracula (Gruia 2005).

14   Nicolae Păduraru, interview. One Romanian tour operator (Alin Todea of Transylvania Live) told me that he thought there were only two Romanian companies offering tours based on the Western vampire Dracula.

operate, continued to develop and offer package tours to Romania themed around both the literary and historical Draculas. Even Romania's neighbours recognized the attraction of Dracula; for example, a Hungarian travel agency developed a four day Transylvanian tour (themed around the life of Vlad the Impaler) aimed at the Western market (Pecoul 1992).

Recognizing that there was almost nothing provided within Romania itself for Western tourists in search of the vampire Dracula, the Transylvanian Society of Dracula also entered the Dracula tourism business in 1992, initially in partnership with a private travel agency and, from 1994, through its own travel 'arm', the Company of Mysterious Journeys (CMJ)[15]. Nicolae Păduraru was able to take advantage of the extensive cultural capital – in the form of knowledge and understanding of the Western vampire Dracula – which he had accumulated during the socialist era (see Ghodsee 2005). Now working in the context of a free market economy Păduraru demonstrated considerable entrepreneurial flair in developing products and packages aimed at Western Dracula enthusiasts that enabled him swiftly to get ahead of his competitors.

Under Păduraru's direction the CMJ played a discrete but formative role in redefining the nature of Dracula tourism in Romania. Through his initiatives entirely new elements were introduced to the Dracula trail. These included evening performances in Aref of traditional dancing and recitations of folk tales regarding Vlad Țepeș around a campfire. This in turn was a major stimulus for the development of *Agroturism* (rural tourism) in Aref, which had a significant impact on the economy of this impoverished village. The CMJ also introduced into the Dracula tour the performance of a witchtrial (in either Sighișoara or Bistrița) along with an investment ceremony into the 'Order of Transylvanian Knights' in Brașov. Păduraru also developed three levels of Dracula tours ranging from the 'Classic Dracula' (an introductory tour combining locations associated with both the historical and literary Draculas) to a more demanding Level Three tour (only offered to 'survivors' of a previous tour) which had a much greater emphasis on Romanian superstitions and folklore (Dalton 1995a). After almost 30 years of Dracula tourism it was only now that a Romanian organization was catering directly for enthusiasts of the vampire Dracula, while at the same time providing a distinctly Romanian interpretation of the whole Dracula phenomenon.

During the mid-1990s the state began to reengage cautiously with Dracula tourism. Although there appears to have been little enthusiasm for promoting Dracula to Western tourists there are nevertheless occasional references to Dracula in *Holidays in Romania*, although their focus was mostly on Vlad Țepeș (for example Ogrinji 1994, 1996). There are also isolated references to Dracula in other promotional materials (including those produced with PHARE support). However, during the mid-1990s the Romanian Ministry of Tourism came to recognize that Dracula was something that continued to bring Western visitors to Romania. In particular, at a time when arrivals of foreign visitors were faltering,

---

15   Nicolae Păduraru, interview.

Matei Agathon Dan, the Minister for Tourism, could not overlook the international interest in the World Dracula Congress in 1995. The Ministry of Tourism (along with the Ministry of Culture) subsequently participated in the organization and sponsorship of the Congress. At a press conference in March 1995 Dan claimed that the international interest generated by the Congress could be used to re-launch international tourism in Romania (Severin and Pavel 1995). He argued that the 'congress offers a new kind of promotion. After 45 years of communism we need new news' (Dalton 1995b:14). For the first time, the Romanian state was prepared to engage directly with the Western myth of Dracula to stimulate tourism demand.

In order to showcase some of Romania's foremost tourist attractions for foreign delegates and journalists the Congress took place at a number of locations and attractions including Sinaia, Poiana Braşov, Târgu Mureş and Bistriţa, ending at Hotel Castle Dracula in the Borgo Pass. The Minister of Tourism also attended and used the occasion to present Romania's offer for international tourism to foreign journalists (Vărzaru 1995, Munteanu and Rusu 1995b). Matei Dan's newly found enthusiasm for the Western vampire Dracula seems to have been boundless and he was reported as remarking to an American newspaper that 'if tourists want hands rising out of coffins, we'll give it to them' (Miller 1997: 109). Nevertheless, the Romanian press was sceptical that the Congress had been an effective showcase for Romanian tourism and suggested instead that it would promote the development of a new form of tourism based on 'kitchness' (Petrescu 1995). The impact of the Congress in re-launching Romania as a tourist destination is difficult to assess: overall, the number of foreign visitors declined by 4.4 per cent between 1995 and 1996 although the number of visitors from America increased by 15 per cent over the same period.[16] However, the Congress seemed to have impressed on Matei Dan what Romania could gain from promoting Dracula tourism. Although he was in opposition after 1996 he returned as the PSDR's Minister for Tourism in 2000 and soon launched ambitious proposals for 'Dracula Land', a Western-style theme park based on the Dracula myth (see the following chapter).

The various locations in Romania that are part of the Dracula trail have also undergone major changes in the post-socialist era. Bran Castle has continued to be the principal focus of Dracula tourism and outside Romania the building is still widely known and promoted as Dracula's Castle. Visitor numbers at the castle have risen steadily in the post-socialist period (see Table 6.1). By 2009 the castle attracted more than half a million visitors, 38 per cent of whom were non-Romanians (Mihail 2010). This makes it the most visited attraction in Romania and gives an indication of the significance of Dracula to Romanian tourism.

In the post-socialist period the building's managers have continued to be ambivalent about the association of Dracula with Bran. Some have attempted to accommodate the castle's erroneous association with Dracula. For example, in 1993 the castle hosted a symposium entitled 'Dracula: History, Literature, Tourism' to coincide with the launch of *Bram Stoker's Dracula*. Various speakers

---

16   These figures are derived from Comisia Naţională pentru Statistică (1997).

Table 6.1   Visitor numbers at Bran Castle (Selected Years)

Year	Number of Visitors
1991	40,000 (a)
1994	180,000 (a)
1995	150,000 (b)
1996	161,820 (b)
1997	172,000 (b)
1998	249,592 (b)
1999	220,000 (b)
2000	261,459 (b)
2004	400,000 (c)
2006	485,000 (d)
2008	480,000 (e)
2009	500,000 (e)

Sources: (a) Adam 1997, (b) Bologa 2004, (c) Narcis Dorin Ion interview, (d) Preda 2007, (e) Mihail (2010)

(including Alexandru Misiuga) argued for the exploitation of Dracula arguing that it represented an opportunity for Romanian tourism. Others (including representatives from the Ministry of Culture) opposed such an initiative on the well-rehearsed grounds that it represented an attack on national dignity and a slur on the name of a national hero (Burileanu 1993). Nevertheless, the castle's custodian (Cornel Taloş) was prepared to experiment and introduced performances and *Son et lumiere* displays in the Castle's interior courtyard. Such events were highly profitable and visitor numbers at the castle rose significantly. However, the Ministry of Culture (which appointed the custodian) intervened to prohibit such events and Taloş was replaced in 1995 (Adam 1997).

Taloş' successor, Raul Mihai, was initially opposed to the Dracula connection and made no attempts to exploit it. The subsequent decline in visitor numbers between 1994 and 1996 was attributed by one newspaper to the failure to exploit fully the opportunities presented by Dracula (Adam 1997). Mihai seems later to have recognized that Dracula could be used to generate income at Bran and introduced Halloween events and 'nights of terror' in 2002 (Şelaru 2002). After 2003 the Castle's manager returned to a position of discouraging the Dracula associations at Bran on the grounds that the presentation and interpretation of the castle should be concerned with historical accuracy and not externally imposed myths.[17] Like ONT staff in the socialist era, the castle's guides continued to acknowledge the Dracula connection but without encouraging it. In short, there

---

17   Narcis Dorin Ion, interview.

continued to be a mismatch between the expectations of many non-Romanian visitors and what they encountered when they arrived at the castle (see Muresan and Smith 1998, Light 2012).

Such is Bran's importance as Romania's foremost visitor attraction that the news in 2006 that the Romanian state was prepared to give up ownership of the castle caused a considerable stir. Romanian legislation of 2001 and 2005 allowed for the restitution of property nationalized by the socialist regime and many former property owners (or their descendents) put in claims. As such, the grandchildren of Queen Marie submitted a claim for the return of Bran Castle. The Ministry of Culture was reluctant to give up ownership of the castle, but in the run up to EU accession Romania needed to demonstrate its commitment to the rule of law and to correcting the injustices of socialism (LeBor 2006). Consequently on 26 May 2006 ownership of the castle returned to Dominic von Habsburg. However, a condition of the restitution was that the castle should remain open as a museum for three years (Travers 2007) and during this period the building remained under the administration of the Romanian Ministry of Culture. There was a period of uncertainty about the status of the museum after 2009 (and at one point the castle was reported as being for sale). However, the new owners decided that the castle should remain a museum open to the public and on 18 May 2009 management passed to a Romanian company established by the new owners.

As a tourist attraction, Bran Castle has changed significantly since 2009. The building is now presented with an entrepreneurial flair that contrasts markedly with the unimaginative approach adopted by previous managements. The castle is unambiguously presented as a royal holiday home from the interwar period and is furnished accordingly. More of the castle has been opened to visitors. Its rooms now contain numerous interpretation panels while the building also includes special exhibition rooms, an audiovisual display, a self-guided audio tour, several shops, and staff in the various rooms to assist visitors. The castle also hosts an increasing number of events and festivals. In short, the building has adopted the strategies of presentation that are commonplace at historical properties in Western Europe and America.

However, the mismatch between the presentation of the building and the expectations of (some) visitors has not disappeared. Those foreign tourists who visit Bran believing it to be Dracula's Castle will continue to be disappointed since what they find is a royal residence, rather than a spooky, haunted castle. Under previous administrations the lack of information and interpretation and the emphasis on old furniture left open the possibilities for fantasy, escapism and imaginative play. As I argued in the previous chapter, visitors in search of Dracula's Castle were able to re-enchant the building and make it (temporarily) what they wanted it to be. However, the professional new management and presentation of the building has rather closed down these possibilities, leaving less space for the imagination. In this sense, Dracula enthusiasts will be less able to make their own meanings for the castle and will continue to be underwhelmed by their visit. On the other hand, there is, for the first time, an engagement with the Dracula connection in the presentation and interpretation of the building. The castle now contains several rooms with interpretive displays that examine Bram Stoker's *Dracula*, Vlad Țepeș, vampires and strigoi.[18] These acknowledge that the building is widely known as Dracula's Castle although they do little more to encourage the association.

The village of Bran itself has expanded considerably in the post-socialist period. The area has become one of the leading centres in Romania for rural tourism and numerous accommodation establishments have opened since 1989. The accessibility of the village from Bucharest means that it has become a popular resort for weekend breaks by both Romanians and foreign workers based in Bucharest. Many local shops, restaurants and hotels have had no reticence in exploiting the Dracula connection and make use of images of Dracula or vampires in their promotion. The village has also established itself as the most popular place in Romania in which to spend Halloween (Bendriș and Ilieș 2009) and many hotels and guest houses in the village arrange special events for the occasion.

In addition, souvenir retailing at Bran has remained a highly lucrative business.[19] As the previous chapter examined, local traders had established their pitches in the car park outside the castle. During the 1990s, as the number of visitors to the castle increased so too did the demand for retailing space. More stalls opened in the car park but this area soon proved inadequate, so that a second market – the 'Dracula Bazar' opened in 2000, a short distance from the castle entrance. Some of the kiosks are owned by members of the same families which have the prime spaces in the car park market, but increasingly the traders are drawn from elsewhere in the county, attracted by the ready money to be made from Dracula. A third retailing space opened close to the entrance of the castle in 2004 with financing from an American businessman. It takes the form of a covered arcade including a number of retailing units, a 'Skeleton Tavern' and a 'haunted castle' where, in true theme park style, costumed ghouls leap out at unsuspecting tourists. By 2004 there were 75 individual retail units around the castle (Light et al. 2005).

The nature of souvenir retailing outside Bran Castle has changed dramatically in the post-socialist period. While the castle's management may have had little interest (until recently) in engaging with Dracula, local traders have had no such reservations. After 1989 the effective state censorship of souvenirs ceased and the local peasants were free to sell what they wanted. While they initially continued to sell locally produced handicrafts they soon embraced the opportunities presented by Dracula. By 1994 souvenirs (particularly T shirts) based on Vlad Țepeș had appeared. By the following year the vampire Dracula had also appeared among

---

18   These displays closely mirror the arguments of *In Search of Dracula* (McNally and Florescu 1972). For example they claim that Bran may have been the inspiration for Bram Stoker's Castle Dracula, while the character of Count Dracula may have been based on Vlad Țepeș.

19   This paragraph is based on interviews with traders at Bran.

the souvenirs on sale.[20] After a cautious start local traders embraced Dracula with enthusiasm and an increasing number of stalls started to sell Dracula-based souvenirs including T-shirts, postcards, mugs, masks, guidebooks and more recently, fridge magnets. This caused considerable friction between the Ministry of Culture (which owned the car park) and the local traders.[21]

During the late 1990s the nature of the souvenirs at Bran changed in other ways. Fewer kiosks continued to sell locally made handicrafts. Instead, their place was taken by a new type of souvenir, seemingly authentic and traditional in appearance but intensively produced and with little relationship to the rural traditions of the Bran area. Such products include painted plates featuring Bran Castle or the face of Vlad Ţepeş; woodcuts of Dracula's face; carved wooden plates and tankards featuring images of Romania or Bran; wooden swords; and wooden spoons, again featuring the Voievode's face. There is also a wide range of generic wooden goods, ceramics and lacework. Most of these souvenirs are apparently mass-produced in factories elsewhere in Transylvania[22] and indeed they are widely available throughout Romania.[23] A survey in 2004 indicated that over 40 per cent of traders were selling such souvenirs with only 12 per cent selling traditional-style products (Light et al. 2005). For the enterprising peasants of Bran it was no longer necessary to sell locally made handicrafts to supplement their incomes. Instead, a comfortable livelihood could be made from fulltime souvenir retailing and from trading goods produced elsewhere in Romania. More recently a new type of souvenir has appeared and an increasing number of stalls are selling goods with a generic horror theme (masks, dolls, hats, swords) without any specific relationship to Bran Castle or even Dracula (see Figure 6.5).[24]

The changing nature of souvenirs at Bran – particularly the apparent decline in locally produced handicrafts – is not an isolated instance. Instead, it has long been argued that the arrival of tourists in large numbers at a destination inevitably leads to an irreversible decline of local and traditional forms of culture (Graburn 1967, Greenwood 1977). The process is driven by the demands by tourists for 'cheap, exotic, portable and durable souvenirs' (Wall and Mathieson 2006: 276). To meet mass demand requires mass production and an emphasis on quantity rather than quality. Thus traditional skills may be lost in the drive towards large scale production of standardized souvenirs. Ultimately, local culture is commercialized and commodified, eventually completely changing its meanings for local people (Greenwood 1977). A related argument states that tourism development erodes the authenticity of local cultures and lifestyles leading to their replacement by a 'staged' (or fake) form of authenticity (MacCannell 1976).

---

20   Elizabeth Miller, personal communication.

21   Narcis Dorin Ion, interview.

22   Narcis Dorin Ion, interview.

23   For example, near-identical souvenirs are on sale at Hotel Castle Dracula and at Poienari Citadel during the summer.

24   Such goods are usually imported and most appear to be made in China.

Figure 6.5   Souvenirs on sale outside Bran Castle

At first sight this appears to be what is happening at Bran: the growth of mass tourism after 1989 has resulted in a significant change in the nature of souvenirs that are sold around the castle, so that locally produced handicrafts in particular are becoming much less common. However, the situation is arguably more complex. Mass tourism is not a recent development at Bran Castle. After all, in 1977 the castle attracted over 220,000 visitors (Anon 1978). Instead, what has changed is the context in which souvenir retailing has taken place. In particular, during the period of state socialism the nature of souvenir retailing was carefully constrained by state ideology. Local traders faced precise restrictions on the types of souvenirs that they could and could not sell. In the post-socialist period, what has happened at Bran is a shift to responding to the demands of the market.

In this context, Bran's canny traders have identified what (Western) tourists are seeking and are providing them with such products. Tourists – whether foreign or Romanian – are unlikely to visit Bran Castle for the purpose of purchasing 'traditional' or 'authentic' Romanian handicrafts. For a start, much of what is sold at Bran is not particularly representative of such traditions.[25] Moreover, those in search of such handicrafts have many opportunities to purchase them elsewhere in Romania. Instead, the majority of foreign tourists at Bran are expecting to find Dracula's Castle. As such, many of them will also expect to be able to purchase souvenirs with a Dracula theme as a means of validating and affirming their visit. The demand for Dracula themed souvenirs has therefore led to the emergence of entirely new craft forms (such as the wide range of carved wooden goods) that are not related to local cultural forms but which are developed in response to market opportunities (Markwick 2001). Such souvenirs may not be authentic in the eyes of their critics (and indeed are frequently derided as kitsch in the Romanian press). However this is unlikely to matter much to most Dracula tourists. What is important is that these souvenirs forge a connection with a place (see Ramsey 2009). They were purchased in Transylvania, themed around Transylvania and were not (usually) available outside Transylvania (Light 2009a). In this sense, the Dracula themed souvenirs at Bran are an authentic memento of a visit to a place that is imagined as being Dracula's Castle and they contribute to an experience of Transylvania that is authentic and meaningful for the tourist (see Wang 1999, Buchman et al. 2010). Indeed, in this way these souvenirs may play an important role in compensating for the disappointment of not finding Dracula in Bran Castle itself.

Elsewhere in the country other locations on the Dracula trail have evolved in less dramatic ways. Poienari Citadel underwent a period of neglect during the austerity of the 1990s but in recent years has undergone something of a revival. In 2009 management of the castle passed from the Curtea de Argeş municipal museum to the county museum (*Muzeul Judeţean)* for Argeş county. This brought about some innovation in the presentation of the citadel: the metal guard rails around the building were repainted: new interpretive panels were added at various stages along the long climb to the castle; floodlighting (that had been long abandoned) was restored; and various models (of impaled bodies and a hanging gibbet) were installed at the entrance to the castle itself. Like Bran, Poienari has adopted the presentation strategies that are commonplace at heritage attractions elsewhere in Europe. The castle continues to be a popular attraction with Romanians (for whom the building is still promoted as a site of national significance) and foreign tourists (many of whom continue to regard the building as the 'real' Dracula's Castle).

In the county of Bistriţa-Năsăud the two hotels which catered for Dracula tourists – the *Coroana de Aur* and Hotel Tihuţa – both experienced a change of management after 1989. The new manager of the *Coroana de Aur* knew little about Dracula and did not promote the Dracula connection.[26] Like many other Romanian hotels in the early 1990s, the *Coroana de Aur* deteriorated due to a prolonged lack of investment and professional management. Alexandru Misiuga, although long retired, refused to renounce his interest in the building and sought to reinstate the Dracula connection. He persuaded the manager to convert a room

---

25   Sabina Ispas, interview.
26   Alexandru Misiuga, interview.

used as a nightclub into a 'Jonathan Harker Breakfast Salon' which opened in 1997. It was decorated with vampire motifs, portraits of Dracula and a collection of animal skins purchased from local hunters.[27] The hotel underwent extensive refurbishment between 2000 and 2003 to restore it to a standard expected by Western Dracula enthusiasts.[28]

In 1990 Hotel Tihuţa was taken over by a manager who, unlike his counterpart at the *Coroana de Aur* was enthusiastic about the Dracula connection. In 1991 the building was renamed Hotel Castle Dracula[29] thereby realizing Alexandru Misiuga's personal dream of seeing a Castle Dracula in the Borgo Pass. The coffin in the cellar also reopened (in a new location) while the hotel became a popular venue for Halloween (and more recently, New Year) parties for Western Dracula enthusiasts. In the mid-2000s the hotel underwent a much needed refurbishment which brought the rooms up to modern standards but also replaced the original rustic interiors that had been designed personally by Misiuga. On Misiuga's initiative a statue of Bram Stoker was erected outside the hotel in November 2006 (Pancevski 2006). The castle has established itself as something of a sightseeing attraction and is a popular stop for coach groups (of both Romanian and foreign tourists) on the Bistriţa-Vatra Dornei road. A number of souvenir stalls have established themselves around the castle selling very much the same souvenirs that are available at Bran Castle. However, the castle-hotel has also been affected by various other post-socialist developments in the Tihuţa Pass. From the late 1990s onwards, numerous new villas and holiday homes have been built in the tiny hamlet of Piatra Fântânele and these have robbed Misiuga's hotel of some of its isolation and grandeur. Moreover, in 2008–9 the Bistriţa-Vatra Dornei road which runs through the Bârgău/Tihuţa pass was resurfaced and widened. It is now a major artery for lorry traffic. As a result, visiting Dracula fans will find that the Pass is much less austere and isolated than its portrayal by Bram Stoker.

Both the *Coroana de Aur* and Hotel Castle Dracula underwent a process of privatization during the early 1990s. Under privatization legislation passed in 1990 all state owned enterprises were transformed into joint-stock companies with the state as the single shareholder. These companies were then subject to autonomous management and were to be prepared for privatization (Stan 1995). Both *Coroana de Aur* and Hotel Castle Dracula were successfully privatized during the Mass

---

27   Alexandru Misiuga, interview.

28   Alexandru Misiuga continued to take a keen interest in the *Coroana de Aur*. He visited the building regularly (particularly to meet visiting groups of Dracula tourists) and he was invariably offered a free glass of beer by the hotel staff. He was made an honorary citizen of Bistriţa for his contribution to bringing foreign tourists to the town. He died unexpectedly of a heart attack in February 2009 aged 84. The fact that his death was reported in the national press (for example Bozbici 2009) indicated recognition of his role in developing Dracula tourism in Bistriţa.

29   Valer Sîmihaian, interview. Sîmihaian was manager of the hotel between 1990 and 1995.

Privatization Programme of 1995 through Management/Employee Buyouts[30] in which employees subscribed ownership coupons (offered to all Romanian citizens by the state) for shares in the hotel. This did not prove to be an effective method of privatization in the tourism sector (Dumbrăveanu 2001) but these two hotels were among the few that were successfully privatized in this way. A local businessman subsequently purchased a majority stake of shares in both hotels.

The county of Bistrița-Năsăud has consolidated its status as a key location on the Dracula trail. However, the relative isolation of this area and its distance from Bucharest means that it still tends to attract dedicated Dracula enthusiasts (those wanting a quick 'soundbite' of Dracula in Transylvania tend to confine their visiting to Bran). Both the *Coroana de Aur* and Hotel Castle Dracula are established destinations for specialist themed Dracula tours, whether run by Romanian or Western operators. There have been some efforts by local travel agencies to create a place identity for Bistrița county as 'Dracula World'.[31] However, this part of Transylvania is increasingly becoming better known among non-Dracula enthusiasts since Bistrița is used as a stopping point on organized excursions to the painted monasteries of Bucovina which are accessed through the Bârgău Pass.

Finally, in recent years Sighișoara has also become an established stop on the Dracula trail (Stephen 2007). Without question, the Dracula Park project of 2001–2 (see the following chapter) played a key role in bringing the town to the attention of Dracula enthusiasts and cultural tourists more broadly. The house where Vlad Țepeș was reputed to have been born is used as a restaurant and is a popular stop for coach parties on Dracula tours. Since 1993 Sighișoara has hosted an annual 'festival of medieval art' which attracted a distinct horror fringe much to the disquiet of local church leaders (Russu 2005). There have been various initiatives to cater for Dracula and horror fans. For example an 'Alchemy bar' opened in the centre of the town in 2004[32] while a small 'torture room' was opened in the town walls. Souvenir stalls in the central square sell the same Dracula and horror-related souvenirs that can be found at Bran and Piatra Fântânele. In the minds of some Dracula enthusiasts Sighișoara has become confused with Castle Dracula.[33]

Conclusion

Since 1989 Dracula tourism has re-established itself as a key segment of Romanian tourism. An increasing number of Romanian travel companies offer Dracula packages of one form or another. Similarly, numerous Western travel companies now offer Dracula tours: an internet search reveals several hundred companies

---

30   Valer Sîmihaian, interview.

31   Valer Sîmihaian, interview.

32   This had closed when I visited in September 2008.

33   An employee in a cultural heritage information centre in Sighișoara recounted wearily that she is asked 50 times a day for directions to Castle Dracula!

offering Dracula-themed holidays in Romania. There are at least eight locations (Bistriţa, Bran, Bucharest, Piatra Fântânele, Poienari, Sighişoara, Târgovişte and Snagov) that are an established part of the Dracula trail. 'Dracula's Castle' (Bran) is the most visited tourist attraction in Romania while souvenirs featuring the word Dracula are the most popular among foreign visitors to Bucharest (Rîncu 2008).

The extent of contemporary Dracula tourism is difficult to quantify. Iordanova (2007) claims (without giving any source) that the volume of Dracula tourism stands at 250,000 visitors a year but this is certainly an exaggeration. Around a quarter of million foreign tourists visit Bran Castle but many are not serious Dracula enthusiasts or visit the castle only for a quick 'soundbite' of Dracula as part of a broader holiday. The number of dedicated or diehard Dracula enthusiasts is certainly much lower. Iancu (2005) suggests that they can be numbered in the tens of thousands[34]. Certainly, visitor numbers at the two hotels intended for Dracula tourists suggest something of this magnitude. In 2007 the *Coroana de Aur* hotel hosted 16,425 visitors of whom 47 per cent were from outside Romania[35]. Similarly, in the same year Hotel Castle Dracula received 4,971 visitors, 40 per cent of whom were non-Romanians[36]. To put this into perspective, 194,418 foreign tourists visited mountain (ski) resorts in 2010 (Institutul Naţional de Statistică 2011). In comparison with other market segments, Dracula tourism is a relatively small segment of Romania's tourism market. However, it is a form of special interest tourism that has shown consistent demand and steady growth in the post-socialist period.

The response in Romania to the demand for Dracula tourism has been mixed. The private sector has been enthusiastic about exploiting Dracula, so that there are now hotels, guest houses, campsites, restaurants, travel agents, casinos and beverages named after Dracula. In many cases it is unclear whether the eponymous Dracula is Stoker's vampire or Vlad the Impaler. However, the Romanian state remains reluctant to embrace Dracula (whether the vampire or the Voievode). During the post-socialist period there have been scattered references to Dracula in Romania's 'official' tourism promotional materials (although the Dracula in question is usually Vlad Ţepeş). There was a brief engagement with Dracula during the World Dracula Congress in 1995 but for most of the post-socialist period the Romanian tourist authorities have shown little interest or enthusiasm for exploiting the commercial possibilities of Dracula. This reluctance is partly grounded in an unwillingness to embrace a form of tourism that is founded on a Western place myth of Romania as a strange, distant and backward place, but also from a continued concern to protect the reputation of Vlad Ţepeş from any

---

34   A more generous estimate was offered by a Romanian tour operator (Alin Todea of Transylvania Live) who suggested to me that the volume of Dracula tourism was less than 100,000 foreign visitors annually.

35   This information was provided by the Direcţia Judeteană pentru Statistică (County Statistics Directorate) for Bistriţa-Năsăud.

36   The information was provided by Hotel Castle Dracula.

association with the vampire Dracula. Indeed, in many ways Romania's stance on Dracula tourism is little different from that of the socialist era. Such tourism is acknowledged and tolerated but there is little encouragement of it since it collides with the identity that the Romanian state wishes to project to the wider world. There has been only one significant attempt by the Romanian state to exploit the commercial possibilities of Dracula. In 2001, the Romanian Minister of Tourism announced proposals to build Dracula Park, a horror theme park to be constructed in Transylvania. The rise and fall of this surprising and controversial proposal is considered in the following chapter.

Chapter 7

'Dracula Park'

The previous chapters have charted Romania's reluctance to engage with the Western Dracula myth, both during the socialist era and in the first post-socialist decade. In this context, perhaps the most surprising and dramatic development in the evolution of Dracula tourism was the announcement in 2001 that Romania intended to construct 'Dracula Land', a theme park based on the vampire Dracula. Billed as the world's first 'horror park', the proposal (later renamed 'Dracula Park') represented the first serious attempt by the Romanian state to exploit the commercial possibilities of the vampire Dracula. In this chapter I chart the rise and fall of Dracula Park, principally through examining the way it was reported in the Romanian and international press. In particular I seek to examine the relationship between the project and Romania's efforts to project an identity to the wider world. At its launch Dracula Park was presented as a confident and forward looking attempt by Romania to exploit the global popularity of Dracula on the country's own terms in order to re-launch Romanian tourism. However, the project rapidly generated controversy and became the focus of a vigorous campaign of both domestic and international opposition that called into question Romania's adherence to wider European norms (and, by extension, its readiness for membership of the European Union). This opposition eventually forced the project to be suspended and, later, abandoned.

The Birth of the Idea

Radu Florescu, speaking at the 1995 World Dracula Congress, first suggested the idea of a theme park based on the Dracula myth. Florescu argued: 'the name of Dracula is magic. Let's exploit it. Why don't we hold a festival of fantastic film or build a theme park based on Dracula' (Terenche 1995: 9). In 1998 a form of Dracula theme park was proposed for the Bistriţa area and although the government apparently showed some interest in the project the idea moved no further.[1]

In November 2000 the opposition PSDR (which in January 2001 renamed itself the Social Democratic Party (SDP)) won parliamentary elections and returned to government with renewed confidence, intent on bringing about economic stability and concluding negotiations for EU membership (Papadimitriou and Phinnemore 2008). It was in this context – a new administration seeking to present itself as dynamic, forward looking and European in outlook – that plans were announced

---

1   Valer Sîmihaian, interview.

to develop a theme park based on Dracula. The project came completely out of the blue: there was no mention of it in any of the tourism plans produced previously (Rus 2000), neither was there any reference to it in the PSDR governing programme produced in late December 2000.[2] Instead, the idea seems to have been a personal initiative of Matei Agathon Dan, the new Minister of Tourism.[3] A charismatic and combative politician, Dan was well aware from his former experience as tourism minister between 1992 and 1996 of the difficulties in reinvigorating Romanian tourism. Moreover, through his involvement with the 1995 World Dracula Congress he was among the few Romanian politicians to appreciate the power of Dracula to attract foreign tourists to Romania. Upon being reappointed as Minister of Tourism Dan demonstrated that he was prepared to use the image of the vampire Dracula to promote Romania and, for example, introduced an actor dressed as Dracula to the Romanian stands at international tourist fairs.

At the Berlin tourism fair of March 2001 Dan formally announced the Dracula Land project (Toader 2001). It was among a number of projects intended to aid in the re-launch of Romanian tourism, which included the construction of a new resort at the Black Sea. There was little initial reaction in the Romanian press. Indeed, pragmatic journalists recognized that Dracula could indeed contribute to reviving Romanian tourism (for example Ceteraş 2001a). Dan gave various explanations of how he had conceived the idea for a Dracula theme park. On one occasion he reported that it was a visit to a Don Quixote theme park in Spain that convinced him that Romania could develop a similar form of literary tourism in Romania (McAleer 2001). He later declared that, during a visit to Switzerland, he had purchased a watch inscribed with the word 'Dracula'. From this he had realized that Romania was missing out on the opportunity to exploit the commercial opportunities of Dracula (Vela 2001a). In announcing the project Dan acknowledged, with more pragmatism than many other Romanians that Dracula was a global phenomenon, whether or not Romania liked the fact. He added: 'it would be a stupidity for the myth to be neglected in its own country and exploited for tourism in other countries which don't have any relationship with Dracula' (Moroianu 2001: 6).

The Ministry of Tourism subsequently commissioned a feasibility study to determine the location of the park. In the following months various locations lobbied for the chance to host Dracula Land. Bistriţa presented its claim on the basis that it was the location of Stoker's novel and that two hotels had already been constructed specifically to cater for Dracula tourists (Sabau 2001). Sighişoara based its claim on its central location and as the birthplace of Vlad Ţepeş (Ceteraş 2001a). Despite the lack of any connections with either Count Dracula or Vlad Ţepeş, Bran's case was based on its long established role as the home of Dracula's

---

2   *Program de Guvernare pe perioda 2001–2004.* [Online] Available at: http://www.cdep.ro/pdfs/prog_guv.pdf [accessed: 8 August 2005].

3   The Ministry of Tourism which had disappeared in a government reorganization in 1998 was re-established in December 2000.

Castle. In June, Matei Dan announced that five locations – Bran, Bucharest, Sighişoara, Târgovişte and the Tihuţa Pass – were on the short list for consideration (Popescu 2001a).

The Choice of Location

In July 2001 the government announced that Sighişoara had been chosen to host Dracula Land. At first sight, Sighişoara had a number of advantages: it was situated in Transylvania and, as the (presumed) birthplace of Vlad Ţepeş, had a direct connection with the historical Dracula. Sighişoara enjoyed a central location in Romania; it was situated on the E60 European road (and close to the route of a projected Bucharest-Budapest motorway) and was relatively close to two airports (Sibiu and Târgu Mureş). This gave it a distinct advantage over Bistriţa (which has much poorer transport connections and is an eight hour drive from Bucharest). Sighişoara also boasted one of the finest medieval citadels in Europe (which was added to the World Heritage List in 1999) that would be showcased by the building of Dracula Land. Moreover, originally built by Transylvania's Saxon population, Sighişoara (Schässburg) was an area with strong historical ties to Germany and Matei Dan was clear that the Romanian government hoped to use these connections to attract German investment for the project (Ceteraş 2001b). Unlike the rival locations of Bistriţa and Bran (where local councils were controlled by the political opposition) Sighişoara was located in a county (Mureş) controlled by the Democratic Union of Hungarians in Romania (which had formed a parliamentary alliance with the SDP). Moreover, the Mayor of Sighişoara was a SDP member and by selecting the town as the home for Dracula Land Matei Dan could ensure that the project enjoyed local support.

Nevertheless, in many ways Sighişoara was a curious choice of location. Although Vlad Ţepeş may have been born in Sighişoara, the Voievode had otherwise few links with Transylvania. But by selecting a site associated with Vlad Ţepeş for a theme park based on the fictional Dracula, the Romanian government was furthering the confusion between the historical and fictional Draculas, something that Romanian historians had opposed for four decades. Moreover, Sighişoara is a small town with little tourist infrastructure (such as hotels and restaurants) to support a major tourism project, while the Citadel itself was fundamentally unsuited to mass tourism. Similarly, Sighişoara's transport connections were not as well developed as initially claimed. Both Sibiu and Târgu Mureş airports were mostly used for domestic flights and Romania's main international airport in Bucharest was a five hour drive (about 190 miles/300 km) away.

The Dracula Land project was initiated through a Government Ordinance of 12 July 2001[4] that approved a 'special programme' of tourism development in the

---

4   Ordonanţă nr 3 din 12 iulie 2001 privind aprobarea şi implementarea Progarmului special de dezvoltare turistiă a zonei Sighişoara [Online] Available at: http://www.cdep.ro/

Sighişoara area. This had, as its principal aim, the 'rehabilitation and revitalization of Sighişoara Citadel ... and the creation in this space of an exclusive touristic-cultural zone'.[5] This was to be achieved through the construction of a theme park (Dracula Land), a golf course and a cable car to connect the park with Sighişoara Citadel. The programme was also intended to bring about the rehabilitation of the public infrastructure in Sighişoara, along with the creation of jobs for local people. Thus, according to the legislation Dracula Land was the means to an end (the revitalization of Sighişoara Citadel) rather than an end in itself. Nevertheless, critics were soon to argue that the outcome and the means proposed to achieve it were incompatible. The Ordinance established a commercial society – *Fondul pentru Dezvoltare Turistică Sighişoara*/FDTS (The Sighişoara Fund for Tourism Development) – to implement the project with the collaboration of Romanian or foreign investors. The project envisaged an investment of €38 million and the creation of 3,000 jobs (Ceteraş 2001b).

From the outset the project encountered problems. The term 'Dracula Land' had already been registered in Bistriţa as a trademark (D. Popa 2001) and immediately after the project was announced enterprising Romanians swiftly registered similar names as trademarks. There was also a rush to register web addresses containing the term 'Draculaland' (Cehan 2001). The holders of the trademarks offered to sell them to the Minister of Tourism who declined the offer. Instead, the project was renamed Dracula Park. This time, however, the government took no chances and the Ministry of Tourism issued a disposition granting exclusive rights of the trademark 'Dracula Park' to FDTS.[6]

Further copyright problems were to follow. The Ministry of Tourism quickly discovered that it did not have the right to exploit the classic image of Dracula since Universal Studios, the producer of the early Dracula films, owned these rights (Poland 2001). Universal expressed its willingness to enter into talks with the Romanian authorities with the view to transferring the copyright to Romania (Anon 2001b). However, the Tourism Minister was reluctant to pay for the copyright rights (and the Ministry almost certainly lacked the financial resources to do so): as a result Dracula Park had to devise an alternative image for its eponymous hero (Anon 2001c).

---

pls/legis/legis_pck.htp_act_text?idt=28842 [accessed: 3 March 2004].

5   Annex to Ordonanţă number 3.

6   Ordin nr. 332 of 19 aprilie 2002 al ministrului turismului pentru cedarea dreptului de proprietate exclusivă către Societatea Comercială "Fondul pentru Dezvoltare Turistică Sighişoara" – S.A. asupra mărcii "Dracula Park" [Online]. Available at: http://www.cdep. ro/pls/legis/legis_pck.htp_act?ida=36184 [accessed: 3 March 2004].

The Launch of the Project

The official launch of Dracula Park took place in Bucharest on 5 November where full details of the project were made public for the first time (Vela 2001b, Burtan 2001a) The 60 ha park was to feature an eclectic range of attractions including a Castle Dracula (with moat), a labyrinth, an Institute of Vampirology with library and lecture rooms, conference facilities, rides in a black caleche, an open air amphitheatre, a golf course, a sport centre, a lake, a riding school, a 'main street' featuring souvenir shops, craft shops, a range of restaurants and various clubs, bars and discos, a wide range of tourist accommodation (including luxury hotels), a conventional amusement park and exhibitions of Romanian history. Dracula Park was to be built on the Breite Plateau, a 130 ha site of ancient oak woodland about one kilometer from the centre of Sighişoara (to which the park would be connected by a cable car).

The total cost of Dracula Park was estimated at $31.5 million and the project was to be financed through a mixture of public and private funding. Central and local government (including the Ministry of Tourism) was putting up $4.5 million. The Sighişoara *Primărie* (town hall), the major shareholder in FDTS, had provided the land (worth $20 million) and intended to generate a further $12 million from a share offer, enabling Romanians to become investors and stakeholders in Dracula Park. The remaining finance would be sought from foreign investors. The park was projected as attracting 400,000 visitors in its first year, subsequently rising to 1.1 million visitors annually. It was expected to generate an annual income of $12 million, much of which would be invested in the restoration of Sighişoara Citadel. Building work was planned to start in March 2002 and the park was expected to be complete by the end of 2003 (Vela 2001a, Constantinescu 2001a, Năstase 2001a).

In scale and concept, Dracula Park was quite unlike any previous tourism development in Romania. It seems to have been intended as a bold and innovative statement of what Romania could achieve. Matei Dan described it as 'the most spectacular tourism project of the start of this millennium' (Constantinescu 2001a: 7) and claimed that it would bring about the re-launch of Romanian tourism. Moreover, Dan was dismissive of suggestions that building a Dracula theme park would cement the association between Romania and Dracula in the Western popular imagination arguing that 'Dracula exists whether we want it or not'. The boldness of the project suggests that it was intended to demonstrate that Romania had fully come to terms with the Western Dracula myth and was confident enough to exploit it in its own way and on its own terms. Thus, Dan argued that the park would 'make fun' of Count Dracula. Dracula Park was presented as a 'national project' and something which was '100 per cent Romanian' (Constantinescu 2001a, Burtan 2001a). Yet, despite such claims, it was clear that the project was essentially importing and mimicking the Western model of the tourism theme park (Shandley et al. 2006).

Within a week of the launch of Dracula Park a rival project was announced! Braşov County Council (controlled by the opposition National Liberal Party) was unhappy with the decision to locate Dracula Park at Sighişoara instead of Bran and clearly feared missing out on the expected economic benefits of the park. As a result, on 9 November the Braşov County authorities approved the construction of an 'alternative' Dracula Park on a 500 ha site at Râşnow, near Bran. The Braşov Liberals argued that Bran Castle had a stronger connection with the Dracula myth and a more developed infrastructure to support the park (Popescu 2001b). Matei Dan immediately dismissed the rival proposal, while the Romanian press speculated about how many Dracula Parks Romania could support.

On 20 November, Dan launched Dracula Park in Sighişoara. Although local opinion in this town of 38,000 people was divided, there was noisy support for the project among those who saw it as a way to create new employment opportunities. Supporters carried banners proclaiming 'Dracula Park at Sighişoara' and 'Agathon, we love you', and a 'Pro-Dracula Foundation' succeeding in gathering 3,600 signatures in support of the project (Burtan 2001b, Anon 2001d). In what one commentator described as a scene reminiscent of the Ceauşescu era in its stage-managed 'spontaneity', a crowd marched from a local factory in support of the project, intent on overawing their opponents who were booed and whistled when they tried to speak (Douglas-Home 2002a, Andrei 2001). Dan reiterated his support for the project and described the decision to locate the park in Sighişoara as 'irrevocable' (Năstase 2001a).

On 12 December the public share offer (the first of its kind in Romania) for Dracula Park was launched. It was the first stage of three such offers through which FDTS intended to raise over $12.1 towards the costs of building the park (Anon 2001e). A total of 15.5 million shares were included in the first offer (aimed at the domestic market) that aimed to generate the $5 million necessary to start building work. An aggressive promotional campaign was launched to encourage Romanians to purchase shares. In order to demonstrate that Dracula Park enjoyed full government support and to promote confidence in the project the Prime Minister (Adrian Năstase) and the Tourism Minister were the first to purchase shares in a high profile and much publicized gesture (Rădulescu 2001).

The Search for Investors

Despite the initial confidence of the Minister of Tourism, foreign investors simply did not consider Dracula Park to be viable. In part this reflected concerns about the uncertain global demand for large theme parks. However, potential investors were also sceptical about the park's business plan, particularly some wildly implausible financial projections contained in the prospectus that accompanied the launch. According to these figures, 80 per cent of visitors to Dracula Park would be Romanians, mostly living within 80 km (50 miles) of the park itself (Crosu 2002). Even more implausibly, the projections assumed that visitors would pay an entry fee of $5 and would each spend $25 when inside the park itself. The press subjected these claims to a withering analysis, arguing that it was unlikely that large numbers of Romanians would visit a theme park based on a Western myth that is little known in Romania, particularly since the catchment area of the park was predominantly rural, where most people did not own cars, and where the average wage was around €50 a month (Fabini 2001, Bako 2002).

While the visitor forecasts failed to stand up to even casual scrutiny, there were other aspects of the project that deterred foreign investors (George 2002). These included the haste with which the project had been pushed forward; the poor infrastructure and transport connections of Sighişoara itself; and the lack of business experience among the management board of the organization charged with running the park (FDTS). Moreover, since the major shareholder of FDTS was Sighşoara town council with the Mayor as a member of the management team, the project was potentially subject to political interference.

While foreign investors avoided direct investment in Dracula Park, Romanians were similarly wary about participating in the domestic share offer. Some in principle wanted nothing to do with Dracula, while others had little confidence in the project as a business opportunity. Several newspapers pointed out the implausibility of the business plan and advised their readers to consider carefully before buying shares in Dracula Park (Anon 2001f, Nistorescu 2002). The National Association of Investors of Romania also expressed its doubts about the viability of the project (Anon 2002a).

But Romanians also had deeper suspicions about Dracula Park. The press made frequent comparisons with two other schemes – Caritas and the National Investment Fund (FNI) – which had promised Romanians quick and easy wealth (Nistorescu 2001, A. Ştefan 2001, C. Ştefan 2002). Caritas, a classic pyramid scheme (to which the PSDR government had turned a blind eye) had collapsed in 1994 costing many people their savings, while FNI, a trust fund offering high-interest returns had similarly collapsed in 2000. Both had been ostensibly private sector initiatives, although the complicity of politicians and former members of the *Securitate* was widely suspected in the case of Caritas (Verdery 1996). Dracula Park, while ostensibly a government project, was promoted by a party – the SDP – that had an established reputation for corruption and many in the party were suspected of having plundered state assets for personal gain, particularly during the privatization programmes of the 1990s (Gallagher 1995, 2005). Many Romanians seem to have interpreted Dracula Park as another scheme designed to enrich senior figures in the governing elite at the expense of the wider population (see Ficeac 2001, A. Ştefan 2001). These suspicions were deepened by the fact that both the Minister of Tourism and the Prime Minister had publicly bought shares in the project. Dan Matei's vocal insistence that Dracula Park would be built at Sighişoara, despite a clearly implausible business plan and the growing domestic and international opposition to the park, further reinforced the belief among many Romanians that the government (or its clients) had vested interests in seeing Dracula Park succeed.[7] The level of distrust in Dracula Park among ordinary Romanians was so great that only 15,000 people bought shares (Avram and Grosu 2003), compared with around four million who invested in Caritas and 300,000 who lost money in FNI (Verdery 1996, Gallagher 2005).

Such was the scepticism of Romanians regarding Dracula Park that, after the initial period of 45 days, only 40 per cent of shares in FDTS had been sold. Consequently the share offer was extended for a further six weeks (Dobre 2002) and Matei Dan made a concerted effort to persuade investors to buy shares. Only two foreign companies did so, both in exchange for the exclusive rights to sell their products in the park (Burtan 2002). When the share offer finally closed in early April, 69 per cent of the shares had been sold. The press reported that one of the financial investment societies created during the 1995 Mass Privatization Programme to manage the public's investments in Romanian companies had 'saved' the project by purchasing a large package of shares (A. Ştefan 2002). Nevertheless, with the share offer having technically been a success Matei Dan announced that the construction work would start in May (Anon 2002b).

Domestic Opposition to Dracula Park

While Matei Dan repeatedly presented Dracula Park as being a national project and in the national interest, it was far from having national support. Although the exploitation of Dracula for tourism did have its supporters (for example Năstase 2001b, Ficeac 2001) Dracula Park quickly proved to be the focus of widespread domestic opposition. Some of the project's critics were opposed in principle to the idea of a Dracula Park; others were concerned about the choice of location; others were concerned about the obviously unsustainable nature of the project and its impact on the environment around Sighişoara (Jamal and Tanase 2005).

The leading objections in principle to a Dracula theme park were expressed in terms of national identity and the impact of building the park on Romania's international image. Press commentators raised issues such as 'what sort of country are we?' and 'how do we want the rest of the world to see us?'. Some argued that the construction of Dracula Park was an inappropriate development for Romania and would simply cement the association between Romania and horror in the Western popular imagination. For example, an editorial in *Evenimentul zilei* (Nistorescu 2001: 1) asked: 'who else could become expert in a pleasure park on a horror theme than the people who gave [the world] Dracula and Nicolae Ceausescu'. In a similar vein, other critics argued that Romania should be promoting itself for tourism on the basis of its culture and history rather than its Dracula associations

---

7   Some Western analysis of Dracula Park (Jamal and Tanase 2005, Tănăsescu 2006) has taken it at face value as a tourism project and overlooked the distinctively post-socialist context in which it was developed. However few people in Romania seemed to have regarded Dracula Park as anything but an elaborate financial scam.

(Andrei 2002a). But these concerns were not confined to the press. A member of the business community claimed: 'superficial speculation in a Hollywood style venture risks the alarming spread in the wider world ... [of] an undignified image of the Romanian people as a 'nation of vampires' and [would give] Romania the undeserved name of Dracula Land' (Anon 2002a: 4).

A similar view was expressed by the historian Neagu Djuvara, speaking at a debate organized by the Group for Social Dialogue. He argued:

> I am a historian and a Romanian patriot and as such I must say that I absolutely oppose 100 per cent this project to create here in Romania a Dracula Park ... why do we bring foreigners to the country in order to show them vampires and to create around our nation a legend of vampirism which doesn't exist? I consider that it is absolutely inadmissible. In principle, I find that a Dracula Land here is aberrant. (cited in Stolea 2002: 9)

Other critics were also opposed to the commodification of a myth – vampirism – regarded as essentially a Western invention and unknown in Romanian culture. Speaking at a conference in Transylvania the Archbishop of Cluj argued 'it is my conviction ... that Dracula Park doesn't have a religious or a cultural justification. In our mythology and culture we don't have the myth of the vampire ... Dracula is an imported image and it does not make sense to adopt it and to turn it into a national emblem' (cited in Valendorfean 2002: 1). Others, particularly from within nationalist circles argued that Dracula Park would further exacerbate the confusion between Count Dracula and Vlad Ţepeş, damaging the image of the Voievode. Matei Dan dismissed such objections with the argument that, as Minister of Tourism, his job was to bring foreign tourists to Romania by any means possible (Constantinescu 2001b).

Many of the Churches in Romania also opposed Dracula Park, arguing that it represented a celebration of the occult entirely inappropriate in a country with a Christian tradition. The pastor of Sighişoara's Lutheran church claimed that 'from the point of view of the Christian religion, 'Dracula-Land' is an aberration but not just that. It is a grave sin in the face of God' (Frölich 2001: 14). The Lutheran Church in Sighişoara subsequently launched an appeal to the other churches in Transylvania to oppose the project. The Roman Catholic Church and most Protestant denominations joined the protest. On the other hand the Romanian Orthodox Church (which has a long history of supporting whichever government is in power) was reluctant to condemn the project (Zubascu 2002) although some individual priests spoke out against it.[8] Indeed, the launch of Dracula Park in Sighişoara opened with a blessing from an Orthodox priest (Andrei 2001), seemingly conferring an additional legitimacy to the project.

---

8   Some analysis (for example Tănăsescu 2006) has greatly overestimated the opposition of the Romanian Orthodox Church to the Dracula Park project.

Other opponents of Dracula Park were concerned less with the concept of the park in principle but with the implications of locating it at Sighişoara. While many in Sighişoara were reported to be enthusiastic about the project, expecting significant economic benefits to the town (Anon 2001d) many Romanian NGOs had serious misgivings. Those concerned with heritage conservation expressed their concerns regarding the impact of Dracula Park on the fabric of Sighişoara Citadel. *Fundaţia Pro-Patrimoniu* (a heritage conservation NGO) argued that the construction of Dracula Park so near to the Citadel was incompatible with the Citadel's status as a World Heritage Site. The organization also expressed concerns that the Citadel was fundamentally unsuited to mass tourism and would be 'suffocated and destroyed' by the extra million visitors expected at Dracula Park (Berza 2002: 8). Others argued that a site such as Sighişoara was ideally suited to cultural tourism but would be degraded by 'vampiric' tourism.

Moreover Sighişoara's remaining Saxon community were resolutely opposed to the Dracula Park project. Their representatives pointed out that the Western vampire myth had no connection with the Germanic heritage of Sighişoara and that superimposing a Dracula theme park upon a medieval Saxon town was an act of cultural aggression against the heritage of Romania's German minority (Stolea 2002). One Saxon argued: 'For us ... a Dracula Land at Sighişoara is like a slap in the face ... We feel attacked and humiliated' (Richter 2001: 14). *Liga Pro-Europa* (The Pro-Europe League), a Transylvanian NGO, described the project as an act of 'cultural vandalism'[9] while others expressed concern that the project might compromise Romanian's obligations to the Council of Europe regarding the protection of the heritage of its ethnic minorities (Stolea 2002). Despite Matei Dan's earlier claims that Dracula Park enjoyed the support of Sighişoara's Saxon community, the political representatives of the Democratic Forum of Germans in Romania declared themselves totally opposed to Dracula Park (Gădea 2001).

However, it was the proposal to build Dracula Park on the Breite Plateau alongside Sighişoara that generated the strongest opposition. Building work would threaten or destroy several hundred ancient oak trees, many more than 400 years old. Protesters argued that to destroy the trees was an act of vandalism equivalent to the destruction of Sighişoara Citadel itself: one silviculturalist described it as 'a barbaric, anti-national and anti-European act' (Stoiculescu 2002: 14). What angered protesters still more was that the Breite Plateau was protected by both local and national legislation and had been included in a register of protected areas under a law passed as recently as 2000 (Stolea 2002). Yet supporters of the project were either unaware of the plateau's protected status or were prepared to ignore it. Moreover the project lacked the approval and authorizations required from other state institutions (each of which had the right to demand modifications). One

---

9   Liga Pro Europa. NU transformării Sighişoarei în Dracula Land [Press conference, 8 November 2001] [Online]. Available at: www.proeuropa.ro/document/CP8noi2001.html [accessed: 30 March 2004].

newspaper reported that Dracula Park required 32 such approvals and had yet to obtain a single one of them (Cehan 2002).

The prospect of a government project openly disregarding both Romanian and international legislation regarding environmental protection and heritage conservation mobilized a sustained campaign of opposition to the Sighişoara location for Dracula Park (Parau 2009). It was coordinated by two non-governmental organizations, *Liga Pro-Europa* and *Sighişoara Durabilă* (Sustainable Sighişoara) which together launched an 'SOS Sighişoara' campaign. The opposition by civil society to Dracula Park was less concerned with the concept in principle but with the manner in which the project had been initiated and the choice of location. As the president of *Liga Pro-Europa* claimed: 'If Dracula Park is built in Sighişoara not a monument or a nature reserve in the country will be safe in future' (Anon 2002c). Most of the press was also opposed to Dracula Park[10] and in February *România liberă* (a resolute opponent of the SDP government) launched a daily full-page feature entitled *Dracularea* (which roughly translates as 'Draculaization'!).

At a time when the SDP government was making Euro-Atlantic integration one of its priorities, much of the opposition from civil society was implicitly or explicitly framed within the context of 'Europe'. As such, opponents sought to present Dracula Park as inappropriate or damaging for a country with aspirations to EU membership. For example, protesters pointed to the lack of transparency and consultation in the development of the project and the choice of its location as indicative of Romania's shortcomings as a democratic state (Derer 2001).[11] In a similar manner, other opponents compared the development of Dracula Park with the extravagant and damaging building projects undertaken by Ceauşescu during the 1980s (Cristea 2002a). Dracula Park was also presented as being discordant with EU norms and practices regarding the sustainable development of cultural or natural heritage resources (Berza 2002, Jamal and Tanase 2005). Others argued that Sighişoara itself was part of the cultural heritage of the whole of Europe, which Romania had obligations to protect (Stolea 2002).

International opposition to Dracula Park

Had the opposition to Dracula Park been confined to Romania the government showed every sign that it was prepared to ignore it. However, Dracula is a highly newsworthy subject and any attempt by Romania to exploit the Dracula myth inevitably caught the attention of the international media. As a result, the Dracula Park proposal was widely reported – often with some amusement – around the

---

10   The Dracula Park project was highly newsworthy and was the subject of over 200 newspaper articles in 2001 and 2002.

11   See also Liga Pro Europa. NU transformării Sighişoarei în Dracula Land [Press conference, 8 November 2001] [Online]. Available at: www.proeuropa.ro/document/ CP8noi2001.html [accessed: 30 March 2004].

world. This of course was exactly the sort of publicity the initiators of the project had hoped for. But as details of Dracula Park became more widely known, a number of international organizations expressed their concern about the project. Eventually the international opposition to Dracula Park reached a pitch that could not be ignored and the Romanian government was compelled to respond to external agendas that it was unable to control (Shandley et al. 2006, Parau 2009).

Among the earliest non-Romanian organization to oppose the scheme was the UK based Mihai Eminescu Trust, a charity promoting conservation and sustainable development in Transylvania. On the day that Dracula Park was launched the Trust published an open letter to President Iliescu expressing concern about the proposal and requesting that an alternative location be found. The president of the Trust was able to use connections within the press to publish a number of articles opposing the project (Douglas-Home 2001a, 2001b, 2002a, 2002b; see also Parau 2009). Thus from the moment of its launch, Dan Matei had to confront a vigorous counter-narrative outside Romania which was firmly opposed to the Sighişoara location for Dracula Park.

Unsurprisingly, UNESCO also expressed concerns. As a signatory to the World Heritage Convention, Romania was obliged to inform UNESCO of any developments which might impact upon a World Heritage Site. Yet the pace at which the Dracula Park project had been pushed forward was such that no notification had been given. At a meeting of the World Heritage Congress in December 2001 the committee noted 'with concern' the project to build a theme park in the vicinity of Sighişoara. It also noted 'with disquiet' that the Romanian authorities had already approved the project. The meeting requested an immediate environmental impact study and urged Romania to consider 'all possible solutions for an alternative location' for the park (UNESCO 2001). A group of UNESCO assessors visited Sighişoara in March 2002 to evaluate for themselves the likely impacts of Dracula Park.

Further opposition came from Greenpeace International. Matei Dan had previously claimed support for Dracula Park from an organization styling itself Greenpeace Romania. Greenpeace International pointed out that the Romanian group had no relationship with Greenpeace and was using the name illegally and requested that Dan refrain from referring to Greenpeace's endorsement of the project (Cristea 2002b). The Central and Eastern European branch of Greenpeace subsequently issued a statement expressing its concern about the environmental impacts of the park and calling for an evaluation of alternative locations. The World Bank also expressed its doubts (Andrei 2002b) while the Cultural Commission of the European Parliament called for a suspension of the project until the publication of the UNESCO evaluation (Andrei 2002c). Coming at a time when Romania was seeking to begin accession negotiations with the EU such a request was difficult to ignore.

However, what seems to have been the decisive intervention came from an unexpected source. Britain's Prince Charles, the patron of the Mihai Eminescu Trust, had visited Transylvania on several occasions and made a private visit in

May 2002 which included a stay in Sighişoara. On his return the Prince issued a statement expressing his reservations about the project: 'Large scale developments in the style of, for example, Dracula Park will definitively destroy the character of this area [Saxon Transylvania]' (Andrei 2002d: 24). President Iliescu (who had previously avoided expressing support for Dracula Park, perhaps unsurprisingly since it was sponsored by the rival 'Năstase' wing of the SDP[12]) immediately distanced himself from the project declaring that, like Prince Charles, he included environmental protection among his hobbies (Iuraşcu and Scărişoreanu 2002).

The Collapse of the Sighişoara Project

By May 2002 the level of domestic – but particularly international – opposition to Dracula Park had reached a level that the SDP government could no longer ignore (Parau 2009). Indeed, as one newspaper wryly noted, the Dracula Park 'scandal' had brought Romania more publicity than any of the tourism promotion undertaken in recent years (Niţu 2002). Far from being a confident and innovative attempt to exploit the Western Dracula myth on Romania's own terms, the project had become a profound embarrassment. Moreover, the international publicity that Dracula Park had received was proving harmful to Romania's global image. The Dracula Park project had inadvertently presented Romania as a state that did not take seriously the protection of its natural environment and historical heritage and did not respect either its own laws or its obligations under international treaties. Furthermore, Romania appeared to demonstrate a lack of respect for the heritage of its ethnic minorities and a preparedness to disregard completely domestic and international objections to the project. In effect, Romania had presented itself as a country completely out of step with the norms of the European Union – all this at a critical moment when it was trying to convince the Union that it was a credible future member. In the context of the long established Balkanist discourse, through its management of Dracula Park Romania had presented itself as being 'not fully European' (Light 2007a).

After the much publicized intervention of Prince Charles it was clear that Dracula Park's days were numbered. Shortly after the Prince's visit Matei Dan admitted for the first time that Dracula Park might not be built at Sighişoara (Drăgotescu et al. 2002). There followed a period of some confusion in which the fate of the park was unclear. Ministry of Tourism officials were reported as being determined to proceed with the Sighişoara project (Radio Free Europe/ Radio Liberty 2002a). Similarly, Mureş County Council issued its formal approval for the building works for Dracula Park (Ceteraş 2002). However, on 29 June the Ministry of Culture formally confirmed the abandonment of the Sighişoara project (Radio Free Europe/Radio Liberty 2002b). Yet Matei Dan was reluctant to admit publicly that he had abandoned Sighişoara as a location

---

12   See Gallagher (2005) on internal rivalries within the SDP.

and declared that the location of the park would depend on a feasibility study to be undertaken by PriceWaterhouseCoopers: until then, he added, the park remained at Sighişoara (Anon 2002d).

The consultancy report was a long time in arriving and until its publication the domestic opposition to the Sighişoara location remained uncertain if their campaign had been successful. When it was finally made public in January 2003 the PriceWaterhouseCoopers report predictably discouraged the government from building the park at Sighişoara (Radio Free Europe/Radio Liberty 2003a). Indeed, many of the highly optimistic forecasts which had accompanied the launch of Dracula Park were now shown to be highly exaggerated (Moise 2003). The news was greeted with jubilation by the project's opponents but with disappointment by those in Sighişoara who had bought shares in the project. On 26 January, Matei Dan announced that the report recommended that Dracula Park should be constructed in, or close to, Bucharest (Radio Free Europe/Radio Liberty 2003b). The following day, at a meeting of FDTS shareholders, Sighişoara Town Council announced its withdrawal from the project (FDTS was subsequently renamed 'Dracula Park SA'). Since the Council was also the owner of the land on the Breite Plateau (which had made up a considerable proportion of FDTS's capital) its withdrawal meant that the value of FDTS shares was expected to fall dramatically (Anon 2003a).

Dracula Park after Sighişoara

In February 2003 Matei Agathon Dan announced that the new location for Dracula Park would be at Snagov, near to Bucharest. In addition to its proximity to Bucharest (the town is 15 miles/25 km north of Romania's international airport) Snagov monastery was the supposed burial place of Vlad Ţepeş. The park was to be built on land owned by the state (a former collective farm). Moreover, its location on the Romanian plain meant that there was little likelihood of objections on ecological grounds. Snagov was also situated in Ilfov county, a long established SDP fiefdom, which also decreased the likelihood of local opposition to the project. On the other hand, it increased speculation that the project was once again intended to bring personal benefits to the ruling party. In addition to a new location, the overall concept of the park was also revised, perhaps as a concession to those who had opposed the idea in principle of a Dracula theme park. In a dramatic change of heart, Dan announced that a theme park exclusively themed around Dracula was unlikely to be a success. Instead, the park was to include a greater emphasis on Romanian culture and history (Anon 2003b) and would include Vlad Ţepeş as well as the vampire Dracula among its attractions. The new Dracula Park was expected to open in late 2004.

In a government reshuffle in June 2003 Matei Agathon Dan lost his position as Minister of Tourism when the Tourism Ministry itself was merged with the Ministry of Transport and Construction.[13] The new minister, Miron Mitrea, announced that the building of Dracula Park was no longer a priority for Romania (Anon 2003c). Little more was heard of the proposal for a rival Dracula Park near Bran. For over a year it appeared that the Snagov proposal had been quietly abandoned until, in September 2004, the project returned to life when the government approved the construction of an 'industrial park' at Snagov.[14] This was to be a substantial complex that would include a wide range of tourism and leisure facilities including a theme park (without any specific mention of the theme!) a water park, hippodrome, a motor racing circuit, carting circuit, golf course, tennis courts, accommodation and restaurants. However, the park was more than simply a tourist attraction, since the complex was to include workshops for Romanian handicrafts and traditional industries as well as facilities for tourism businesses and for the training of staff for employment in the tourism industry, along with exhibition facilities. The total cost was to be between €40 million and €70 million (Palade and Roibu 2004). The complex was to be entitled 'Snagov Tourism and Pleasure Park', an indication that the government seemed to have little desire or intention to revive Dracula Park in its original form. Nevertheless 'Dracula Park SA' was to be the administrator of the theme park section (Bechir 2004).

Even now the project still had the potential to generate controversy. Snagov Park was to be managed by a newly established commercial company which had been granted the free use of the 450 ha site for a 49 year period. An investigation by one newspaper suggested that the major shareholders in this company had close links to various members of the government (Savin 2004, Boeru 2004) leading inevitably to speculation that the project was, once again, intended for the enrichment of the ruling elite. Moreover, the opposition National Liberal Party subsequently started a legal process to annul the government decision that had established Snagov Park on the grounds that the ceding of public land to a private firm was forbidden by the Romanian constitution. As a result of the legal proceedings the country's capital market regulator refused to allow Dracula Park SA to list its shares on the capital market Anon 2005a).

Since Dracula Park was so closely associated with one political party it was inevitably vulnerable to a change of government. When the SDP lost parliamentary elections in November 2004 it came as no surprise that the new administration, seeking to distance itself from its predecessor, showed little enthusiasm for Dracula Park. In January 2005 President Băsescu called for the government decision establishing Snagov Park to be cancelled. The following month the president of the National Authority for Tourism declared that the Authority would no longer promote, develop or invest in Dracula Park (Anon 2005b) seemingly marking the final nail in the coffin for the park as a government project. The government

---

13   Dan did not subsequently stand in the parliamentary elections of November 2004.

14   Hotărâre Guvernului nr. 1560 privind aprobarea construirii parcului industrial "Parcul touristic şi de agrement Snagov" [Online]. Available at www.guv.ro/notefundam/afis-nota.php?id=894 [accessed 5 December 2004].

formally annulled the Snagov project in July 2006[15] although Dracula Park SA remained in existence and had still not given up its intention to construct a Dracula theme park somewhere in Romania (Neacşu 2006). In 2011 one newspaper reported that the small investors who had purchased shares in Dracula Park had yet to secure the return of their original investments (Păvălaşc 2011).

Conclusions

Dracula Park was the first attempt by the Romanian state to exploit seriously the financial possibilities of Dracula. It was launched as a bold and innovative initiative that was intended to bring about a dramatic re-launch of tourism in Romania. In many ways it was a surprising development since a high profile project such as Dracula Park could only have the effect of cementing further the association between Romania and Dracula in the Western imagination, an association that Romania had resisted for more than three decades. However, arising at a time when Romania was engaged in negotiations for EU membership Dracula Park seems to have been intended to make a statement about post-socialist Romania. That the project enjoyed government support could be interpreted as presenting Romania as an energetic and ambitious country which was confident enough to engage with the Western myth of Dracula on its own terms. As Matei Agathon Dan announced at the launch of the project, Romania was now ready to 'make fun' of Dracula. Nevertheless, Dracula Park rapidly came to be seen not as a demonstration of Romania's confidence and innovation but instead as a profound embarrassment for the Romanian government. The saga illustrates once again how Dracula has the capability to harm the international image of Romania!

Dracula Park was a project promoted by a political elite (Shandley et al. 2006) but it conspicuously failed to attract a broader base of support. However it was significant in that it stimulated a vigorous debate within Romania about the exploitation of Dracula, particularly for the purposes of tourism. Some in the press regarded such exploitation as acceptable and a means to promote the many other resources Romania can offer tourists. But many others were deeply sceptical about the promotion of Dracula as Romania's principal tourist attraction, preferring instead that Romania should promote the many attractions it could offer for cultural tourism. Underpinning this debate were questions of national identity, such as 'what sort of a country are we?' and 'what do we want to say about ourselves through tourism?'. Romanians recognized that tourism was a means for the country to present itself to the wider international community but many were unhappy that Dracula should be a central element of such a presentation. As the

---

15   Hotărâre Guvernului nr 878 privind anularea constituirii parcului industrial „Parc Turistic şi de Agrement Snagov", aprobata prin Hotărârea Guvernului nr 1560/2004. [online] Available at: www.guv.ro/notefundam/afis-nota.php?id=2480 [accessed 29 June 2008].

project vividly illustrated, there was no consensus within Romania about whether to embrace and exploit the Western Dracula or to continue the strategy of denial.

Nevertheless, there were positive outcomes of the Dracula Park story. In particular, it demonstrated the success of civil society in mobilizing opposition to a mega-project that had been imposed on Sighişoara without public consultation and in a manner clumsily resonant of Nicolae Ceauşescu (see Gallagher 2005). The opponents of the park demonstrated that they could attract international support and compel the government to reconsider. Thus, their success in overturning the Sighişoara project was a significant moment for Romania's post-socialist democracy, testifying to an increased assertiveness on the part of civil society and demonstrating that the government was no longer guaranteed success when pushing ahead with unpopular projects (Parau 2009). In addition, the remarkable charm of Sighişoara has become more widely known as a result of the international press coverage of Dracula Park. Cultural tourism has increased significantly in the town as a result.[16] Moreover, Dracula Park drew Romania to the world's attention, and successfully highlighted what – other than Dracula – it had to offer tourists.

---

16   Nicolae Păduraru, interview.

Chapter 8
Conclusions

Bram Stoker was not the first Western author to write about Transylvania (Miller 1997) but he was certainly the most influential. In writing *Dracula* he needed an appropriate home for his vampire and Transylvania – a region he had never visited and knew little about – suited his purposes perfectly. It was a real place but at the same time it was almost completely unknown among his readers. It was identifiably European but at the same time was situated in an uncertain, liminal position on the very edge of Europe. It was close enough to be recognizable but distant enough to be threatening. Stoker portrayed Transylvania as a terrifying place and therefore an entirely plausible home for a predatory Eastern vampire that posed a real menace to the West. Stoker gave full rein to his imagination and seems to have relished writing about Transylvania: the parts of the novel that are set there are often considered to be the most inspired and they have certainly been the most influential. Bram Stoker effectively invented Transylvania as we understand it today. In writing *Dracula* he set in motion a distinctive, alluring and enduring place myth of Transylvania that has now taken on a momentum of its own. In the Western imagination the word 'Transylvania' effortlessly conjures up images of a dark, mountainous and forested land, peopled by fearful, superstitious peasants, where sinister vampires and other supernatural creatures reign unchecked.

While at first glance, *Dracula* was just another Victorian pot-boiler, the novel is also significant for the way that it encoded much broader ideas in the West about the nature of Europe itself. In particular, *Dracula* expresses a long-standing belief about the division of Europe into two halves: a modern, progressive and 'civilized' West, and a backward, primitive and unpredictable East that lags behind the West in terms of economic and social development (Wolff 1994, Dittmer 2002/3). Todorova has labelled this Western discourse about southeast Europe as 'Balkanism' and Balkanist tropes are ever-present in *Dracula*. The novel is insistent on the contrast between Transylvania and Britain, and *Dracula* effectively maps Transylvania and its surroundings – what is now the state of Romania – as being firmly within the West's 'first circle of Otherness' (Boia 2001b: 186). Indeed, Dittmer (2002/3) argues that Stoker's *Dracula* plays a key role in reproducing and naturalizing the imaginative division of Europe into East and West and turning it into a taken-for-granted fact. It is the role of *Dracula* in reproducing and reinforcing such Balkanist ideas about Transylvania (and Romania more generally) that lie at the heart of Romania's dilemma with Dracula.

Nevertheless, if *Dracula* had enjoyed the same popularity as Stoker's other novels Transylvania would probably be as little known in the West as Oltenia, Moldova, Muntenia or Crisana (other regions of contemporary Romania). But

Dracula has enjoyed a spectacular global success during the twentieth century and moreover has been embraced by many forms of Western popular culture, particularly cinema. The result is that Stoker's portrayal of Transylvania has circulated among a global audience. From the 1970s onwards *Dracula* has also inspired a distinct vampire subculture which has proved to be hugely popular and enduring. Vampires have mutated and shifted in all sorts of ways. Even if contemporary vampires are rather softer creatures than those of the nineteenth century they still can trace their lineage back to Count Dracula. And Transylvania continues to be firmly established in the Western imagination as the seemingly natural home of vampires.

Given the way that Stoker's novel represents Transylvania – a region that many Romanians consider to be the cradle of their culture and identity – it is hardly surprising that Romanians have shown little interest in embracing Count Dracula. After all, *Dracula* is hardly a flattering portrait of their country! Romanians are quick to point out that there is no factual underpinning to the Transylvania place myth and that vampires are unknown in their folklore and traditions. Ordinary Romanians are acutely conscious of the way that their country is seen by the wider world and they have no desire to be known as a nation of vampires. Similarly Romania's political leaders have long been concerned about the international image of their country. Like most contemporary nation-states Romania seeks to project a sense of its own political and cultural identity to the wider world on its own terms. Yet the Balkanist underpinnings of *Dracula* – which insist that Romania is situated in a part of Europe that lags behind the West – are fundamentally in collision with Romania's sense of its own identity. When Dracula attained new heights of popularity during the 1970s Romania was a socialist state, founded on an agenda of modernization, development and progress. Socialist Romania therefore had nothing to gain by embracing an international cultural icon that reproduces a place myth of Transylvania as primitive, underdeveloped and haunted by the supernatural. Similarly, from the mid-1990s onwards post-socialist Romania has striven to convince the West that it is not the semi-European Other portrayed in *Dracula* but instead a modern, developed European state that is ready to take its place in the European Union. In different ways in different political and historical contexts the Balkanist discourse that is expressed in *Dracula* is fundamentally antithetical to Romania's sense of its own identity but also the face that it wishes to present to the wider world.

But the reluctance of Romania and Romanians to embrace Dracula is not just about the Balkanist underpinnings of the Transylvania place myth. There is also the matter of Romania's own Dracula, Vlad Ţepeş. Despite his brutality, Vlad III is held in high esteem in contemporary Romania where many seem to regard him as a model of authoritarian leadership. Every country has its national heroes and the process of nation-building involves venerating such figures and placing them in the national pantheon of those who defended and built the modern nation-state. No country would wish to see one of its national heroes denigrated from outside. For this reason Romanians are, unsurprisingly, irritated when people from outside

Romania equate Vlad Țepeș with a vampire. Indeed, there is a longstanding argument in Romania which questions how Americans would feel if the rest of the world considered George Washington to be a vampire. There is little basis for the confusion between Count Dracula and Vlad Țepeș and, as Elizabeth Miller and others have argued, the claims presented by McNally and Florescu in *In Search of Dracula* (1972) now look increasingly tenuous. However, like the Transylvania place myth, the claim that Vlad Țepeș is the inspiration for Count Dracula has taken on a momentum of its own within Western popular culture. Romania no longer has control over the appropriation of one of its national heroes.

However, while Romanians may be unhappy about their country being associated with the supernatural or about Vlad Țepeș being regarded as a vampire, Romania has little influence over the way that Transylvania or Vlad Țepeș are represented in Western (and increasingly global) popular culture. This situation illustrates global inequalities and asymmetries in cultural power, particularly the power to represent. In particular, many countries and peoples are not represented as they would choose to represent themselves but instead through the myths, clichés and stereotypes which more powerful states – particularly in the West – choose to attribute to them (Morgan and Pritchard 1998). Romania would certainly not choose to present itself as the 'land of Dracula' to the Western world. Yet while Romania might reject Dracula as an externally-imposed stereotype there is little it can do to change this situation. As such, Dracula represents a site of cultural struggle between Romania and the West (Light 2007a). At the root of this issue is the collision between the ongoing appropriation of Transylvania within Western popular culture and Romania's efforts to define itself in its own way and on its own terms.

The popularity of Dracula in the West and the resonance of the Transylvania place myth have long drawn tourists to Romania. Such travel – which I have termed Dracula tourism in this study – is a form of special interest tourism that is generated outside Romania. In fact, Dracula tourism is not a uniform phenomenon but instead comprises a range of motives and expectations although there is considerable overlap between them. Some tourists are seeking the literary roots of the Dracula myth in Transylvania, and such travel is, in fact, little different from many other forms of literary tourism throughout the world. Other tourists are seeking the locations in Transylvania portrayed in Dracula films and as a form of screen tourism this is again unexceptional. Another group of tourists are drawn to Romania in search of the supernatural roots of Stoker's novel and are perhaps anticipating an experience of the supernatural and ineffable in Transylvania. This is an unusual form of special interest tourism that is currently little understood. There are relatively few places in the world that are believed to offer such enchantment, so that such tourism is specific to Romania (although it is worth noting that a form of Dracula tourism did develop on a smaller scale in the Yorkshire town of Whitby from the 1970s onwards). There is also another group of tourists who visit Romania to see places associated with Vlad Țepeș. What underpins these various forms of Dracula tourism is a fascination with the Western myth of Transylvania and a desire to experience at first hand the locations and landscapes that are associated with the Dracula myth.

In itself, Dracula tourism is not an especially large segment of Romania's tourist market – the number of serious Dracula enthusiasts visiting Romania can probably be numbered in the tens of thousands. However there are many more tourists who have visited Romania for reasons other than Dracula but who, nonetheless, are eager to engage briefly with the Dracula myth whilst in Transylvania. Thus, for many foreign tourists – especially those from Western countries – some form of encounter with Dracula is a key element of a holiday in Romania. Such tourism is problematic for Romania which, like many other nation-states, uses tourism as a means to present itself on its own terms to the wider world. Through its tourism agencies the state promotes and supports the development of forms of tourism that flatter and affirm the identity that it wishes to show to visitors. Hence, since the 1960s tourism planners have promoted forms of tourism based on the country's natural landscapes (the Carpathians and Danube Delta), beach resorts and the rural and cultural heritage of Transylvania. However, Dracula tourism with its focus on vampires and the supernatural is at odds with this project since it is underpinned by an insistence on the Otherness of Romania. There is an additional problem in that such tourism furthers the confusion between a fictional vampire and a historical figure that many in Romania regard as a national hero. Overall then, for Romania Dracula tourism is a form of cultural appropriation that brings little reciprocal benefit or understanding (see Burns 2005).

How, then, has Romania responded to Dracula tourism? To understand this response it is essential to recognize the role of the state (a frequently overlooked actor in analyses of tourism) in regulating and controlling tourism development in what is conceived to be the national interest. When Western tourists began to visit Romania in search of Dracula in the 1960 the initial response of the socialist state was to do nothing. This was not due to any ideological objections to Dracula but simply because Stoker's novel was unknown in Romania so that the tourism authorities did not understand Dracula tourism as a distinct segment of Romanian tourism. In the absence of anything in Transylvania to cater for their needs and interests Dracula enthusiasts found what they wanted at Bran Castle which rapidly gained the name (outside Romania) of Dracula's Castle. In this sense tourists were active participants in the ongoing appropriation of Transylvania so that it accorded with the expectations generated by Western popular culture.

It was not until the 1970s when an American travel company developed the first Dracula tour (*Spotlight on Dracula*) that Romania's tourism planners came to recognize the significance of the Western Dracula myth in generating inbound tourism to Romania. There was a cautious acknowledgement of Dracula tourism in 1973 but the socialist tourism authorities decided that this was not something that they wished to encourage. Instead, the Romanian state sought to manage Dracula tourism on its own terms through its own Dracula tour – *Dracula: Legend and Truth* – themed around the life of Vlad the Impaler who was enjoying unexpected global fame at the time. This tour was strictly focused on the historical Dracula and was overtly intended to refute any association between Vlad Țepeș and the vampire Dracula of Western popular culture. While it was effective in catering for those interested in the life and deeds of Vlad Țepeș this tour did little to satisfy the growing numbers of Western visitors in search of the vampire Dracula in Transylvania. Thereafter the socialist state fell back to a position of tolerating Dracula tourism (with little enthusiasm) but doing nothing to encourage it. Indeed, Romania became increasingly hostile towards the Western Dracula during the 1980s.

However, while Romania's only concession to Dracula tourism was the *Dracula: Legend and Truth* tour, individual Romanians were able to take matters into their own hands to provide Western Dracula fans with the experiences they sought in Transylvania. For example, Nicolae Păduraru and the handful of other ONT guides who understood the Western Dracula myth were able unobtrusively to offer short excursions to the places in northern Transylvania associated with Stoker's novel to those tourists who had completed the *Legend and Truth* tour. In America, Andrei Raiescu discretely made use of the high profile of the vampire Dracula to promote Romania as a tourist destination. And in Bistrița, Alexandru Misiuga, a natural innovator and entrepreneur in a socialist state that discouraged such traits, was able to persuade the local state and Communist Party authorities to support the development of two hotels intended for Western Dracula enthusiasts. In each of these cases, knowledge of the Dracula story proved to be a crucial asset in a country where Stoker's novel was almost entirely unknown. This knowledge was a form of cultural capital that those in the know could use to their advantage. Some were able to convert it into economic capital through earning extra income (in the form of hard currency tips) from Western tourists. Others were able to use this knowledge as a means to consolidate and safeguard their positions within the state hierarchy. And this, in turn, illustrates that socialist Romania was not the monolithic, perfect surveillance machine that it is sometimes imagined to be. Instead, the Romanian state was much weaker than is often supposed. Those who were able to identify and work around these 'gaps' in state power were able to exploit this weakness for their own benefit – but also to the benefit of foreign Dracula fans.

After the collapse of state socialism in 1989 Romania's approach towards Dracula has slowly changed. The state largely withdrew from providing tourism services and this role was taken over by the emerging private sector which swiftly recognized the money to be made from Dracula. Some of those who had built up an understanding of the Western Dracula myth during the socialist period were now able to use this cultural capital to their advantage in the context of a market economy (see Ghodsee 2005). Hence, the state's tourism planners showed little interest in exploiting Dracula to attract foreign tourists to Romania and, apart from the continued promotion of a Vlad Țepeș trail, Dracula barely featured in Romania's tourism promotion. As in the socialist period, this situation is underpinned by a concern to protect Romania's international image from associations with the supernatural and also from a desire to protect the reputation of Vlad Țepeș. And, as in the socialist period, there has been a continued mismatch between the expectations of Western Dracula tourists who visit Transylvania and what Romania is willing to offer them.

Post-socialist Romania's only serious attempt to exploit Dracula for tourism was the Dracula Park project of 2001–2. Some outside Romania have interpreted Dracula Park as indicating that Romania had finally recognized that it had no choice but to 'give in' to the international interest in Dracula and to embrace an unwanted stereotype that has been imposed upon it from outside. However, I am unconvinced by this argument. Instead, Dracula Park seems to have been intended to project a message about Romania to the wider world. The theme park project was presented as an energetic and self-confident attempt by Romania to embrace and exploit the Western Dracula myth in its own way and on its own terms. And the timing of the project – in the run up to EU accession – also seems intended to make such a statement about Romania to the wider world. Dracula Park certainly did send out a message about Romania but one that was exactly the opposite that that which was intended. An implausible business plan and suspicions that the project was some form of complicated financial scam were enough to deter potential investors. The unwise choice of location and the rushed manner in which the project was implemented provoked comparisons with the Ceauşescu era. Moreover, Romania's apparent willingness to disregard its own laws and international commitments regarding environmental protection and heritage conservation generated a domestic and international campaign of opposition. Romania's international image was damaged by the global media coverage of the project to the extent that Dracula Park was unceremoniously abandoned.

Indeed, having had its fingers badly burnt with Dracula Park there has subsequently been little interest by the Romanian Ministry of Tourism in any further attempts to exploit Dracula. For example, the 2006 tourism masterplan contains hardly any reference to Dracula (Pop et al. 2007) beyond a few scattered acknowledgements that Dracula attracts visitors to Romania. Elena Udrea, Romania's Minister of Tourism between 2008 and 2012, declared at the start of her mandate that she had no interest in using Dracula to create a tourist brand for Romania (Pricope 2009). Similarly Romania's recent national branding strategy (Ministerul Dezvoltării Regionale şi Turismului 2011) makes no mention at all of Dracula. The Romanian National Tourist Office website[1] does now feature a page on Dracula tourism but it is not given a high profile and is listed as just one of a number of forms of special interest tourism. There are increasing voices within Romania that advocate the use of Dracula to promote Romanian tourism (see for example Pop et al. 2007, Oprea 2010, Dan cited in Rădulescu 2010, Cosma et al. 2007) but they do not seem to be finding a receptive audience in the Ministry of Tourism.

What, then, does the future hold? Romania could continue to ignore Dracula. I am unconvinced by claims that Romania simply has no choice but to accept the inevitable and embrace the vampire Dracula for easy profits. For more than four

---

1   www.romaniantourism.com

decades Romania has done its best to ignore Count Dracula completely and there is no reason why it should not continue to do so. Moreover, tourism in Romania appears to be undergoing a revival without there having been any need to embrace Dracula. Since Romania joined the European Union it has increasingly come to be seen as a safe and stable destination. Sibiu's status as European Capital of Culture in 2007 did much to generate interest in Romania as a destination. Standards and services at the major tourist destinations are now little different from tourist centres in the rest of Europe. Moreover, Romania is increasingly gaining a reputation as a destination for ecotourism and cultural tourism, much of which is centred on the lifestyles and traditions of Transylvania and Maramureş. Romania's rural heritage is becoming the country's unique selling point for tourism without any need to resort to Dracula.

On the other hand, Count Dracula is clearly not going to go away. The association between Transylvania and vampires is deeply rooted in the Western popular imagination and Dracula enthusiasts will continue to visit Transylvania in search of the literary, cinematic and supernatural roots of the Western Dracula myth. In these circumstances perhaps Romania can start to use Dracula to its advantage. Count Dracula is, after all, a globally recognized cultural icon that is immediately associated with Romania. There is little need to brand Romania as the 'land of Dracula' since this brand identity is already well developed. Instead, Count Dracula could play a role in a branding and promotional strategy that utilizes a cliché or stereotype as the starting point to project much broader messages about a destination and its people (see Morgan and Pritchard 2002). If Dracula can be used to entice tourists to visit Romania this is also an opportunity to redefine their imaginative geographies of Transylvania by demonstrating that there is much more to the region than vampires, haunted castles and superstitious peasants. Instead, Dracula can become a starting point for a much broader cultural tourism experience of Transylvania. A promotional strategy that clearly differentiated between the fictional vampire and the historical Voievode would be acceptable to most Romanians. And Romania could continue to cater for diehard Dracula enthusiasts (especially at Halloween) without compromising the other forms of cultural tourism that it can offer. Indeed, such a strategy has been discreetly employed by some private sector organizations (such as the Transylvanian Society of Dracula) for more than a decade. However, for it to be adopted as tourism policy would require a significant change in the approach of Romania's tourism authorities.

Count Dracula has been Romania's unwanted problem for more than four decades but this situation need not persist indefinitely. Since January 2007 Romania has been a member of the European Union. In political terms, it is no longer part of an Eastern European Other but instead part of a united Europe, on equal terms with other member states. If Romania is successful in assuming the duties and responsibilities of membership it has an opportunity to counter – even negate – the Balkanist stereotypes about the country that exist in the West. As Romania takes its place in the Union it will become less part of a strange and unpredictable Other Europe and instead something increasingly known and familiar in the West. As more tourists from other EU countries see Transylvania for themselves they will recognize that it is not a vampire-haunted netherworld on the margins of Europe but instead just another region of Central Europe, within the European Union. If Romania comes to be less 'strange' and 'different' in the Western popular imagination the country's long-standing dilemma with Dracula will gradually diminish. Indeed, over time Romanians may even come to embrace Count Dracula or, at the very least, to accept their most famous (fictional) compatriot and put him to work for their advantage.

References

Abram, S. and Waldren, J. 1997. Introduction: Tourists and tourism – identifying with people and places, in *Tourists and Tourism: Identifying with People and Places*, edited by S. Abram, J. Waldren and D.V.L. Macleod. Oxford: Berg, 1–11.

Adam, B. 1997. Nu vă fi frică de Dracula! *România liberă*, 8 May, 20.

Agniel L. 1975. Real Dracula was no tourist attraction. *Smithsonian*, 5(22), 108–13.

Aitchison, C., MacLeod, N.E. and Shaw, S.J. 2000. *Leisure and Tourism Landscapes: Social and Cultural Geographies*. London: Routledge.

Allcock, J.B. 1995. International tourism and the appropriation of history in the Balkans, in *International Tourism: Identity and Change*, edited by M. Lanfant, J.B. Allcock and E. Bruner. London: Sage, 100–112.

Anderson, B. 2006. *Imagined Communities: Reflections on the Origins and Spread of Nationalism*. Revised Edition [First published in 1983]. London: Verso.

Andreescu, Ş. 1976. *Vlad Ţepeş (Dracula): Între legendă şi adevăr istoric*. Bucureşti: Editura Minerva.

Andreescu Ş. and McNally, R.T. 1989. Exactly where was Dracula captured in 1462?, *East European Quarterly*, XXIII (3), 269–81.

Andrei, C. 2001. Dracula Park: O 'distractie' la propriu şi la figurat. *România liberă*, 23 November, 14.

Andrei, C. 2002a. Turism cultural, şi nu turism vampiric. *România liberă*, 21 February, 14.

Andrei, C. 2002b. Banca Mondială a anunţat că nu va sprijin financiar Dracula Park. *România liberă*, 16 March, 1.

Andrei, C. 2002c. Parlamentul Europei cere oprirea lucrărilor la 'Dracula Park' până la prezentarea raportului UNESCO. *România liberă*, 29 April, 1.

Andrei, C. 2002d. În locul Dracula Park vom promova un plan global pentru dezvoltarea zonei Sighişoara. *România liberă*, 9 May, 24.

Anholt, S. 2010. Nation-brands and the value of provenance, in *Destination Branding: Creating the Unique Destination Proposition*. Revised 2nd Edition, edited by N. Morgan, A. Pritchard and R. Pride. Oxford: Butterworth Heinemann, 26–39.

Anon (A Fellow of the Carpathian Society) 1881. *Magyarland: Being the Narrative of our Travels Through the Highlands and Lowlands of Hungary (2 vols)*. London: Sampson Low, Marston, Searle and Rivington.

Anon. 1962. Tourists from 36 countries on the Rumanian Black Sea coast. *Rumania for Tourists*, 2–3(17), 25.

Anon. 1966. *Romania in Brief*. Bucharest: Meridiane Publishing House.

Anon. 1971. *Romania: An Encyclopedia Guide-book*. Bucharest: Meridiane Publishing House.

Anon. 1972. 'Cetatea lui Ţepeş' din Bîrgău. *Scînteia*, 1 September, 2.

Anon. 1973. Rumania improving Draculas image. *New York Times*, 30 September, 15.

Anon. 1974. Ce zi. *Scînteia*, 16 May, 2.

Anon. 1975. The members of British Dracula Society on Pilgrimage. *Holidays in Romania*, 42 (June), 14–15.

Anon. 1978. Bran. *România pitorească*, VII (4), 10.

Anon. 1979. *Romania: Facts and Figures*. Bucharest: Editura Ştiinţifică şi Enciclopedică.

Anon. 1984a. *Romania: An Encyclopedic Survey*. Bucharest: Editura Ştiinţifică şi Enciclopedică.

Anon. 1984b. La întrebarea ce este nou în turismul bistriţean? Răspundem Complexul hotelier 'Tihuţa', in *Almanah Turistic 1984*. Bucureşti: ONT Carpaţi, 149.

Anon. 1985. Hotel-castel 'Tihuţa', in *Almanah Turistic 1985*. Bucureşti: ONT Carpaţi, no pagination.

Anon. 1990. Untitled, *Holidays in Romania*, 3–4, 39.

Anon. 2001a. Obiectele de artă au fost sustrase cu bonuri de mână. *România liberă*, 31 August, 2.

Anon. 2001b. Agathon vrea să importe Dracula din America. *Ziua*, 23 August, 8.

Anon. 2001c. Ministerul Turismului nu este dispus să plătească pentru achiziţionarea imaginii contelui Dracula de la Universal Studios. *Adevărul*, 13 September, 14.

Anon. 2001d. Dracula salveaza Sighişoara. *Ziua*, 21 November, 7.

Anon. 2001e. Emisiune de acţiune pentru finanţarea proiectului Dracula Park. *Adevărul*, 6 December, 15.

Anon. 2001f. Elementele 'ofertei-şoc' a României. *Adevărul*, 12 December, 7.

Anon. 2002a. Dracula Park…în…Dracula Land. *România liberă*, 23 January, 4.

Anon. 2002b. Mereu surprinzătorul Agathon a strâns în trei zile 11 miliard lei pentru 'Dracula Park'. *România liberă*, 5 April, 10.

Anon. 2002c. Precedent periculos prin încălcarea legii mediului şi a patrimoniului. *România liberă*, 19 April, 8.

Anon. 2002d. Locaţia Dracula Park este deocamdată acolo unde s-a stabilit. *Adevărul* 2 July, 20.

Anon. 2003a. Bucureşti – noua locaţie recomandata de PWC pentru 'Dracula Park'. *România liberă* 27 January, 1.

Anon. 2003b. Dracula Park se va construi la Snagov pe terenul RA-APPS. *Adevărul*, 6 February, 1.

Anon. 2003c. Proiectul Dracula Park nu reprezinta o prioritate pentru România. *România liberă*, 30 June, 1.

Anon. 2004a. *Istoria Castelului Dracula*. Bucureşti: Societatea Transilvană Dracula.

Anon. 2004b. Dracula are 4 ani şi e oltean. *Libertatea*, 26 March, 1.

Anon. 2005a. Dracula Park mai aşteapta listarea la Bursa. *Ziua*, 25 January, 10.

Anon. 2005b. Şeful turismului promite vacanţe sociale în vârf de sezon. *Adevărul*, 18 February, 14.

Anon. 2006. Get ready for the Romanian invasion. *Daily Express*, 23 August, 1.

Anon. 2010. Dracula beats new blood to top vampire poll. *Daily Telegraph* [Online, 22 August] Available at: http://www.telegraph.co.uk/news/ celebritynews/7958468/Dracula-beats-new-blood-to-top-vampire-poll.html [accessed: 30 May 2011].

Anon. Undated. *Romania Offers You*. Braşov: ONT Carpaţi.

Apostol, M. 2010. Vampirii din Twilight imploraţi să vină la Bucureşti. *Adevărul* [Online, 2 July]. Available at: http://www.adevarul.ro/locale/ bucuresti/Bucuresti-_Vampirii_din_Twilight-implorati_sa_vina_la_ Bucuresti_0_290971131.html. [accessed: 16 June 2011].

Arata, S.D. 1990. The occidental tourist: *Dracula* and the anxiety of reverse colonisation. *Victorian Studies*, 33(4), 621–45.

Ateljevic, I. and Doorne, S. 2002. Representing New Zealand: Tourism imagery and ideology. *Annals of Tourism Research*, 29(3), 648–67.

Atkinson, D. 2007. Kitsch geographies and the everyday spaces of social memory. *Environment and Planning A*, 39(3), 521–40.

Auerbach, N. 1995. *Our Vampires, Ourselves*. Chicago: University of Chicago Press.

Auerbach, N. and Skal, D.J. 1997. Preface, in *Dracula* by Bram Stoker [first published in 1897] edited by N. Auerbach and D.J. Skal. New York: W.W. Norton and Company, ix–xiii.

Avram, L. and Grosu, C. 2003. Dracula Park a supt miliarde de la bugetul de stat. *Adevărul*, 2 July, 1 and 10.

Azaryahu, M. 1996. The power of commemorative street names. *Environment and Planning D: Society and Space*, 14(3), 311–30.

Bako, A. 2002. Consideraţii critice cu privire la eficienţa şi finanţarea 'Dracula Park' lângă Sighişoara. *România liberă*, 22 March, 11.

Balkan Holidays Limited. 2004. *Bulgaria, Slovenia, Serbia, Romania, Ski and Snowboard 2004–5* [Brochure]. London: Balkan Holidays Limited.

Bandyopadhyay, R. and Morais, D. 2005. Representative dissonance: India's Self and Western image. *Annals of Tourism Research*, 32(4), 1006–21.

Banyai, M. 2010. Dracula's image in tourism: Western bloggers versus tour guides. *European Journal of Tourism Research*, 3(1), 5–22.

Barbu, M. 1993. Patru veacuri de singurătate în Castelul din Carpaţi. *România literară*, XXVI (18–24 July), 17.

Barry, J. 1997. In search of Dracula, in *Dracula: Celebrating 100 Years*, edited by L. Shephard, and A. Power. Dublin: Mentor Press, 84–95.

Barsan, V.C. 1975. Dracula: a warped image of escapism and insanity. *Romanian Sources*, 1(2), 44–54.

Basarab, A. 1980. Bran on the threshold of half a millennium. *Holidays in Romania*, 106 (October), 2–3 and 5.

Bechir, M. 2004. Fundaţia invizibilă. *Evenimentul zilei*, 13 October, 5.

Beeton, S. 2005. *Film-Induced Tourism*. Clevedon: Channel View.

Behr, E. 1991. *Kiss the Hand you Cannot Bite: The Rise and Fall of the* Ceausescus. London: Hamish Hamilton.

Bendriş, T. and Ilieş, D. 2009. Dracula a petrecut o noapte la Castelul Bran. *Adevărul* [Online, 2 November]. Available at: http://www.adevarul.ro/actualitate/eveniment/Castelul-Dracula-Bran-petrecut-noapte_0_145785490.html [accessed: 9 July 2011].

Beresford, M. 2008. *From Demons to Dracula: The Creation of the Modern Vampire Myth*. London: Reaktion.

Berza, M. 2002. Proiectual şi efectele sale nocive asupra Sighişoarei au ajuns pe ordinea de zi a Comitetului Patrimoniului Mondial. *România liberă*, 1 March, 8.

Bibeau, P. 2007. *Sundays with Vlad*. London: Constable.

Binkley, S. Kitsch as a repetitive system: A problem for the theory of taste hierarchy. *Journal of Material Culture*, 5(2), 131–52.

Bjelić, D.I. 2002. Introduction: Blowing up the 'bridge', in *Balkan as Metaphor: Between Globalization and Fragmentation*, edited by D.I. Bjelić and O. Savić. London: MIT Press, 1–22.

Boeru, M. 2004. Bartolomeu Finiş, boss-ul afacerii 'Dracula Park de Snagov'. *Evenimentul zilei*, 20 October, 5.

Bogdan, I. (1896) *Vlad Ţepeş şi naraţiunile germane şi ruseşti asupra lui*, Editura Librăriei Soceco, Bucureşti.

Boia, L. 1999. *Mitologia ştinţifică a comunismului*. Bucureşti: Humanitas.

Boia, L. 2000. *Pentru o istoria a imaginarului*. Bucureşti: Humanitas.

Boia, L. 2001a. *Romania: Borderland of Europe*. London: Reaktion.

Boia, L. 2001b. *History and Myth in Romanian Consciousness* [first published in Romanian in 1997]. Budapest: Central European University Press.

Bolan, P., Boy, S. and Bell, J. 2011. 'We've seen it in the movies, let's see if it's true': Authenticity and displacement in film-induced tourism. *Worldwide Hospitality and Tourism Themes*, 3(2), 102–16.

Bologa, R. 2004. Impactul internet-ului asupra afluxului de vizitatori spre muzee. *Informatica Economica*. [Online], 1(29), 55–9. Available at: www.revistaie.ase.ro/content/29/bologa.pdf [accessed: 24 June 2008].

Boner, C. 1865. *Transylvania: Its Products and its People*. London: Longmans, Green, Reader and Dyer.

Bonifaciu, S. (ed.) 1985. *Romania Tourist Guide*. Bucureşti: Editura Sport-turism.

Bonifaciu, S., Docsănescu, N. and Vasiuliu-Ciotoiu, I. 1974. *Romania Tourist Guide*. Bucharest: The Tourism Publishing House.

Bozbici, S. 2009. Baronul Casei Dracula a trecut la cele veşnice. *Adevărul* [Online, 22 February]. Available at: http://www.adevarul.ro/actualitate/Baronul-Casei-Dracula-trecut-vesnice_0_22799217.html. [accessed: 20 June 2011].

Bozdog, N. 1968. Balanţ rodnic. in *Almanah touristic1968*. Bucureşti: Oficiul Naţional de Turism, 6–7.

Braun, A. 1978. *Romanian Foreign Policy Since 1965: The Political and Military Limits of Autonomy*. London: Praeger.

Bray, R. and Raitz V. 2001. *Flight to the Sun: The Story of the Holiday Revolution*. London: Continuum.

Bristow, R.S. and Newman, M. 2005. Myth vs. fact: An exploration of fright tourism, in *Proceedings of the 2004 Northeastern Recreation Research Symposium*, edited by K. Bricker and S.J. Millington. [Online: USDA Forest Service, Northeastern Research Station General Technical Report NE-326, 215–21]. Available at: http://www.fs.fed.us/ne/newtown_square/publications/ technical_reports/pdfs/2005/326papers/bristow326.pdf [accessed: 12 March 2008].

Brokaw, K. 1976. *A Night in Transylvania: The Dracula Scrapbook*. New York: Grosset and Dunlap.

Brown, J. 1997. Draculafilm: 'high' and 'low' until the end of the world, in *Bram Stoker's Dracula: Sucking Through the Century, 1897–1997*, edited by C.M. Davison. Toronto: Dundurn, 269–82.

Browning, J.E. and Picart, C.J. 2011. *Dracula in Visual Media: Film, Television, Comic Book and Electronic Game Appearances, 1921–2010*. Jefferson: McFarland and Company.

Buchmann, A. 2006. From Erewhon to Edoras: Tourism and myths in New Zealand. *Tourism Culture and Communication*, 6(3), 181–9.

Buchmann, A., Moore, K. and Fisher, D. 2010. Experiencing film tourism: Authenticity and fellowship. *Annals of Tourism Research*, 37(1), 229–48.

Bunea, I. and Rădulescu, G. 2010. Noul brand: 'Explorează grădina carpatină'. *Adevărul* [Online, 29 July 2010]. Available at: http://www. adevarul.ro/actualitate/eveniment/Noul_brand-_Exploreaza_gradina_ carpatina_0_306569877.html [accessed: 17 June 2011].

Burford, T. 1996. *Hiking Guide to Romania*. 2nd Edition. Chalfont St Peter: Bradt Publications.

Burford, T. and Longley, N. 2011. *Romania: the Rough Guide*. 6th Edition. London: Rough Guides.

Burileanu, B. 1993. Dracula, pe lista neagră. *România liberă*, 12 July, 16.

Burns, P.M. 2005. Social identities, globalisation and the cultural politics of tourism, in *Global Tourism*. 3rd Edition, edited by W.F. Theobald. Amsterdam: Elsevier, 391–405.

Burns, P.M. and Novelli, M. 2006. *Tourism and Social identities: Global Frameworks and Local Realities*. Oxford: Elsevier.

Burtan, N. 2001a. Casa Groazei şi ţeapa-jet în Dracula Park. *Evenimentul zilei*, 6 November, 12.

Burtan, N. 2001b. Sighişoreanul s-a făcut frate cu Dracula. *Evenimentul zilei* 21 November, 10.

Burtan, N. 2002. 96 miliarde de lei pentru 'Dracula Park'. *Evenimentul zilei*, 2 April, 11.

Busby, G. and Klug, J. 2001. Movie-induced tourism: The challenge of measurement and other issues. *Journal of Vacation Marketing*, 7(4), 316–32.

Caloian, O. 2009. Halloween de România, pe urmele lui Dracula. *Adevărul* [Online 24 October]. Available at: http://www.adevarul.ro/financiar/analiza_/_special/ Halloween-Romania-Dracula-urmele-lui_0_140385989.html [accessed: 9 July 2011].

Câmpina, B.T. 1954. Complotul boierilor şi răscoala din Ţară Românească din iulie-noiembrie 1462. *Studii şi referate privind istoria României*, Part 1, 599–624.

Canciovici, M.A. 1995. Congresul 'Dracula', *România liberă*, 2 June, 2.

Cano, L. M. and Mysyk A. 2004. Cultural tourism, the state and the day of the dead. *Annals of Tourism Research*, 31(4), 879–98.

Cantacuzino, G.I. 1971. Cetatea Poenari. *Studii şi cercetări de istorie veche*, 22(2), 263–89.

Caraciuc, T. 1983. Invitatie la cel mai nou 'Castel', Hotelul 'Tihuta'. *România pitorească*, 9 (September), 19.

Carl, D., Kindon, S. and Smith, K. 2007. Tourists' experiences of film locations: New Zealand as '*Middle Earth*'. *Tourism Geographies*, 9(1), 49–63.

Carter, M.L. (ed.) 1988a. *Dracula: The Vampire and the Critics*. Ann Arbor: UNI Research Press.

Carter, M.L. 1988b. Introduction, in *Dracula: The Vampire and the Critics*, edited by M.L. Carter. Ann Arbor: UMI Research Press, 1–10.

Catrina C. and Lupu I. (eds) 1981. *Judeţele Patriei: Braşov*. Bucureşti: Editura Sport-Turism.

Cazacu, M. 2008. *Dracula* [first published in French in 2004]. Bucureşti: Humanitas.

Căzănişteanu, C. 1976. O personalitate proeminentă a istoriei naţionale, întruchipare a voinţei poporului român de a trăi liber în vatra strămoşească. *Scînteia*, 14 December 1976, 4.

Cehan, S. 2001. 'Dracula Land' revendicat de 'sugătorii de măduvă'. *Evenimentul zilei*, 10 July, 5.

Cehan, S. 2002. 'Dracula Park' o polemică abia la început. *Evenimentul zilei*, 19 January, 14.

Cernovodeanu, P. 1977. A new approach towards Vlad Ţepeş. *Revue Roumaine d'Histoire*, XVII(2), 335–45.

Ceteraş, Ş. 2001a. Cetatea Sighişoara, un posibil 'Dracula Land'. *România liberă*, 20 March, 24.

Ceteraş, Ş. 2001b. Draculaland. *România liberă*, 13 July, 14.

Ceteraş, Ş. 2002. Consiliul Judeţean a aprobat PUZ şi PUD. *România liberă*, 13 June, 1.

Chwiałkowska, L. (ed.) 1995. *Let's Go: The Budget Guide to Eastern Europe 1995*. London: MacMillan.

Ciobanu, R.Ş. 1979. *Pe urmele lui Vlad Ţepeş*. Bucureşti: Editura Sport-Turism.

Ciobanu, M., Noisescu, N. and Ciobanu, R.Ş. 1984. *Cetatea Poienari*. Bucureşti: Editura Sport Turism.

Cioculescu, B. 1990. Metamorfozele unui mit (introduction to Romanian version of *Dracula* by Bram Stoker). Bucureşti: Editura Univers, 5–19.

Cioculescu, Ş. 1971. Istorie şi literatura, *România Literară*, 29 July, 5 and 8.

Cioculescu, Ş., Sadoveanu, I.M., Bonifaciu, S., Grigorescu, M., Vasiliu, I. and Mihalache, M. 1967. *Romania: A Guidebook*. Bucharest: Meridiane Publishing House.

Cioranescu, G. 1977. Vlad the Impaler – current parallels with a medieval Romanian prince. *Radio Free Europe Research, Background Report (Romania)* 23 (31 January), 1–10.

Clarke, N. 2004. Free independent travellers? British working holiday makers in Australia. *Transactions of the Institute of British Geographers*, 29(4), 499–509.

Comisia Naţională pentru Statistică. 1995. *Anuarul turistic al româniei 1995*. Bucureşti: Comisia Naţională pentru Statistică.

Comisia Naţională pentru Statistică. 1997. *Turismul în România 1997*. Bucureşti: Comisia Naţională pentru Statistică, Bucureşti.

Connell, J. and Meyer, D. 2009. Balamory revisited: An evaluation of the screen tourism destination-tourist nexus. *Tourism Management*, 30(2), 194–207.

Consiliul Naţional pentru Studierea Arhivelor Securităţii. 2004. *Membrii C.C. al P.C.R. 1945–1989, Dicţionar*. Bucureşti: Editura Enciclopedică.

Constantinescu, M. 2001a, Dan Matei Agathon este gata să se întălneasca cu contestatarii 'Dracula Park'. *Cotidianul*, 6 November, 7.

Constantinescu, M. 2001b. Cei care denigrează acest proiect nu ştiu ce vrem să facem noi. *Cotidianul* 6 November, 7.

Cosma, I. 1973. Dezvoltarea turismului în România: Sarcini actuale şi în următorii 5–10 ani. *Terra*, V(4), 9–16.

Cosma, S., Pop, C. and Negrusa, A. 2007. Should Dracula myth be a brand to promote Romania as a tourist destination? *Interdisciplinary Management Research* [online] 3, 39–56. Available at: http://www.efos.hr/repec/osi/journl/ PDF/InterdisciplinaryManagementResearchIII/IMR3a2.pdf [accessed: 12 May 2010].

Craik, J. 1997. The culture of tourism, in *Touring Cultures: Transformations of Travel and Theory*, edited by J. Urry and C. Rojek. London: Routledge, 113–36.

Crang, M. 1998. *Cultural Geography*. London: Routledge.

Cremer, R. 1976. *Lugosi: The Man Behind the Cape*. Chicago: Henry Regnery Company.

Cresswell, T. 2004. *Place: A Short Introduction*. Oxford: Blackwell.

Crişan, M. 2008. The models for Castle Dracula in Stoker's sources on Transylvania, *Journal of Dracula Studies* [Online], 10. Available at: www.blooferland.com/ drc/index.php?title=journal_of_dracula_studies [accessed: 29 May 2011].

Cristea, R. 2002a. Sighişoara, singurul oraş aflat pe lista patrimoniului universal, nu are nevoie de o sosie kitsch. *România liberă*, 25 February, 17.

Cristea, R. 2002b. Ministerul Turismului a fost somat să nu mai folosească numele GREENPEACE pentru susținerea programului. *România liberă*, 27 February, 10.

Crosse, A.F. 1878. *Round About the Carpathians*. Edinburgh: William Blackwood and Sons.

Crosu, C. 2002. Dormi liniștit: Dracula te suge mai bine. *Adevărul*, 1 February, 1.

Cruceru A. (ed.) 1986. *Romania*. București: Ministerul Turismului.

Curticapean, A. 2007. 'Are you Hungarian or Romanian?' On the study of national and ethnic identity in Central and Eastern Europe. *Nationalities Papers* 35(3), 411–27.

Cuthill, V. 2004. Little England's global conference centre: Harrogate, in *Tourism Mobilities: Places to Play, Places in Play*, edited by M. Sheller and J. Urry. London: Routledge, 55–66.

Dalton, J. 1995a. From a Romanian point of view, Dracula is a blessing of sorts. *Travel Weekly*, 54(60), 1, 11 and 12.

Dalton, J. 1995b. 'Dracula Congress' draws scholars and attention. Travel Weekly, 54(60), 14.

Dann, G.M.S. 1996. *The Language of Tourism: A Sociolinguistic Perspective*. Wallingford: CABI.

Dann, G. 1999. Writing out the tourist in space and time. *Annals of Tourism Research*, 26(1), 159–87.

Davies, B. 1997. The Dracula Society, London, England, in *Bram Stoker's Dracula: Sucking Through the Century, 1897–1997*, edited by C.M. Davison. Toronto: Dundurn Press, 383–86.

Deletant, D. 1991. Rewriting the past: Trends in contemporary Romania. *Ethnic and Racial Studies*, 14(1), 64–86.

Deletant, D. 1995. *Ceaușescu and the Securitate: Coercion and Dissent in Romania, 1965–1989*. London: Hurst and Company.

Deletant, D. 1999. *Romania under Communist Rule*. Iași: Center for Romanian Studies.

de Ludes, Count Ignatius. 1981. *The Tourist's Guide to Transylvania*. London: Octopus Books.

Derer, P. 2001. Dracula Park – o altă perspectivă. *22*, XII (51) (18–24 November), 8.

Desforges, L. 2002. Travelling the world: Identity and travel biography. *Annals of Tourism Research*, 27(4), 926–45.

D'Harlingue, B. 2010. Specters of the U.S. prison regime: Haunting tourism and the penal gaze, in *Popular Ghosts: The Haunted Spaces of Everyday Culture*, edited by M. Blanco and E. Peeren. New York: Continuum, 133–46.

Diana, A. 1979. Would you like your picture with Dracula. *Holidays in Romania*, XXI (November), 22.

Dittmer, J. 2002/2003. *Dracula* and the cultural construction of Europe. *Connotations*, [Online], 12(2–3), 233–248. Available at: www.uni-tuebingen. de.connotations/dittmer1223.htm [accessed: 15 July 2005].

Djuvara, N. and Oltean, R. 2003. *De la Vlad Ţepeş la Dracula Vampirul*. Bucureşti: Humanitas.

Dobre, D. 2002. Emisiunea de acţiuni Dracula Park a fost prelungită până pe 3 Aprilie. *România liberă*, 19 February, 1.

Dogaru, M. 1994. *Dracula: Mit şi realitate istorică*. Bucureşti: Editura Ianus Inf.

Dogaru, M. 1995. *Dracula: Împăratul răsăritului*. Bucureşti: Editura Globus.

Dolea, A. and Ţăruş, A. 2009. *Branding Romania: Cum (ne) promovăm imaginea de ţară*. Bucureşti: Curtea Veche.

Douglas-Home, J. 2001a. Dracula goes Disney. *The Times (Part 2)*, 6 November, 5.

Douglas-Home, 2001b. A new Dracula horror in Romania. *Wall Street Journal*, 28 December, 7.

Douglas-Home, J. 2002a. Fangs but no thanks. *The Spectator* [Online, 12 January 2002]. Available at: www.spectator.co.uk/article.php3?table=old&section=bac k&issue=2002-01-12&id=1477 [accessed: 11 December 2003].

Douglas-Home, J. 2002b. Dream parks and theme parks. *Building Conservation Journal*, Summer, 5–7.

Drăgotescu, C., Niţu, M. and Modreanu, C. 2002. Ministerul Turismului e gata să mute Dracula Park de la Sighişoara. *Adevărul*, 9 May, 1.

Drăguşanu, A. 1997. Simboluri istorice în filatelie (1944–1989), in *Miturile comunismului românesc Vol II*, edited by L. Boia. Bucureşti: Editura Universitătii din Bucureşti, 31–44.

Dresser, N. 1989. *American Vampires*. New York: Vintage Books.

Dukes, P. 1982. Dracula: Fact, legend and fiction. *History Today*, 32(7), 44–7.

Dumbrăveanu, D. 2001. The challenge of privatisation: the tourist accommodation industry in transition, in *Post-Communist Romania: Coming to Terms with Transition*, edited by D. Light and D. Phinnemore. Basingstoke: Palgrave, 207–23.

Dumbrăveanu, D. 2009. Place branding: A challenging process for Romania. *Human Geographies: Journal of Studies and Research in Human Geography*, 3(2), 39–48.

Duţu, A. 1991. Portraits of Vlad Ţepeş: Literature, pictures and images of the ideal man, in *Dracula: Essays on the Life and Times of Vlad Ţepes* edited by K.W. Treptow. New York: Columbia University Press (East European Monographs Nr 323), 209–45.

Echtner, C.M. and Prasad, P. 2003. The context of third world tourism marketing. *Annals of Tourism Research*, 30(3), 660–82.

Edensor, T. 1997. National identity and the politics of memory: remembering Bruce and Wallace in symbolic space. *Environment and Planning D: Society and Space*, 15(2), 175–94.

Edensor, T. 1998. *Tourists at the Taj: Performance and Meaning at a Symbolic Site*. London: Routledge.

Edensor, T. 2001. Performing tourism, staging tourism: (Re)producing tourist space and practice. *Tourist Studies*, 1(1), 59–81.

Edensor, T. 2002. *National Identity, Popular Culture and Everyday Life*. Oxford: Berg.

Eighteen-Bisang, R. and Miller, E. 2008. *Bram Stoker's Notes for Dracula*. Jefferson, North Carolina: McFarland and Company Inc.

Elliot, H. 1993. Recovering from Dracula's legacy. *The Times,* 2 October, 20.

Enache, Ş. 1976. ONT are 40 de ani. *România pitorească,* V(April), 4.

Enache, Ş. 1978. Politica de perspectivă a partidului communist roman în domeniul turismului, in *Oglinzile viitorului în turism*, edited by I. Berbecaru. Bucureşti: Editura Sport-Turism, 7–22.

Ene, G. 1976. Romanian folklore about Vlad Tepes. *Revue des etudes sud-est Europénnes*, XIV(4), 581–90.

Epuran, G. and Bonifaciu, S. 1966. *A Short Tour in Romania: The Prahova Valley and the Olt Defile*. Bucharest: Meridiane Publishing House.

Fabini, H. 2001. Dracula Park Sighisoara: O analiza critica a proiectului. *România liberă,* 24 November, 11.

Fagge, N. and Whitehead, T. 2006. Romanian £8 flights to Britain. *Daily Express,* 26 September, 1.

Ficeac, B. 1999. *Cenzura comunistă şi formarea 'omului nou'*. Bucureşti: Editura Nemira.

Ficeac, B. 2001. Turism în ţară lui Dracula. *România liberă,* 22 November, 1.

Florescu, I. 1993. Vampiri de pe meleagurile noastre. *România liberă,* 16 July, 2.

Florescu, R. 1997. Dracula: The True Story? *In Review Romania,* 2(1) (February 1997), 45.

Florescu, R. 1998. What's in a name: Dracula or Vlad the Impaler, in *Dracula: The Shade and the Shadow*, edited by E. Miller. Westcliffe-on-Sea: Desert Island Books, 192–201.

Florescu, R. and McNally, R.T. 1973. *Dracula: A Biography of Vlad the Impaler 1431–1476*. New York: Hawthorn Books.

Florescu, R. and McNally, R. 1976. Introduction, in K. Brokaw, *A Night in Transylvania: The Dracula Scrapbook*. New York: Grosset and Dunlap, 1–4.

Florescu, R. and McNally, R.T. 1989. *Dracula: Prince of Many Faces*. Boston: Little, Brown and Company.

Foucault, M. 1977. *Discipline and Punish: The Birth of the Prison*. Harmondsworth: Penguin.

Fowler, P.J. 1992. *The Past in Contemporary Society: Then, Now*. London: Routledge.

Franklin, A. 2003. *Tourism: An Introduction*. London: Sage.

Frayling, C. 1991. *Vampires: Lord Byron to Count Dracula*. London: Faber and Faber.

Frölich, H.B. 2001. Nu avem nevoie de un Draculaland. *România liberă,* 5 November, 14.

Gao, B.W., Zhang, H. and Decosta, P.E. 2012. Phantasmal destination: A postmodernist perspective, *Annals of Tourism Research,* 39(1), 197–220.

Gallagher, T. 1995. *Romania after Ceauşescu.* Edinburgh: Edinburgh University Press.

Gallagher, T. 1997. To be or not to be Balkan: Romania's quest for self-definition. *Daedalus*, 126(3), 63–83.

Gallagher, T. 2005. *Theft of a Nation: Romania since Communism.* London: Hurst.

Gădea, F. 2001. Dracula Park un proiect contestat. *România liberă*, 14 December, 14.

Gelder, K. 1994. *Reading the Vampire.* London: Routledge.

Gencarella, S.O. 2007. Touring history: Guidebooks and the commodification of the Salem Witch Trials. *The Journal of American Culture*, 30(3), 271–84.

General Tours/Pan-Am. 1972. *Spotlight on Dracula (Pan-Am Holiday 494)* (promotional leaflet). New York: General Tours.

Gentry, G.W. 2007. Walking with the dead: the place of ghost walk tourism in Savannah, Georgia. *Southeastern Geographer*, 47(2), 222–38.

George, R. 2002. Mickey Mouse with fangs. *Independent on Sunday*, 27 January, 18–21.

Gerard, E. 1885. Transylvanian superstitions. *XIX Century*, XVIII (July), 130–50.

Georgescu, V. 1991. *Politica şi istorie: Cazul comuniştilor români 1944–1977.* Bucureşti: Humanitas.

Gheorghiu, L. 1995. Draculiada organizată de amatori. *Cotidianul*, 31 May 1995, 3.

Ghodsee, K. 2005. *The Red Riviera: Gender, Tourism and Postsocialism on the Black Sea.* Durham: Duke University Press.

Gibson, M. 2006. *Dracula and the Eastern Question: British and French Vampire Narratives of the Nineteenth-Century Near East.* Basingstoke: Palgrave.

Giurescu, C.C. 1937. *Istoria românilor Vol II, Parte întâi.* Bucureşti: Fundaţia pentru literatură şi artă 'Regele Carol II'.

Giurescu, C.C. 1971. *Jurnal de călătorie: Impresii din Statele Unite, Paris şi Londra.* Bucureşti: Editura Cartea Românească.

Giurescu, C.C. 1974. Viteazul şi temutul Vlad Ţepeş. *Magazin istoric*, VIII(3), 3–12.

Giurescu, C.C. 1977. *Jurnal de călătorie.* 2nd edition. Bucureşti: Editura Sport-Turism.

Giurescu, C.C. 1991. The historical Dracula, in *Dracula: Essays on the Life and Times of Vlad Ţepes* edited by K.W. Treptow. New York: Columbia University Press (East European Monographs Nr 323), 13–27.

Goldsworthy, V. 1998. *Inventing Ruritania: The Imperialism of the Imagination.* London: Yale University Press.

Goulding, C. and Domic, D. 2009. Heritage, identity and ideological manipulation: the case of Croatia. *Annals of Tourism Research*, 36(1), 85–102.

Graburn, N. 1967. The Eskimo and airport art. *Trans-Action*, 4(10), 28–33.

Graham, B. 2000. The past in place: historical geographies of identity, in *Modern Historical Geographies*, edited by B. Graham and C. Nash. Harlow: Pearson, 70–99.

Graml, G. 2004. (Re)mapping the nation: *Sound of Music* tourism and national identity in Austria, ca 2000CE. *Tourist Studies*, 4(1), 137–59.

Grecu, R. 2009. Vampirii din seria 'Twilight' cuceresc România. *Adevărul* [Online: 26 November]. Available at: http://www.adevarul.ro/cultura/Vampirii_din_ seria_-Twilight-_cuceresc_Romania_0_160184384.html. [accessed 16 June 2011].

Greenwood, D.J. 1977. Culture by the pound: an anthropological perspective on tourism as cultural commoditization, in *Hosts and Guests: The Anthropology of Tourism*, edited by V. Smith. Oxford: Blackwell, 129–39.

Grossberg, L. 1996. Identity and Cultural Studies: Is that all there is?, in *Questions of Cultural Identity*, edited by S. Hall and P. du Gay. London: Sage, 87–107.

Grufudd, P. 1994. Back to the land: historiography, rurality and the nation in interwar Wales. *Transactions of the Institute of British Geographers*, 19(1), 61–77.

Gruia, C. 2005. Ce facem cu Dracula. *National Geographic România*, November, 24–45.

Guiley, R.E. 1991. *Vampires Among Us*. New York: Pocket Books.

Hainagiu, M. 2008. Une légend á des fins touristiques dans la Roumanie communiste. Les circuits á theme 'Dracula, Vérité et Légende'. *Civilisations: Revue internationale d'anthropologie et de sciences humaines*, 57(1–2), 109–25.

Haining, P. (ed.) 1976. *The Dracula Scrapbook*. London: New English Library.

Haining, P. and Tremayne, P. 1997. *The Un-Dead: The Legend of Bram Stoker and Dracula*. London: Constable.

Hall, C.M. 1994. *Tourism and Politics: Policy, Power and Place*. Chichester: Wiley.

Hall, C.M. 2000. *Tourism Planning: Policies, Processes and Relationships*. Harlow: Pearson.

Hall, C.M. 2005. *Tourism: Rethinking the Social Science of Mobility*. Harlow: Pearson.

Hall, D.R. 1984. Foreign tourism under socialism: The Albanian 'Stalinist' model. *Annals of Tourism Research*, 11(4), 539–55.

Hall, D.R. 1990. Stalinism and tourism: A study of Albania and North Korea. *Annals of Tourism Research*, 17(1), 36–54.

Hall, D.R. 1991. Evolutionary patterns of tourism development in Eastern Europe and the Soviet Union, in *Tourism and Economic Development in Eastern Europe and the Soviet Union*, edited by D. R. Hall. London: Belhaven, 79–115.

Hall, D. 1999. Destination branding, niche marketing and national image projection in Central and Eastern Europe. *Journal of Vacation Marketing*, 5(3), 227–37.

Hall, D. 2001. Brand development, tourism and national identity: The re-imaging of former Yugoslavia. *Brand Management*, 9(4–5), 323–34.

Hall, D. 2010. Branding and national identity: The case of Central and Eastern Europe, in *Destination Branding: Creating the Unique Destination Proposition*.

Revised 2nd Edition, edited by N. Morgan, A. Pritchard, and R. Pride. Oxford: Butterworth Heinemann, 111–27.

Hall, S. 1996. Who needs identity?, in *Questions of Cultural Identity*, edited by S. Hall and P. du Gay. London: Sage, 1–17.

Harris, A. 2008. *Breaking Borders: One Man's Journey to Erase the Lines that Divide*. Bloomington, IN: iUniverse.

Hammond, A. 2004. Introduction, in *The Balkans and the West: Constructing the European Other 1945–2003*, edited by A. Hammond. Aldershot: Ashgate, xi–xxiii.

Harrop, K. and McMillan, J. 2002. Government, Governance and Tourism, in *The Tourist Business: An Introduction*, edited by R. Sharpley. Sunderland: Business Educational Publishers, 243–62.

Henegariu, A.M. 1963. *Cetatea Bran*. Bucureşti: Editura Meridiane.

Hennig, C. 2002. Tourism: Enacting modern myths, in *The Tourist as a Metaphor of the Social World*, edited by G.M.S. Dann. Wallingford: CABI, 169–87.

Herbert, D.T. 1996. Artistic and literary places in France as tourist attractions. *Tourism Management*, 17(2), 77–85.

Herbert, D. 2001. Literary places, tourism and the heritage experience. *Annals of Tourism Research*, 28(2), 312–33.

Hillyer, V. 1988. *Vampires*. Los Banos: Loose Change Publications.

Holloway, J. 2010. Legend-tripping in spooky spaces: ghost tourism and infrastructures of enchantment. *Environment and Planning D: Society and Space*, 28(4), 618–37.

Horne, D. 1984. *The Great Museum: The Re-presentation of history*. London: Pluto.

Hossu-Longin, V. 1980. Momente în istoria turismului românesc. *România pitorească*, 6 (June), 14–15.

Hovi, T. 2008a. Dracula tourism and Romania, in *Europe as Viewed from the Margins: An East-Central European Perspective from World War I to Present*, edited by S. Miloiu. Târgovişte: Valachia University Press, 73–84.

Hovi, T. 2008b. Tradition and history as building blocks for tourism: The Middle Ages as a modern tourist attraction. *Valahian Journal of Historical Studies* 10, 75–85.

Hughes, G. 1992. Tourism and the geographical imagination. *Leisure Studies*, 11(1), 31–42.

Hurezean, G. 1993. Când se îndragosteşte Dracula. *Tineretul liber*, 20 July, 7.

Iancu, L. 2005. Cât ne datorează Dracula? *Business Magazin*, 21 (2–8 March), 36–41.

Inglis, D. and Holmes, M. 2003. Highlands and other haunts: Ghosts in Scottish Tourism. *Annals of Tourism Research*, 30(1), 50–63.

Institutul Naţional de Statistică. 2003a. *Anuarul Statistic al României 2003 (serii de timp 1990–2002)* (CD Rom). Bucureşti: Institutul Naţional de Statistică.

Institutul Naţional de Statistică. 2003b. *Turismul României: Breviar Statistic*. Bucureşti: Institutul Naţional de Statistică.

Institutul Naţional de Statistică. 2006. *Turismul României: Breviar Statistic (ediţia 2006)*. Bucureşti: Institutul Naţional de Statistică.

Institutul Naţional de Statistică. 2008. *Turismul României: Breviar Statistic (ediţia 2008)*. Bucureşti: Institutul Naţional de Statistică.

Institutul Naţional de Statistică. 2011. *Turismul României:Breviar Statistic (ediţia 2011)*. Bucureşti: Institutul Naţional de Statistică.

Ionescu, D. 1986. Who's afraid of Dracula? *Radio Free Europe: Romania Situation Report 6* (26 May), 19–22.

Iordanova, D. 2007. Cashing in on Dracula: Eastern Europe's hard sells. *Framework* 48(1), 46–63.

Iorga, N. 1937. *Istoria românilor Vol IV*. Bucureşti: Monitorul Oficial şi imprimeriile statului imprimeria naţională.

Istrate, I. 1986. *Romania: A Traveller's Handbook*. Bucharest: Editura Ştiinţifică şi Enciclopedica.

Iulian, R. 2004. *Dracula sau triumful modern al vampirului*. Bucureşti: Compania.

Iuraşcu, O. and Scărişoreanu, M. 2002. Ion Iliescu şi Prinţul Charles şi-au împărtăşit reţinerile faţă de Dracula Park. *Adevărul* 8 May, 1.

Jamal, T. and Tanase, A. 2005. Impacts and conflicts surrounding Dracula Park, Romania: The role of sustainable tourism principles. *Journal of Sustainable Tourism*, 13(5), 440–55.

Jeffries, D. 2001. *Governments and Tourism*. Oxford: Butterworth Heinemann.

Johns, N. and Clarke, V. 2001. Mythological analysis of boating tourism. *Annals of Tourism Research*, 28(3), 334–59.

Johnson, E.C. 1885. *On the Track of the Crescent: Erratic Notes from the Piraus to Pesth*. London: Hurst and Blackett.

Johnson, N.C. 1994. Sculpting heroic histories: celebrating the centenary of the 1798 rebellion in Ireland. *Transactions of the Institute of British Geographers*, 19(1), 78–93.

Kaneva, N. and Popescu, D. 2011. National identity lite: Nation branding in post-communist Romania and Bulgaria. *International Journal of Cultural Studies*, 14(2), 191–207.

Kaplan, R.D. 1993. *Balkan Ghosts: A Journey Through History*. London: Papermac.

Karg, B., Spaite, A. and Sutherland, R. 2009. *The Everything Vampire Book*. Avon MA: F+W Media.

Kim, H. and Richardson, S.L. 2003. Motion picture impacts on destinations images. *Annals of Tourism Research*, 30(1), 216–37.

King, R.R. 1980. *A History of the Romanian Communist Party*. Stanford: Hoover Institution Press.

Kirtley, B. 1958. Dracula, The Monastic Chronicles and Slavic Folklore, in *Dracula: The Vampire and the Critics*, edited by M.L. Carter (1988). Ann Arbor: UMI Research Press, 11–17.

Kokker, S. and Kemp, C. 2004. *Romania and Moldova (Lonely Planet Guide)*. 3rd Edition. Melbourne: Lonely Planet Publications.

Kostova, E. 2005. *The Historian*. London: Little, Brown.

Krebbs, L. 2006. Spook tourists: We don't want 'em but they keep on coming. Paper to the Association of American Geographers Annual Meeting: Chicago, 9 March 2006.

Lanfant, M-F 1995. International tourism, internationalization and the challenge to identity, in *International Tourism: Identity and Change*, edited by M-F. Lanfant, J.B. Allcock and E.M. Bruner. London: Sage, 24–43.

Leatherdale, C. 1987. *The Origins of Dracula*. London: William Kimber.

Leatherdale, C. 1993. *Dracula: The Novel and the Legend*. Revised Edition. Brighton: Desert Island Books.

Leatherdale, C. 2000. Introduction, in E. Miller, *Dracula: Sense and Nonsense*. Westcliffe-on-Sea: Desert Island Books, 6–11.

LeBor, A. 2006. Dracula's castle goes back to a family of royal blood. *The Times*, 26 May, 39.

Lennig, A. 2003. *The Immortal Count: The Life and Films of Bela Lugosi*. Lexington: University Press of Kentucky.

Lennon, J. and Foley, M. 2000. *Dark Tourism: The Attraction of Death and Disaster*. London: Continuum.

Leu, C. 1986. Istoria şi o anume istorie literară. *Contemporanul*, 12 (21 March 1986), 12.

Leviţschi, L. and Bantaş, A. (eds) 2004. *Eminescu: Poezii/Poems*. Bucureşti: Teora.

Light, D. 2000. Gazing on communism: heritage tourism and post-communist identities in Germany, Hungary and Romania. *Tourism Geographies*, 2(2), 157–76.

Light, D. 2001. 'Facing the future': tourism and identity-building in post-socialist Romania. *Political Geography*, 20(8), 1053–74.

Light, D. 2005. The people of Bram Stoker's Transylvania. *Journal of Dracula Studies*, 7, 38–44.

Light, D. 2006. Romania: national identity, tourism promotion and European integration, in *Tourism in the New Europe: The Challenges and Opportunities of EU Enlargement*, edited by D. Hall, M. Smith and B. Marciszewska. Wallingford: CABI, 256–69.

Light, D. 2007a. Dracula tourism in Romania: Cultural identity and the state. *Annals of Tourism Research*, 34(3), 746–65.

Light, D. 2007b. The status of Vlad Ţepeş in Communist Romania: A Reassessment. *Journal of Dracula Studies*, 9, 9–21.

Light, D. 2008. Imaginative geographies, *Dracula* and the Transylvania place myth. *Human Geographies: Journal of Studies and Research in Human Geography*, 2(2), 5–16.

Light, D. 2009a. Performing Transylvania: Tourism, fantasy and play in a liminal place. *Tourist Studies* 9(3), 240–58.

Light, D. 2009b. When was *Dracula* first translated into Romanian? *Journal of Dracula Studies*, 11, 42–50.

Light, D. 2009c. Halloween in Transylvania, in *Trick or Treat? Halloween in a Globalising World*, edited by M. Foley and H. O'Donnell. Newcastle upon Tyne: Cambridge Scholars Publishing, 186–200.

Light, D. 2012. Taking Dracula on holiday: The presence of 'home' in the tourist encounter, in *The Cultural Moment in Tourism*, edited by L. Smith, E. Waterton and S. Watson. London: Routledge, 59–78.

Light, D. and Dumbrăveanu, D. 1999. Romanian tourism in the post-communist period. *Annals of Tourism Research*, 26(4), 898–927.

Light, D., Dumbrăveanu, D., Ciobanu, C. and Chiva, V. 2005. Tourism, Geography and souvenir retailing at Bran Castle. *Universitate din Bucureşti, Facultatea de Geografie, Comunicari de Geografie*, IX, 465–72.

Light, D., Nicolae, I. and Suditu, B, 2002. Toponymy and the communist city: Street names in Bucharest 1947–1965. *Geojournal*, 56(2), 135–44.

Light, D. and Young, C. 2009. European Union enlargement, post-accession migration and imaginative geographies of the 'New Europe': Media discourses in Romania and the United Kingdom. *Journal of Cultural Geography*, 26(3), 281–303.

Ludlam, H. 1962. *A Biography of Dracula: The Life Story of Bram Stoker*. London: Quality Book Club.

McAleer, P. 2001. Dracula emerges from his tomb. *Financial Times* 14/15 July 2001, xx.

MacCannell, D. 1976. *The Tourist: A New Theory of the Leisure Class*. New York: Schocken Books, New York.

McGrath, P. 1997. Preface: Bram Stoker and his vampire, in *Bram Stoker's Dracula: Sucking Through the Century, 1897–1997*, edited by C.M. Davidson. Toronto: Dundurn Press, 41–8.

Mackenzie, A. 1977. *Dracula Country*. London: Arthur Barker Ltd.

Mackenzie A. 1983. *Romanian Journey*. London: Robert Hale.

McNally, R.T. 1983. *Dracula was a Woman*. New York: McGrew-Hill.

McNally, R.T. 1991. An historical appraisal of the image of Vlad Ţepeş in contemporary Romanian folklore, in *Dracula: Essays on the Life and Times of Vlad Ţepes* edited by K.W. Treptow. New York: Columbia University Press (East European Monographs Nr 323), 197–228.

McNally, R. 1999. Separation granted; divorce denied; annulment unlikely. *Journal of Dracula Studies*, 1, 25–7.

McNally, R.T. and Florescu, R.T. 1969. În căutarea lui Vlad Ţepeş. *Magazin istoric*, III(12), 43–5.

McNally, R.T. and Florescu, R 1972. *In Search of Dracula: A True History of Dracula and Vampire Legends*. Greenwich: New York Graphic Society.

McNally, R.T. and Florescu, R. 1994. *In Search of Dracula: The History of Dracula and Vampires*. 2nd Edition. Boston: Houghton Mifflin Co.

Marigney, J. 1994. *Vampires: Restless Creatures of the Night*. New York: Harry N Abrams.

Marinescu, D. 1986. 50 de ani de la crearea oficiului naţional de turism. *Actualităţii în turism*, 2–3, 1–5.

Markwick, M.C. 2001. Tourism and the development of handicraft production in the Maltese islands. *Tourism Geographies*, 3(1), 29–51.

Marx, K. and Engels, F. 1992. *The Communist Manifesto* [first published 1848]. Oxford: Oxford University Press.

Mânzat, I. (2008) *Ecouri din zig-zag-urile vieţii*. Bistriţa: Editura Mesagerul.

Melton, J.G. undated. *All things Dracula: A bibliography of editions, reprints, adaptations and translations of Dracula* [online]. Available at: http://www.cesnur.org/2003/dracula/default.htm [accessed: 30 May 2011].

Melton, J.G. 1999. *The Vampire Book: The Encyclopedia of the Undead*. 2nd Edition. Detroit: Visible Ink Press.

Melton, J.G. 2011. *The Vampire Book: The Encyclopedia of the Undead*. 3rd Edition. Detroit: Visible Ink Press.

Mihail, S. 2010. Familia Habsburg a adus profitul la Castelul Bran. *Capital* [Online, 6 June]. Available at: http://www.capital.ro/detalii-articole/stiri/familia-habsburg-a-adus-profitul-la-castelul-bran-135507.html [accessed: 17 June 2011].

Miller, E. 1997. *Reflections on Dracula: Ten Essays*. White Rock BC: Transylvania Press.

Miller, E. 1998 Filing for divorce: Count Dracula vs Vlad Tepes, in *Dracula: The Shade and the Shadow*, edited by E. Miller. Westcliffe on Sea: Desert Island Books, 167–79.

Miller, E. 2000. *Dracula: Sense and Nonsense*. Westcliff on Sea: Desert Island Books.

Miller, E. 2003. *A Dracula Handbook*. Bucureşti: Editura GEROT.

Ministerul Dezvoltării Regionale şi Turismului 2011. *România: Exploraţi Grădina Carpaţilor*. Bucureşti: Ministerul Dezvoltării Regionale şi Turismului.

Misiuga, A. 1995. Cum am ajuns Draculişti la Bistrita. Paper to the First World Dracula Congress: Bistriţa, 28 May 1995.

Moise, L. 2003. „Dracula Park' se mută la Bucureşti. *Evenimentul zilei*, 27 January, 2.

Moisescu, C. 1979. *Tîrgovişte, monumente istorice şi de artă*. Bucureşti: Editura Meridiane.

Moore, T. 2007. The past perfect. *The Times (Travel Section)*, 29 Jan, 6.

Morgan, N. and A. Pritchard (1998) *Tourism Promotion and Power: Creating Images, Creating Identities*. Chichester: Wiley.

Morgan, N. and Pritchard, A. 2002. Conceptualizing destination branding, in *Destination Branding: Creating the Unique Destination Proposition*, edited by N. Morgan, A. Pritchard and R. Pride. Oxford: Butterworth Heinemann, 11–41.

Moroianu, G. 2001. Dracula va avea residinţa oficială la Sighişoara. *Ziua*, 9 July, 6.

Mowforth, M. and Munt, I. 2009. *Tourism and Sustainability: Development, Globalisation and New Tourism in the Third World*. 3rd Edition. London: Routledge.

Munt, I. 1994. The 'Other' postmodern tourism: Culture, Travel and the New Middle Classes. *Theory, Culture and Society*, 11(3), 101–23.

Munteanu, L. and Rusu, V. 1995a. Draculofilismul va salva turismul. *Adevărul*, 29 May, 8.

Munteanu, L. and Rusu, V. 1995b. Ministerul Agathon patronează o penibilă şuşanea turistică. *Adevărul* 30 May, 12.

Muresan, A. and Smith, K.A. 1998. Dracula's Castle in Transylvania: Conflicting heritage marketing strategies. *International Journal of Heritage Studies*, 4(2), 73–85.

Nandris, G. 1969. The historical Dracula: The theme of his legend in the Western and in the Eastern literatures of Europe, in *Comparative Literature: Matter and Method*, edited by A.O. Aldridge. Urbana: University of Illinois Press, 109–43.

Năstase, G. 2001a. Decizia de a construi Dracula Park la Sighişoara este irevocablilă. *Cotidianul*, 22 November, 7.

Năstase, G. 2001b. Dracula – produs touristic. *Cotidianul*, 15 November, 10.

Neacşu, C. 2006. Untitled. *Adevărul* 7 July, B1.

Neagoe, M. 1976. The truth about Dracula. *Holidays in Romania*, 60 (December), 8–9.

Negrici, E. 1999. *Literature and Propaganda in Communist Romania*. Bucharest: Romanian Cultural Foundation Publishing House.

Nelson, D.N. 1980. *Democratic Centralism in Romania: A Study of Local Communist Politics*. New York: Columbia University Press/East European Monographs no. LXIX.

Neumann, I.B. 1999. *Uses of the Other: 'The East' in European Identity Formation*. Minneapolis: University of Minnesota Press.

Newby, P.T. 1981. Literature and the fashioning of tourist taste, in *Humanistic Geography and Literature: Essays on the Experience of Place*, edited by P.C.D. Pocock. London: Croom Helm, 130–41.

Nistorescu, C. 2001. Dracula Show. *Evenimentul zilei*, 14 November, 1.

Nistorescu, C. 2002. Păzea cu 'Dracula Park'. *Evenimentul zilei*, 16 January, 1.

Niţu, M. 2002. Vampirul mai scoate o mână din coşciug. *Adevărul* 2 July, 1.

Novelli, M. (ed.) 2005. *Niche Tourism: Contemporary Issues, Trends and Cases*. London: Elsevier.

O'Connor, B. 1993. Myths and mirrors: tourist images and national identity, in *Tourism in Ireland: A Critical Analysis*, edited by B. O'Connor and M. Cronin. Cork: Cork University Press, 68–85.

Ogrinji M. 1994. Meet Dracula. *Holidays in Romania*, 238, 18–19.

Ogrinji, M. 1996. The immortal Dracula. *Holidays in Romania*, 246, 31.

Oprea, B. 2010. Dracula şi frunza de brand. *Adevărul* [Online, 23 August] Available at:

http://www.adevarul.ro/locale/bucuresti/Dracula-Transilvania-pastila-Bogdan_ Oprea-funza-brand_0_322167857.html [accessed: 9 July 2011].

Oţetea, A., Popescu-Puţuri, I., Nestor,I., Berza, M., and Maciu, V. 1970. *Istoria poporului roman*. Bucureşti: Editura Ştiinţifica.

Overing, J. 1997. The role of myth: An anthropological perspective, or: 'The reality of the really made-up', in *Myths and Nationhood*, edited by G. Hosking and G. Schöpflin. London: Hurst, 1–18.

Pacepa, I.M. 1988. *Red Horizons*. London: Heinemann.

Palade, G. and Roibu, I. 2004. Preţurile terenurilor explodeaza. *Evenimentul zilei*, 13 October, 5.

Paler, O. 1995. Patriotic, nu? *România liberă*, 21 March, 1.

Palmer, C. 1999. Tourism and the symbols of identity. *Tourism Management* 20(3), 313–21.

Palmer, C. 2003. Tourism Churchill's England: Rituals of kinships and belonging. *Annals of Tourism Research*, 30(2), 426–45.

Palmer, C. 2005. An ethnography of Englishness: Experiencing identity through tourism. *Annals of Tourism Research*, 32(1), 7–27.

Panait, P.I. and Ştefănescu, A. 1973. *Museul Curtea Veche, Palatul Voievodal*. Bucureşti: Muzeul de istorie a municipiului Bucureşti.

Pancevski, B. 2006. Bram Stoker is honoured for services to tourism in Transylvania. *The Times* [Online, 9 November].Available at: http://entertainment.timesonline. co.uk/tol/arts_and_entertainment/article630975.ece [accessed: 19 June 2011].

Papadimitriou, D. and Phinnemore, D. 2008. *Romania and the European Union: From Marginalisation to Membership*. London: Routledge.

Parau, C.E. 2009. Impaling Dracula: How EU accession empowered civil society in Romania. *West European Politics*, 32(1), 119–41.

Park, H. 2010. Heritage tourism: Emotional journeys into nationhood. *Annals of Tourism Research*, 37(1), 116–35.

Partidul Comunist Român. 1969.*Congresul al X-lea al Partidul Comunist Român*. Bucureşti: Editura politica.

Partidul Muncitoresc Român. 1960. *Directivele Congresului al III-lea al PMR pentru Planul de Dezvoltare a Economiei Naţionale pe anii 1960–1965 şi pentru programul economic de perspective*. Bucureşti: Editura Politica.

Pavel D. 2000. The textbooks scandal and rewriting history in Romania. *East European Politics and Societies*, 14(2),179–89.

Păduraru, N. 1970. Dracula, in *Almanah Turistic, 1970*. Bucureşti: ONT Carpaţi, 51 and 53.

Păduraru, N. 1972a. Dracula: I. Cultul lui Dracula. *România pitorească*, I (July), 30–1.

Păduraru, N. 1972b. Dracula: II necunoscute.*România pitorească*, I (August), 30.

Păduraru, N. 1973. Ultimele descoperiri în pasul Bîrgăului. *România pitorească*, II(February), 13.

Păduraru, N. 1986. Halloween. *Holidays in Romania*, XXVII (April), 8–10.

Păunescu, A. 1986. O minciună: Dracula. *Contemporanul*, 10 (7 March 1986), 13.

Păvălaşc, M. 2011. Proiectul Dracula Park i-a lăsat pe români fără bani. Prejudiciul este estimat la peste un million de euro. *Adevărul* [Online, 8 February]. Available at: http://www.adevarul.ro/locale/galati/Proiectul_Dracula_Park_i-a_lasat_ pe_romani_fara_bani_si_dupa_zece_ani_de_la_lansarea_sa_0_423557712. html [accessed: 9 July 2011].

Pecoul, P. 1992. A Vlady good holiday, *The Guardian*, 5 June, 26.

Peleggi, M. 1996. National heritage and global tourism in Thailand. *Annals of Tourism Research*, 23(2), 432–48.

Petrescu, C.D. 1971. România şi fluxul turistic internaţional. *Terra*, III (3), 9–18.

Petrescu, L. 1995. Ce ne mai lipsea: 'Congresul Mondial Dracula'. *Cotidianul* 25 May, 6.

Petru, C. and Năstase, A. 2004. Hotelul lui Dracula de la Tihuţa. *Jurnalul Naţional*, 12 July, 7.

Phinnemore, D. 2001. Romania and Euro-Atlantic integration since 1989: A decade of frustration, in *Post-Communist Romania: Coming to Terms with Transition*, edited by D. Light and D. Phinnemore. Basingstoke: Palgrave, 245–69.

Pile, S. 2005. *Real Cities: Modernity, Space and the Phantasmagorias of City Life*. London: Sage.

Pitchford, S. 2008. *Identity Tourism: Imaging and Imagining the Nation*. Bingley: Emerald.

Pitt, L.F., Opoku, R., Hultman, M., Abratt, R. and Spyropoulou, S. 2007. What I say about myself: Communication of brand personality by African countries. *Tourism Management*, 28(3), 835–44.

Pocock, D.C.D. 1987. Haworth: The experience of literary place, in *Geography and Literature: A Meeting of the Disciplines*, edited by W.E. Mallory and P. Simpson-Housley. New York: Syracuse University Press, 135–42.

Pocock, D. 1992. Catherine Cookson Country: Tourist Expectation and Experience. *Geography*, 77(3), 236–43.

Poland, K. 2001. Romania has no stake in Dracula. BBC News [Online: 30 September]. Available at: http://news.bbc.co.uk/hi/english/world/europe/ newsid_1571000/1571560.stm [accessed: 5 July 2002].

Pop, C., Cosma, S., Negrusa, A., Ionescu, C. and Marinescu, N. 2007. *Romania as a Tourist Destination and the Romanian Hotel Industry*. Newcastle: Cambridge Scholars Publishing.

Popa, D. 2001. Marca Dracula Land este proprietatea unei personae fizice! *România liberă*, 17 November, 1.

Popa M.R. 2007. Understanding the urban past: The transformation of Bucharest in the late socialist period, in *Testimonies of the City: Identity, Community and Change in a Contemporary Urban World*, edited by R. Rodger and J. Herbert. Aldershot: Ashgate, 159–86.

Popescu, A. 2001a. Amplasamentul pentru Dracula Land va fi decis în maximum o lună de zile. *Adevărul*, 27 June, 15.

Popescu, A. 2001b. Pesediştii din C.J. Braşov au votat un 'Dracula Land alternativ' la Bran-Rîşnov. *Adevărul*, 12 November, 13.

Pozzi, T. 2003. Any special requests. *The Guardian* [Online, 14 June]. Available at: http://www.guardian.co.uk/travel/2003/jun/14/hotels.guardiansaturdaytrav elsection?INTCMP=SRCH [accessed: 26 May 2008].

Prahoveanu, I. 1999. *Bran Castle*. Braşov: Editura C2 Design.

Prahoveanu, I. and Coşuleţ, S. 1985. *Muzeul Bran, Ghid*. Braşov: Comitetul de Cultură şi Educaţie Socialistă al Judeţului Braşov.

Preda, A. 2007. In plin scandal, Branul a fost muzeul cel mai vizitat in 2006. 9am [Online, 13 February]. Available at: http://www.9am.ro/stiri-revista-presei/2007-02-13/in-plin-scandal-branul-a-fost-muzeul-cel-mai-vizitat-in-2006.html [accessed: 17 June 2011].

Pretes, M. 2003. Tourism and nationalism. *Annals of Tourism Research*, 30(1), 125–42.

Pricope, D. 2009. Udrea îl îngroapa pe Dracula. *România liberă* [Online, 16 January. Available at: www.romanialibera.ro/a143808/udrea-il-ingroapa-pe-dracula.html. [accessed: 19 January 2009].

Pritchard, A. and Morgan, N. 2001. Culture, identity and tourism representation: marketing Cymru or Wales? *Tourism Management*, 22(1), 167–79.

Pritchard, A. and Morgan N. 2006. 'Hotel Babylon?' Exploring hotels as liminal sites of transition and transgression. *Tourism Management*, 27(5), 762–72.

Pruteanu, G. 1993. La Craiova apare o ediţie-pirat a romanului 'Dracula'. *Evenimentul zilei*, 23 July, 6.

Pryke, S. 2009. *Nationalism in a Global World*. Basingstoke: Palgrave.

Radio Free Europe/Radio Liberty. 2002a. Romanian tourism minister vows to struggle for Dracula Park. *Radio Free Europe/Radio Liberty Newsline*, 6 (112), Part II (17 June 2002).

Radio Free Europe/Radio Liberty. 2002b. Opponents win concession in dispute over Dracula theme park. *Radio Free Europe/Radio Liberty Newsline* 6(124), Part II (1 July 2002).

Radio Free Europe/Radio Liberty, 2003a. Western consultants oppose Romanian Dracula Park project. *Radio Free Europe/Radio Liberty Newsline*, 7(11), Part II (17 January 2003)

Radio Free Europe/Radio Liberty, 2003b. Dracula to be Bucharest resident. *Radio Free Europe/Radio Liberty Newsline* 7(17) Part II (27 January 2003).

Rădulescu, D. 2001. Cu 120 milioane de lei Adrian Năstase devine primul investitor la Dracula Park. *România liberă*, 13 December, 1.

Rădulescu, G. 2010. Dan Matei Agathon: „Dracula trebuie folosit obligatoriu". *Adevărul* [Online: 19 September]. Available at: http://www.adevarul. ro/la_masa_adevarului/Dan_Matei_Agathon-_Dracula_trebuie_folosit_ obligatoriu_0_332367217.html [accessed: 1 July 2011].

Rady, M. 1992. *Romania in Turmoil*. London: I.B. Tauris.

Rady, M. 1995. Nationalism and nationality in Romania, in *Contemporary Nationalism in East Central Europe*, edited by P. Latiawski. New York: St Martin's Press, 127–42.

Raento, P. and Brunn, S.D. 2005. Visualising Finland: Postage Stamps as political messengers. *Geografiska Annaler B*, 87(2), 145–64.

Raicu, A. 1975. A chime for the shadows of yore. *Holidays in Romania*, XVIII (October), 3 and 5.

Raica, A. 1978. If you go to Bistritza. *Holidays in Romania*, 83(November), 18–20.

Ramsay, N. 2009. Taking-place: Refracted enchantment and the habitual spaces of the tourist souvenir. *Social and Cultural Geography*, 10(2), 197–217.

Reijnders, S. 2010. Places of the imagination: An ethnography of the TV detective tour. *Cultural Geographies*, 17(1), 37–52.

Reijnders, S. 2011a. Stalking the Count: Dracula, fandom and tourism. *Annals of Tourism Research*, 38(1), 231–48.

Reijnders, S. 2011b. *Places of the Imagination: Media, Tourism, Culture*. Ashgate: London.

Rice, A. 1976. *Interview with the Vampire*. London: Time Warner Paperbacks.

Richardson, D. and Denton, J. 1988. *The Rough Guide to Eastern Europe: Hungary, Romania and Bulgaria*. London: Harrap-Columbus.

Richardson, D. and Burford, T. 1995. *Romania: The Rough Guide*. London: Rough Guides Ltd.

Richter, C. 2001. Dracula vine dintr-o zonă obscură, nu noi. *România liberă*, 5 November, 14.

Riley, R.W. 1994. Movie-induced tourism, in *Tourism: The State of the Art*, edited by A.V. Seaton, C.L. Jenkins, R.C. Wood, P.U.C. Dieke, M.M. Bennett, L.R. MacLellan and R. Smith. Chichester: Wiley, 453–8.

Riley, R., Baker, D. and Van Doren C.S. 1998. Movie-induced tourism. *Annals of Tourism Research*, 25(4), 919–35.

Rîncu, I. 2008. Dracula şi Casa Poporului vând bine capitala. *Evenimentul zilei* [Online, 30 April].Available at: http://www.evz.ro/detalii/stiri/dracula-si-casa-poporului-vand-bine-capitala-801597.html. [accessed: 28 June 2008].

Robb, J.G. 1998. Tourism and legends: Archaeology of Heritage. *Annals of Tourism Research*, 25(3), 579–96.

Roberts, K. 2004. *The Leisure Industries*. Basingstoke: Palgrave.

Roberts, L. 1996. Barriers to the development of rural tourism in the Bran area of Transylvania, in *Tourism and Culture: Image, Identity and Marketing*, edited by M. Robinson, N. Evans, and P.M. Callaghan. Sunderland: Business Education Publishers, 185–97.

Robinson, M. 2002. Between and beyond the pages: Literature-tourism relationships, in *Literature and Tourism: Reading and Writing Tourism Texts*, edited by H-C. Andersen and M. Robinson. London: Continuum, 39–79.

Robinson, M. and Andersen, H-C. 2002a. Reading between the lines: Literature and the creation of touristic spaces, in *Literature and Tourism: Reading and Writing Tourism Texts*, edited by H-C. Andersen and M. Robinson. London: Continuum, 1–38.

Robinson, M. and Andersen, H-C. 2002b. Introduction, in *Literature and Tourism: Reading and Writing Tourism Texts*, edited by H-C. Andersen and M. Robinson. London: Continuum, xiii–xix.

Roesch, S. 2009. *The Experience of Film Location Tourists*. Bristol: Channel View.

Rojek, C. 1993. *Ways of Escape: Modern Transformations of Leisure and Travel*. Basingstoke: MacMillan.

Rojek, C. 1997. Indexing, dragging and the social construction of tourist sights, in *Touring Cultures: Transformations of Travel and Theory*, edited by C. Rojek and J. Urry. London: Routledge, 52–74.

Ronay, G. 1972. *The Dracula Myth*. London: W.H. Allen.

Rowling, J.K. 1997. *Harry Potter and the Philosopher's Stone*. London: Bloomsbury.

Rowling, J.K. 2001. *Harry Potter şi Piatra Filozofală*. Bucureşti: Editura Egmont Romania.

Rumania for Tourists. 1963, 6(3), back cover.

Rus, C. 2000 Evolutions and trends in the Romanian tourism. *Romanian Business Journal*, 7(23) (9–15 June), 16.

Russu, V. 2005. La Sighişoara se vor arde vrăjitoare. *Adevărul* 5 July, 15.

Sabau, C. 2001. Afacerea Dracula. *Ziua*, 26 April, 8.

Said, E.W. 1995. *Orientalism: Western Conceptions of the Orient* [first published 1978]. Harmondsworth: Penguin.

Sanchez, P.M and Adams, K.M. 2008. The Janus-faced character of tourism in Cuba. *Annals of Tourism Research*, 35(1), 27–46.

Savin, N. 2004. Acţionarii firmei, prieteni cu guvernanţii. *Evenimentul zilei*, 12 October, 3.

Seaton, A.V. 2000. The worst of journeys, the best of journeys: Travel and the concept of the periphery in European culture, in *Expressions of Culture, Identity and Meaning in Tourism*, edited by M. Robinson, P. Long, N. Evans, R. Sharpley and J. Swarbrooke. Sunderland: Centre for Travel and Tourism/ Business Educational Publishers, 321–46.

Şelaru, V. 2002. La castelul Bran timp de o noapte vor locui...vampirii. *România liberă*, 1 November, 15.

Selwyn, T. 1996. Introduction, in *The Tourist Image: Myths and Myth Making in Tourism*, edited by T. Selwyn. Chichester: Wiley, 1–32.

Severin, M. and Pavel, R.M. 1995. Dracula a fost numit agentul publicitar nr 1 al României. *Ziua*, 10 March, 5.

Shackley, M. 2001. The legend of Robin Hood: Myth, inauthenticity, and tourism development in Nottingham, England, in *Hosts and Guests Revisited: Tourism Issues of the 21st Century*, edited by V.L. Smith and M. Brent. New York: Cognizant Communication Corporation, 315–22.

Shandley, R., Jamal, T. and Tanase, A. 2006. Location shooting and the filmic destination: Transylvanian myths and the post-colonial tourism enterprise. *Journal of Tourism and Cultural Change*, 4(3), 137–58.

Shearings Holidays Ltd 2001. *Europe: Coach, Air, Rail & Cruise Holidays* [Brochure] Wigan: Shearings Holidays.

Shields, R. 1991. *Places on the Margin: Alternative Geographies of Modernity.* London: Routledge.

Skal, D.J. 1996. *V is for Vampire.* London: Robson Books.

Skal, D.J. 1997. 'His hour upon the stage': Theatrical Adaptations of Dracula, in *Dracula* by Bram Stoker, edited by N. Auerbach and D.J. Skal. New York: W.W. Norton and Company, 371–81.

Skal, D. 2004. *Hollywood Gothic: The Tangled Web of Dracula from Novel to Stage to Screen.* Revised Edition. New York: Faber and Faber.

Smith, A. 2001. The transition to a market economy in Romania and the competitiveness of exports, in *Post-Communist Romania: Coming to Terms with Transition*, edited by D. Light and D. Phinnemore. Basingstoke: Palgrave, 127–49.

Smith, A. 2006. The Romanian economy since 1989, in *The EU and Romania: Accession and Beyond*, edited by D. Phinnemore. London: Federal Trust, 29–37.

Smith, A.D. 1988. *The Ethnic Origin of Nations.* Oxford: Blackwell.

Smith, A.D. 1991. *National Identity.* Harmondsworth: Penguin.

Smith, M.K. 2009. *Issues in Cultural Tourism Studies.* 2nd Edition. London: Routledge.

Smith, M. and Puczkó, L. 2011. National identity construction and tourism in Hungary: A multi-level approach, in *Tourism and National Identity: An International Perspective*, edited by E. Frew and L. White, London: Routledge, 38-51.

Snak, O. 1976. *Economia şi organizarea turismului.* Bucureşti: Editura Sport-Turism.

Sobaru, A. 1971. Ora bilanţului, in *Almanah turistic 1971.* Bucureşti: Oficiul Naţional de Turism, 5–10.

Squire, S.J. 1988. Wordsworth and Lake District tourism: Romantic reshaping of landscape. *Canadian Geographer*, 32(3), 237–47.

Squire, S.J. 1993. Valuing countryside: reflections on Beatrix Potter tourism. *Area*, 25(1), 5–10.

Squire, S.J. 1994. The cultural values of literary tourism. *Annals of Tourism Research*, 21(1), 103–20.

Stan, L. 1995. Romanian privatisation: Assessment of the First Five Years. *Communist and Post-Communist Studies*, 28(4), 427–35.

Stanca, D. 1995. Dracula bântuie vârtos în România tranziţiei. *România liberă*, 15 March 1995, 2.

Stănescu, S. 1993. Vampireala. *Adevărul*, 17 July, 3.

Stăvăruş, I. 1978. *Povestiri medievale despre Vlad Ţepeş-Draculea.* Bucureşti: Editura Univers.

Ştefan, A. 2001. Dracula Park, o filială a Trezoreriei. *România liberă*, 15 December, 1.

Ştefan, A. 2002. Românul, între Dracula Park şi FNI. *România liberă*, 16 February, 1.

Ştefan, C. 2002. SIF-urile au salvat, totuşi, Dracula Park. *Adevărul* 5 April, 13.

Ştefănescu, Ş. 2001. Vlad Ţepeş, in *Istoria românilor (Vol 4)*, edited by Ş. Ştefănescu, and C. Mureşanu. Bucureşti: Editura Enciclopedica, 349–64.

Stephen, C. 2007. Romania sinks its teeth into the tourist trade. *The Scotsman* [Online, 7 January]. Available at:http://news.Scotsman.com/latestnews/ Romania-sinks-its-teeth-into.3335835.jpm. [accessed: 25 June 2008].

Stoian, E. 1980. Cetatea Bran şi destinul lui Vlad Tepes. *Magazin istoric*, XIV(9), 33.

Stoian, E. 1989. *Vlad Ţepeş: Mit şi realitatea istorică*. Bucureşti: Editura Albatros.

Stoicescu, N. 1976. *Vlad Ţepeş*. Bucureşti: Editura Academiei Republicii Socialiste Române.

Stoicescu, N. 1978. *Vlad Ţepeş: Prince of Wallachia*. Bucureşti: Editura Academiei Republicii Socialiste România.

Stoicescu, N. 1979. *Vlad Ţepeş*. Bucureşti: Editura Militară.

Stoicescu, N. 1986. Vlad Tepes şi Dracula: Între adevăr şi legendă II. *Contemporanul*, 14 (4 April 1986), 10.

Stoiculescu, C.D. 2002. Se distruge identitate naţională a romaniei. *România liberă*, 28 February, 14.

Stoker, B. 1990. *Dracula* (translated by B. Cioculescu and I. Verzea). Bucureşti: Editura Univers.

Stoker, B. 1997. *Dracula* edited by N. Auerbach and D. Skal. [First published 1897]. New York: W.W. Norton and Company.

Stolea, A. 2002. Untitled. *România liberă*, 23 February, 9.

Sweeney, J. 1991. *The Life and Evil Times of Nicolae Ceausescu*. London: Hutchinson.

Szondi, G. 2007. The role and challenges of country branding in transition countries: The Central and Eastern European experience. *Place Branding and Public Diplomacy*, 3(1), 8–20.

Tănăsescu, A. 2006. Tourism, nationalism and post-communist Romania: The life and death of Dracula Park. *Journal of Tourism and Cultural Change*, 4(3), 159–76.

Teller, M. and Ratcliffe, L. 2006. *The Rough Guide to the Italian Lakes*. London: Rough Guides.

Terenche, C. 1995. Primul Congress Mondial despre Dracula stropit cu 'Draculina' de 'Drăculeşti'. *România liberă*, 27 May, 9.

Tetley, S. and Bramwell, B. 2002. Tourists and the cultural construction of Haworth's literary landscape, in *Literature and Tourism: Reading and Writing Tourism Texts*, edited by H-C. Andersen and M. Robinson. London: Continuum, 155–70.

Tismăneanu, V. 1999. Understanding national Stalinism: reflections on Ceauşescu's socialism. *Communist and Post-Communist Studies*, 32(2), 155–73.

Tismăneanu, V. 2003. *Stalinism for All Seasons: A Political History of Romanian Communism*. Berkeley: University of California Press.

Toader, A. 2001. România îsi prezinta la Berlin proiectele turistice. *Ziua*, 3 March, 12.

Todorova, M. 1997. *Imagining the Balkans*. Oxford: Oxford University Press.

Todorova, M. 2009. *Imagining the Balkans*. Updated Edition. Oxford: Oxford University Press.

Tooke, N. and Baker, M. 1996. Seeing is believing: The effect of film on visitor numbers to screened locations. *Tourism Management*, 17(2), 87–94.

Travers, B. 2007. Vlad the unique selling point. *Daily Telegraph* [Online, 6 January]. Available at: http://www.telegraph.co.uk/property/overseasproperty/3355514/Vlad-the-unique-selling-point.html [accessed: 27 June 2008].

Treptow, K.W. 2000. *Vlad III Dracula: The Life and Times of the Historical Dracula*. Iaşi: Center for Romanian Studies.

Trofin, R. 1979. Norman Burton in Romania. *Holidays in Romania*, XXI (August), 17.

Troncotă, T. 2006. *România comunistă: Propagandă şi cenzură*. Bucureşti: Tritonic.

Trow, M.J. 2003. *Vlad the Impaler: In Search of the Real Dracula*. Stroud: Sutton Publishing.

Tunbridge, J. 1994. 1994 Whose Heritage? Global Problem, European Nightmare, in *Building a New Heritage: Tourism, Culture and Identity in the New Europe*, edited by G. Ashworth and P. Larkham. London: Routledge, 123–34.

Turnock, D. 1974. *An Economic Geography of Romania*. London: G. Bell and Sons Ltd.

Turnock, D. 1989. *Eastern Europe: An Economic and Political Geography*. London: Routledge.

Turnock, D. 1991a. Romania, in *Tourism and Economic Development in Eastern Europe and the Soviet Union*, edited by D. Hall. London: Belhaven, 203–19.

Turnock, D. 1991b. Romanian villages: rural planning under communism. *Rural History*, 2(1), 81–112.

Turnock, D. 1991c. The planning of rural settlement in Romania. *The Geographical Journal* 157(3), 251–264.

Turnock, D. 2007. *Aspects of Independent Romania's Economic History with Particular Reference to Transition for EU Accession*. Aldershot: Ashgate.

Tyler, H.A. 1978. Dracula was a hero, not a vampire. *Chicago Tribune*, 31 October, 1 and 4.

Tzanelli, R. 2004. Constructing the 'cinematic tourist': The 'sign industry' of The Lord of the Rings. *Tourist Studies*, 4(1), 21–42.

Ungheanu, M. 1992. *Răstălmăcirea lui Ţepeş*. Bucureşti: Editura Globus.

UNESCO. 2001. *World Heritage Committee, Twenty-fifth session, Helsinki, Finland, 11–16 December 2001: Report* [Online: UNESCO]. Available at http://whc.unesco.org/toc/mainf10.htm [accessed: 30 March 2004].

United States Department of Commerce. 1973. *1970 Census of Population: Supplementary Report: Country of Origin, Mother Tongue, and Citizenship for the United States: 1970* [Online: US Department of Commerce] Available at: http://www2.census.gov/prod2/decennial/documents/31679801n1-40ch04. pdf [accessed: 17 March 2008].

Unwin, T. and Hewitt. V. 2001. Banknotes and national identity in central and eastern Europe. *Political Geography*, 20(8), 1005–28.

Urma, V. 1985. Guests count on thrills at Hotel Dracula. *Los Angeles Times*, 20 December, 7.

Urry, J. 1994. Cultural change and contemporary tourism. *Leisure Studies*, 13(4), 233–8.

Urry, J. 1995. *Consuming Places*. London: Routledge.

Urry, J. 2002. *The Tourist Gaze*. 2nd Edition. London: Sage.

Valendorfean 2002. Oameni de cultură i-au spus răspicat lui Iliescu că nu avem nevoie de Dracula Park. *România liberă*, 4 April, 1.

Vansant, J. 1999. Robert Wise's *The Sound of Music* and the 'Denazification' of Austria in American Cinema, in *From World War to Waldheim Volume 2*, edited by D.F. Good and R. Wodak. New York: Berghahn, 165–86.

Varma, D.P. 1976. The genesis of Dracula: A Revisit, in *The Vampire's Bedside Companion: The Amazing World of Vampires in Fact and Fiction*, edited by P. Underwood. London: Coronet Books, 44–54.

Vărzaru, C. 1995. Dracula reprezinta România în întreagă lumea. *Ziua*, 26 May, 1.

Vela, A. 2001a. Dracula Park – la 6 km de Sighisoara pe Platoul Breite. *Adevărul* 21 November, 13.

Vela, A. 2001b. Lânga Sighişoara – Dracula Park. *Adevărul*, 6 November, 16.

Verdery, K. 1991. *National Ideology under Socialism: Identity and Cultural Politics in Ceauşescu's Romania*. Berkeley: University of California Press.

Verdery, K. 1996. *What was Socialism and What Comes Next?* Princeton: Princeton University Press.

Verdery, K. 1999. *The Political Lives of Dead Bodies: Reburial and Postsocialist Change*. New York: Columbia University Press.

Verdery, K. 2004. Anthropological adventures with Romania's Wizard of Oz, 1973–1989. *Focaal-European Journal of Anthropology*, 43,134–45.

Verne, J. 2001. *The Castle of the Carpathians* [first published in French in 1893]. Amsterdam: Fredonia Books.

Vulpe, M. and Chilianu, D. 2007. Ţepele PD, distruse de Ziua bărbatului. *Adevărul*, 8 May, 7.

Wall, G. and Mathieson, A. 2006. *Tourism: Change, Impacts and Opportunities*. Harlow: Pearson.

Wallace, J.M.T. 2001. Putting 'culture' into sustainable tourism: Negotiating tourism at Lake Balaton, Hungary, in *Hosts and Guests Revisited: Tourism Issues of the 21st Century* edited by V.L. Smith and M. Brent. New York: Cognizant Communication Corporation, 298–314.

Wang, N. 1999. Rethinking authenticity in tourism experience. *Annals of Tourism Research*, 26(2), 349–70.

Wasson, R. 1966. The politics of Dracula. *English Language in Transition*, 9(1), 24–7.

Waterfall, C. 1997. Reality bites. *Geographical Magazine*, LXIX(2), 34–5.

Wearing, S., Stevenson, D. and Young, T. 2010. *Tourist Cultures: Identity, Place and the Traveller*. London: Sage.

White, L. and Frew, E. 2011. Tourism and national identities: Connections and conceptualisations, in *Tourism and National Identity: An International Perspective*, edited by E. Frew and L. White, London: London, 1-10.

Wilkinson, W. 1820. *An Account of the Principalities of Wallachia and Moldavia.* London: Longman

Williams, D. 2002. In fair Verona, answers for the lovelorn. *The Washington Post*, 14 February] Available at: www.washintonpost.com [accessed 21 August 2006].

Williams, N. 1998. *Romania and Moldova (Lonely Planet Guide)*. Hawthorne (Australia): Lonely Planet.

Williams, N. and Wildman, K. 2001. *Romania and Moldova (Lonely Planet Guide)*. 2nd edition. Melbourne: Lonely Planet Publications.

Wingrove, D. 1997. Dracula: The true story? *In Review Romania* 2(1), February, 45.

Wolff, L. 1994. *Inventing Eastern Europe: The Map of Civilization on the Mind of the Enlightenment*. Stanford: Stanford University Press.

Wood, R. 1984. Ethnic tourism, the state, and cultural change in Southeast Asia. *Annals of Tourism Research*, 11(3), 353–74.

World Travel and Tourism Council. 2011. *Travel and Tourism Economic Impact 2011: Romania*. [Online: World Travel and Tourism Council]. Available at: http://www.wttc.org/bin/file/original_file/romania_report_2011-pdf.pdf [accessed: 4 June 2011].

Yan, H. and Bramwell, B. 2009. Cultural tourism, ceremony and the state in China. *Annals of Tourism Research*, 35(4), 969–89.

Yan, G. and Santos, C.A. 2009. 'China, Forever': Tourism Discourse and Self-Orientalism. *Annals of Tourism Research*, 36(2), 295–315.

Young, C. and Hörschelmann, K. 2007. Identity under communism and post-communism, in T. Herrschel, *Global Geographies of Post-Socialist Transition: Geographies, Societies, Policies*, London: Routledge, 209–23.

Zubascu, I. 2002. Biserică Ortodoxă Română şi-a dat accordul pentru proiectul 'Parcul lui Dracula'. *România liberă*, 5 March, 14.

Films

Bram Stoker's Dracula (dir. Francis Ford Coppola, 1992)

Dracula (dir. Tod Browning, 1931) (Re-released as part of *Dracula: The Legacy Collection* [Universal], DVD, 2004)
In Search of Dracula (dir. Calvin Floyd, 1974)
The Dracula Business (dir. Anthony de Lotbiniere, 1974)

Index

For Product Safety Concerns and Information please contact our
EU representative GPSR@taylorandfrancis.com Taylor & Francis
Verlag GmbH, Kaufingerstraße 24, 80331 München, Germany